Becoming Westerly

Jamie Brisick

Outpost19 I San Francisco
outpost19.com

Brisick, Jamie
        Becoming Westerly/ Jamie Brisick
        ISBN 9781937402747 (pbk)
        ISBN 9781937402754 (ebk)

Library of Congress Control Number: 2015902714

cover design: Julian Chavez

OUTPOST19

PROVOCATIVE READING
SAN FRANCISCO
NEW YORK
OUTPOST19.COM

"BECOMING WESTERLY is much more than a book about a celebrated surfer who becomes a woman—in this case, a dude who becomes a diva. Brisick presents us with a case study of narcissism, of the pathology of celebrity, and a detailed look at the complex world of competitive surfing. It is a funny and painful book, too, and one I greatly enjoyed."

— Paul Theroux, author of *Mr. Bones: Twenty Stories, The Last Train to Zona Verde, The Great Railway Bazaar* and *Mosquito Coast*

"BECOMING WESTERLY is a haunting and important book—a reminder of what it means to be human, flawed, and occasionally fabulous."

— Karl Taro Greenfeld, author of *Speed Tribes* and *The Subprimes*

"Brisick's BECOMING WESTERLY is as compelling and magnificent as Westerly Windina herself—so charming and formidable, lonely and controlling, fierce and coquettish, and, like Marilyn Monroe, the woman with whom she most identifies, always far larger than life. In his intimate and amazing portrait of this formerly renowned male Australian surf champion now turned female entertainer, Brisick has undertaken a remarkable and riveting investigation of human identity in all of its complexities."

— Richard McCann, author of *Mother of Sorrows*

"Brisick shines a brilliant light on the fascinating Ms. Windina, at once damsel in distress and Superwoman. The surfing scenes are riveting—written with an excitement and an immediacy that only a lifelong wave rider can pull off."

— James Frey, author of *A Million Little Pieces*

"In BECOMING WESTERLY, Jamie Brisick sketches with exasperated subtlety an antihero/antiheroine who is both maddening and captivating. The book describes how surfing itself moved from obscurity to the mainstream, and how one surfer moved from his place in the surfing mainstream into her highly personal obscurity. It is often hilarious, and also, ultimately, deeply empathetic and touching."

— Andrew Solomon, author of *Far From The Tree*

"You've never read anything like BECOMING WESTERLY. Peter Drouyn is a character beyond the capacities of almost any novelist to imagine—and then he turns into someone else. Jamie Brisick traces the emergence of Westerly Windina with so much empathy, eloquence, and patience. His book is dazzling, devastating, funny, and surpassingly strange."

— William Finnegan, author of *Barbarian Days*

"Jamie Brisick tells the unlikely story of how Peter Drouyn, one of Australia's greatest surfers, morphed into the chanteuse Westerly Windina. At once candid autobiography, participatory anthropology, and cultural history, the tale of Drouyn's metamorphosis is told with compassion, humility, and authority. BECOMING WESTERLY is a remarkable book, proving once again that the truth is usually stranger than fiction."

— Dr. Peter Maguire, author of *Law and War, Facing Death in Cambodia* and *Thai Stick*

"BECOMING WESTERLY examines a difficult life with clear-eyed compassion, a story that helps us better understand how we all can become authors of authentic lives."

— Kem Nunn, author of *Chance*

"From deep inside the barrel, Jamie Brisick recounts the tale of the waverider who revolutionized pro surfing with man-on-man heats and then became a woman—having thought of herself as Marilyn Monroe all along. With this compassionate, funny, and wrenching book, Brisick has taken his impressive body of work to a new level, establishing himself as a fine observer of life's currents, on land, sea, and inside the heart."

— Deanne Stillman, author of *Twentynine Palms, Mustang*, and *Desert Reckoning*

"What a wild and wonderful and fascinating journey our lives can be! BECOMING WESTERLY stands as beautiful evidence of this—gorgeous proof of the ever-unfolding transformations many of us undergo—and Jamie Brisick brings these changes to vivid and heart-rending life. A sometimes-brutal book, every page is marked with care, affection, friendship, and pure honesty."

— William Lychack, author of *The Architect of Flowers*

"Whitman wrote, 'I contain multitudes,' and he might have had this book in mind. BECOMING WESTERLY is the story of surfing great, Peter Drouyn, and his subsequent transformation, via a sex change operation, into aspiring diva Westerly Windina. But it's also a tale of the writer, Jamie Brisick, and his efforts to understand what—for lack of a more specific term—it all means. In the process, this engrossing narrative raises a series of questions rather more profound than you might expect: Who are we? Where do we begin? Where do we end? Is there such a thing as destiny? Are we riding the wave or a part of it? And as with the best books, in the end it's our own lives we examine."

— Jim Krusoe, author of *Parsifal*

"Surfers are rightly proud of their tradition of rebellion and nonconformity, but when it comes to matters of sexuality and gender, surf culture is no better than the mainstream—and in some respects even worse. In BECOMING WESTERLY, Jamie Brisick has written a profound, astonishingly vivid, intimate portrait of one of the sport's true originals, and in a single stroke brought surfing out of the dark ages and into the light of the truly sublime."

— Thad Ziolkowski, author of *On a Wave*

"A strange, exhilarating, ultimately uplifting ride. Jamie Brisick is the perfect guide into the life of an amazing ninja-level surfer, provocateur, and diva."

— Matt Warshaw, author of *Encyclopedia of Surfing*

"Surf is beige. Never the act and not the characters but the representation. It is monochromatic, conservative, bland. Feathers are better left unruffled, I suppose, but son of a bitch, thank God for Jamie Brisick. He decided to write about an ex-pro surf legend that has decided to become a woman. BECOMING WESTERLY is, above all, a great story but it is a difficult story and Jamie tells it perfectly. Peter Drouyn/Westerly Windina is, at turns, inspiring, brave, massively selfish, narcissistic and Jamie never pulls a punch. He lets all the variables of an extremely complex person breathe. He ushers the reader in to a bizarre world and allows for multiple possible conclusions. And the way he paints the surf backdrop is amazing. The interviews, descriptions, historical and modern nuances…. It is journalistic art. If I were ever to become a woman, or male model or Vegas showman, I would want Jamie Brisick along for the ride. Shall we dance, darling?"

— Chas Smith, author of *Welcome to Paradise, Now Go to Hell*

"In BECOMING WESTERLY Jamie Brisick transports the reader deep into the fascinating journey of an iconic surf-champion, Peter Drouyn, who has decided to become a woman. Calling himself Westerly in his new identity, Peter/Westerly is a Willy Loman-like tragic hero, and Brisick captures the struggle—the highs and lows, the comedy and the sorrow—deftly mining a compelling, universal story that is ultimately about human nature. Superbly written, Brisick has crafted a beautiful book."

— Norman Ollestad, author of *Crazy for the Storm*

"What happens after the endless summer? BECOMING WESTERLY is what happens. Jamie Brisick has given readers one shaggy, tasty gift: not only the history of surfing, as seen from inside that raging, curling wave (quite an accomplishment in itself), but the more intimate struggle that comes from being alone with your aloneness. The transformation of Peter Drouyn—troubled narcissist, influential surfing genius—into wannabe starlet Westerly Windina is every bit as absorbing as it is frustrating, as charming as it is essential."

— Charles Bock, author of *Beautiful Children*

Becoming
Westerly

To Gisela Matta,
for lessons in love.
To Mom and Dad,
for lessons in life.

"A man who views the world the same at fifty as he did at twenty has wasted thirty years of his life."

—Muhammad Ali

"I'm selfish, impatient and a little insecure. I make mistakes, I am out of control and at times hard to handle. But if you can't handle me at my worst, then you sure as hell don't deserve me at my best."

—Marilyn Monroe

"She went into the movies. She's been there ever since."

—Hüsker Dü

PART ONE

A PERFORMER FOR ALL GENERATIONS

NOVEMBER 2012

"DO I LOOK ALL RIGHT?" ASKS WESTERLY WINDINA for what must be the fifth time in the last hour.

Hunched forward in seat 39F of Thai Airways flight 474, she looks vulnerable, shrunken. Her platinum blonde hair curls around her furrowed face. Her mascaraed, smoky eyes beg for validation. She wears white swing shoes, white hip-hugger capri pants, a frilly powder blue cardigan—the sort of outfit Marilyn Monroe might have worn on a Pan Am flight in the fifties.

"Stunning, Westerly. You look absolutely stunning."

"Aw, c'mon, Jamie. You can't just say it. You've got to look me in the eyes and mean it."

This is the thing about Westerly. She's insecure. She needs constant reassurance. And the more you feed it, the bigger her appetite grows. But it's more than that. It's a power play. It's one-upmanship. She's a spoiled Southern belle very purposely dropping her handkerchief in the mud and taking great delight in seeing me dive for it.

I gaze up from my book. "You look beautiful, Westerly."

She smiles warmly. "Oh, that was nice! That was like Peter O'Toole or Cary Grant. That was perfect."

The game's been going on for three years now. In 2009 I traveled to Australia to interview Ms. Westerly Windina, formerly Peter Drouyn, champion surfer. What started as a 5,000-word profile for *The Surfer's Journal* has swollen into the greatest love/hate rela-

1

tionship of my entire life—under the guise of a documentary film. Westerly is en route to Bangkok, where a certain scalpel-wielding Dr. Chettawut awaits her. I am, as she calls it, her "wingman."

She opens her purse and out spills a couple of drawers' worth of cheap cosmetics. A waft of perfumes that belong to fifty years ago hits me in the face.

"Can you get that?" she says of a tube of lipstick that is easily within her reach.

Without looking up I grab it off the floor, pass it to her.

When a stewardess hands her headphones, she pretends to be unable to find the plughole glaring at her from the inside of the armrest.

I help her with that, too.

Now she's humming along to whatever song's playing and rocking just enough to shoulder bump me and make it impossible for me to read.

We've yet to leave the ground and it feels like we've been traveling for ten hours.

A jingle comes over the speakers. First in Thai, then in English, a recorded, babyish female voice explains how to fasten seatbelts, where the emergency exits are located, how to strap on oxygen masks and life jackets. All of this is pantomimed by the porcelain-skinned stewardess standing at the end of our row.

"Look at that femininity," whispers Westerly. "Look at how graceful and delicate she is. That's what I keep trying to tell you, Jamie. A woman's touch is finer than 16,000 magic carpets from Aladdin's lamp! It can change the world."

A few minutes later the engines fire up and we barrel down the runway. The cabin vibrates, the overhead compartments quake. Westerly's sun-beaten, manicured hands clutch the armrest. Her ruby-red lips quiver slightly. Her eyes go glassy. As the plane angles skyward she wipes away a tear.

.

The trip almost didn't happen. Days before Nick, the director of photography, and I were scheduled to fly first to Brisbane, then on to Bangkok with Westerly, I called her from my home in New York to confirm our itinerary.

"Aw, look, Jamie," she said despondently, "I'm thinking I might put the surgery off for a bit."

"Why? What's happening?"

"Well, I've been trying to get a bloody answer out of you guys for months."

"An answer to what?"

"The showcase finale."

The idea of the showcase finale first surfaced in December 2011, when my co-director Alan White and I were in Australia shooting a sizzle reel of Westerly. A sizzle reel is a sort of teaser used to acquire funding for a film. While interviewing Westerly at her home she insisted on singing us a song. It was a slow, melodramatic version of "River of No Return," much of it delivered with eyes shut and hand on heart. When she finished we applauded. She proceeded to tell us her plans for the film's climax scene, in which she would "sing, dance and tell a few jokes" in front of a large audience. "We'll see," said Alan.

That *we'll see* snowballed into the showcase finale.

"The showcase finale is the most crucial element of the film. You've got to understand this, Jamie. The story is not about Peter. Peter's gone. Peter was a caterpillar who turned into a butterfly. And without a showcase finale, we're nowhere."

"Wait a minute, Westerly. Now you're misquoting yourself. Before it was 'Peter was a caterpillar, who turned into a butterfly, but she can't fly without her operation.' You've been obsessing over your operation for as long as I've known you. You've begged me to help you find someone to help you out financially. I do that, and now you tack on this showcase finale."

"This is my last hope, Jamie. This is for my son. Without a platform to showcase my talents I'll just be Peter with a vagina!"

She went on and on about the great stress she was under. I

told her to relax, that the film did not hinge on her surgery, that we were interested in her story regardless. She said she needed a definitive answer about the showcase finale. I told her I'd talk to the team and get back to her within twenty-four hours. That night she sent a group email to us Westerly filmmakers stating that "the showcase finale will reveal the resurrected goddess Westerly Windina magnified tenfold by her completion." She made us promise in writing that the showcase finale would happen. Then she sent a second email with a Microsoft Word attachment that went as follows:

The Westerly Windina SHOWCASE FINALE
Starring the new singing and comedy sensation:
WESTERLY WINDINA
See this amazing lady break
all the boundaries of live performance:
she's a new star for everyone:
a performer for all generations!
A vision and voice that will knock you out!
She will change you forever!

.

Westerly and I arrive into New Bangkok International, clear customs, and find Nick in the waiting area.

"Welcome, guys. Here, Westerly, let me grab that for you."

Thirty years old, born and bred on the Gold Coast, a surfer turned ace shooter, Nick Atkins is jovial, easygoing. He has a dark scruffy beard and a reassuring, rosy-cheeked smile. Most importantly, he and Westerly get along well.

We'd originally planned to all travel together, but when Westerly told us that she was seriously considering postponing her surgery, we made an executive decision and cancelled the Bangkok leg of our trip. When she changed her mind the following day it was too late; there was only one seat left on Westerly's flight, so

Nick had to fly a day earlier. Not only that, but her hotel had no vacancies.

The Bangkok night air is sweet and humid. We hail a taxi, zip through a maze of narrow lanes. On the main highway, in thick traffic, we pass ramshackle slums draped with laundry. Shadowy, bowlegged figures in shorts and T-shirts amble dangerously close to the road. Locusts of motorcycles buzz between cars.

Situated at the end of a long brick driveway, the Bangkok Rama Hotel is a white three-story building that looks generic, office-like. Our taxi driver pulls up in front of the entrance, hops out, opens the door for Westerly. She exits languorously, one foot at a time. Nick and I carry her bags across the tiled lobby to the front desk. Frayed maps and portraits of smiling monks decorate the pale pink walls. A cloth mandala hangs above a pair of old computers. The room smells vaguely of sewage.

Clad in a purple and pink uniform, the receptionist, Lamai, greets us with a stress-dissolving smile. We check Westerly in, walk her to the elevator.

"I have my debriefing tomorrow morning at ten," she says.

"You want us to join you?" I ask.

"Yes. That'd be nice."

"Okay. We'll call you when we wake up."

Nick and I say goodnight.

She gives us a scared-child look. "You boys aren't going to disappear on me, are you?"

.

The following morning we meet Westerly at her hotel, eat a hurried breakfast of fruit, yogurt and weak coffee from the buffet, and hail a taxi. Traffic is heavy. The streets bristle with shops and signage and street vendors.

"I can't wait to meet Dr. Chettawut," says Westerly, dossier in lap. She wears a candy-apple red skirt, white lace top, and black-and-white Chanel-style ballet flats. "I felt like I should dress up, in case he asks me for a dance. I sure wasn't going to show up looking like a bum. How can this Hollywood girl show up looking like a bum?"

"What exactly does this meeting entail?" asks Nick, camera trained on Westerly.

Westerly peers into a sequined hand mirror. She applies lipstick. "It's an obligatory consultation. I show him cardiovascular tests, a million blood tests, referential letters. My cholesterol was something like four out of ten—super, I guess."

The taxi driver pulls into a driveway. Flanked by a plumbing parts manufacturer and a satellite-dish retailer, Dr. Chettawut's brick facade is plain and windowless. Thai letters stripe the two-story building. Below them: DR. CHETTAWUT PLASTIC SURGERY CENTER.

We enter the spartan waiting room. Som, Dr. Chettawut's Thai assistant, rises from a wooden desk and shakes our hands. She is middle-aged, kind but formal, speaks perfect English. "No filming inside," she says.

Westerly takes a seat across from her. Som pulls out a series of documents and spreads them across the desk. Pointing with her pen, she takes Westerly through the details of the surgery. Nick and I loll on the couch, flip through Thai fashion magazines splashed with cheery models, take it all in.

As ordinary as the place looks, there is something vaguely sinister about it. Perhaps I know too much. Dr. Chettawut's facility is where both the surgery and convalescence take place. Westerly describes the surgery as "a sort of butterflying, like you'd do with a shrimp." Afterward, for at least a week, the patient is forced to lay supine, legs restrained in a spread-eagle position so as not to disturb "the sculpture." Peering down the tiled hallway at the double doors, I'm reminded of *The Shining*. I feel like little Danny on his Big Wheel pondering the door to Room 237.

After twenty minutes or so Westerly walks over. "Well, that was a piece of cake," she says.

"It says for the next three days I can eat broths and yogurt, but absolutely nothing solid. No pad Thai, no green papaya salad, none of that beautiful yellow curry over rice."

We're at a little outdoor café around the corner from Westerly's hotel, Westerly, Nick and I. It's high lunchtime, the place is buzzing. Westerly flips through the information packet that Som had given her.

"They have to make sure I'm completely empty. They're obviously concerned about infection—the geography of the whole thing makes it relevant. I'll have a catheter. They pack the vagina with ice, like tuna. Like a tuna catch in the North Sea." She giggles in a studied fashion. I can almost see her rewinding whatever Marilyn film, imitating her in the mirror.

A few feet from us is a glass display case full of roasted ducks. They're lined up in perfect symmetry, heads torqued painfully to the right. In the kitchen behind it a sweating chef chops whole chickens with a cleaver—whack! whack! whack!

A rotund, apron-clad lady comes over to take our order. She's elderly, gap-toothed. We speak not a single word of Thai. At the table next to us a group of workers in pale blue coveralls slurps down bowls of pinkish soup with various tendrils poking out. Their waitress arrives and distributes plates heaped with long strips of chicken atop a mound of rice and what looks like bean sprouts, red peppers, peanuts, coriander. It smells ridiculously good.

"Same," we say, pointing at their plates.

Westerly makes a bowl with her hands. "Broth," she says.

"No meat."

Somehow the waitress gets it.

Westerly shows us a page from her information packet. Item #7 shows a diagram of an enema. Item #8: Do not sit cross-legged or squat. "Chettawut's an artist," she says. "He does full vulva constructions."

The food arrives quickly. Nick's and my dishes, whatever they're called, are excellent. The soup is a coconut/fish mixture; the dark chicken meat is tender and smoky. Spicy, sweet and sour tumble across the tastebuds.

Westerly, on the other hand, grimaces with every spoonful. "This looks like the soup they gave Steve McQueen in *Papillon* when they pushed it in his cell."

After we finish eating Westerly goes back to her information packet. She reads us the harrowing details of the actual surgery. She looks up. "Oh, I almost forgot to tell you. Som said that I need to get a final evaluation before the surgery. I thought I only needed two—I saw these psychologists in Brisbane, one of them's a real specialist when it comes to gender dysphoria. But Som says I need three. She set up an appointment for tomorrow."

.

Nick and I wait in the lobby of Westerly's hotel. She returns from her evaluation in bright sundress, black faux-Dior sunglasses, face aglow.

"I had him laughing. It was, 'You're in the navy now!'" She giggles. "He took one look at me and he just knew. He said, 'Right, you're a prime candidate.'"

"That's great news," I say.

"Sometimes I get in a mode where everything feels just right. I just look and feel right." She removes her sunglasses, looks me square in the eye. "She's coming out of me, you know."

In an earlier interview I'd asked Westerly if she ever had doubts. "I've made myself have doubts," she said. "I've had to force myself to question it. But that's just it, that's how I know. I've had to force myself to see it from the male perspective, I've had to go backwards in time and cross back over that line. You see, I see everything from a woman's perspective now ... I've had nearly six years of knowing it can happen. I have never wavered from the fact that I just want to be completed."

For the next day and a half Westerly is radiant. In the trashy, gi-normous shopping center she tries on discount jeans, poses like a pin-up girl for Nick and me, bursts into a tango with the smiling salesgirl. Through the gardens near the Royal Palace she literally smells roses, chats up tourists. When Nick asks her to walk across a long footbridge that stretches over a busy intersection again and again and again so he can shoot various angles of it, she is happy to oblige.

"You should have seen Peter when he was here in '74," she offers as we amble through Patpong, the epicenter of Bangkok's red-light district. "He was in heaven!"

Music thumps out of go-go bars with names like "Bada Bing" and "Superpussy." Lingerie-clad girls hover under neon signs. Pot-bellied men drink beer in cafés.

"Peter was never satisfied with just one," she says with a Marilyn giggle. "He had to have two or three or even four. And the girls just loved him."

Westerly's affection for Peter comes in many forms. Most of the time it's wistful and forlorn. When she talks about his awkwardness, his pretending to be something he was not, she sounds like a mother remembering her deceased child. Always there is great love. I find this fascinating. It's as if Peter could not love himself as Peter, but hop across the gender gap, and with that distance and objectivity, the love gushes.

When we were shooting the sizzle reel Westerly took us through her wardrobe. "This is my evening dress," she said, holding up a pearl-colored cocktail dress, "if ever I'm asked out."

"What kind of guy would you like to date?" I asked her.

"Someone kind. He'd have to be a real gentleman . . . Someone who understands me." She paused, brought her hand to her chin.

"Someone like Peter."

(Later, in a separate conversation, she would say: "Peter was always looking for a princess, he wanted to find his princess. Unfortunately, the princess was me. I'm the princess that Peter always wanted but never met.")

.

On the third morning Westerly, Nick and I eat breakfast in the dining room of Westerly's hotel. In walks a butch and beefy man in dress and high heels. Her thinning ginger hair is combed forward. She looks at least Westerly's age. She clutches a black purse.

"We're all on deck," whispers Westerly.

She proceeds to tell us that the Bangkok Rama is part of the Dr. Chettawut SRS (Sexual Reassignment Surgery) package deal. You stay four or five nights at the hotel, go in for surgery at Chez Chettawut, convalesce there for roughly one week, then move back to the Bangkok Rama for a few days, where Dr. Chettawut's nurses do house calls.

On cue a svelte transgender woman saunters in. She's tall, wears a long, slinky peach-colored dress. Her face is lean and beautiful. She looks no older than thirty.

"I think she's French," says Westerly.

"Have you talked to her?"

"No, but I heard her talking to the receptionist."

The newcomer takes a seat on the other side of the room, as far as possible from the first woman. They are alone. They wear game faces.

"You're all here for the same thing. Why not at least say hi to each other?" I ask Westerly.

"Oh god no, Jamie. I don't want to talk to them."

At first I find this strange, but on second thought it makes perfect sense. Clearly there's a heavy psyche-up going on. They are about to say goodbye forever to their former selves. They're giving each other space.

.

Westerly spends a lot of time thinking about her future as an entertainer. Much of this thinking is done aloud. About a month before we came to Bangkok she, or rather Peter Drouyn, was invited to the fiftieth-anniversary celebrations for Surfing Australia, a government-funded organization that oversees the Australian Surfing Hall of Fame, into which Peter was inducted in 1991. At this red-carpet gala they will be naming Australia's Ten Most Influential Surfers. Peter has a good shot of making the list. Here's the email she sent back (to Andrew Stark, Surfing Australia CEO):

Dear Andrew,

Hope you are in fine spirits as I write this.

I have an entertainment segment ready to launch at the 50th Anniversary Surfing Awards ceremony.

I would like to be invited onto the stage under spotlight (from backstage if possible), in my gala outfit and with a large white birthday cake topped with 50 lit candles rolled in beside me, by two stewards, one either side of the trolley.

Then I will sing a special arrangement of the "Happy Birthday" song. I will sing that alone and then blow out the candles.

Then, after the hip-hip-hoorays! times three, all will fall quiet and I will sing my flagship song (won't tell you yet).

It would be gracious of you if you provided a Spanish guitarist to accompany me. He will sit on a stool beside me (standing with mike).

So there you have it: a "special" appearance by Westerly Windina—no fees asked!

This will help launch my "showbiz" career in this country.

Let me know ASAP if you find my offer to your liking.

Have a really good afternoon!

Sincerely,

Westerly Windina

·

"You've said many times that Peter is dead. Maybe you want to say a proper goodbye? We could do some kind of send-off."

Westerly smiles. "Oh, Jamie, that's a lovely idea. Peter always loved flowers."

"Golden hour'll be just sparkling on the river," adds Nick, consummate director of photography.

This is on the eve of her surgery. The three of us are seated on a leather couch in a Western-style café drinking weak coffee. Since we met up with her at the breakfast buffet a few hours earlier, Westerly has been all grins and giggles.

"I think I'll wear my slim-fitting red dress," she says.

At 3 pm we catch a taxi and make a beeline for the Chao Phraya River, Bangkok's largest waterway. Only it's less a beeline than a plod. Traffic is all honking horns and brake lights. Exhaust fumes are chokingly thick.

Clad in white high heels and red vintage sheath dress with black lace bra strap poking out at the shoulders, Westerly rides in the backseat. She holds a bouquet of white roses on her lap. She babbles on about her showcase finale.

"... a nice gentleman on the piano gets up and then the guitarist will sort of chime in on that composition of mine, and it will be all solid and tight. An old microphone, fifties-style. And a glittering gown, tight-fitting—"

"Can I ask you something for the camera real quick?"

"Sure, Jamie."

"Tomorrow's the big day. Are you anxious?"

"No. I'm calm. I'm blissful actually."

"By this time tomorrow you'll have an entirely new apparatus."

"And I'm over the moon about it!" Westerly laughs. "And it's not just there to look pretty. It'll be fully functional. It says in the little booklet that it might even be more sensitive than what's there now."

Hot sun stabs through the windows, casting Westerly in a dramatic amber glow. Her face looks leathery, grandma-ish. Cherry-red lipstick mottles her teeth. A motorcycle clips our rearview mirror and the elderly taxi driver curses in Thai. Nick points to the low sun and gives me a furtive, we're-going-to-miss-the-good-light look.

We arrive at the pier with not a minute to spare. Westerly and Nick, camera over shoulder, break into a trot. I lug backpacks, a tripod. The river is wide and mirror-smooth, a row of buildings and vestige of setting sun on the other side. Westerly stands at the water's edge. Her made-up face looks sad, almost clownish. Conscious of the camera, she bows her head, shuts her eyes, mutters something inaudible.

At that very moment a water taxi comes charging around the bend, aimed for the exact spot where we're perched. It's long and light blue and packed with tourists. Its wake chops the glassy water and rocks the floating pier, forcing high-heeled Westerly to bend her knees and extend her arms to keep from falling. Bobbing up and down, she looks like she's surfing. The water taxi pulls up inches from us, its leaf-blower drone blaspheming our private moment. Waves slosh onto the deck. Nick quickly lifts his gear to keep it from getting soaked. It's impossible not to think of that scene in *The Big Lebowski* in which Walter, with a Folger's coffee can doubling for an urn, commits Donny's "mortal remains to the bosom of the Pacific Ocean." A gust of onshore wind blows the ashes straight into the Dude's face. *"Everything's a fucking travesty with you, maaan!"*

We walk from the pier to a narrow lane packed with restaurants and shops. The night sky has a rose hue; the air is soft and humid. Smoke from a hundred street food vendors—pork broth, pad Thai, omelettes, shrimp, samosas—wafts cartoonishly up our nasal passages and insists that we eat. Immediately.

We find a little corner restaurant, take a seat at a picnic table under a blue plastic tarp. Nick and I eat crunchy green papaya salad and absurdly tasty *pla pao* (roasted fish stuffed with crushed lemongrass stalks, coated in a thick layer of salt, dipped in sweet and sour chili sauce).

"How good are the little prawns in the salad?" says Nick.

"I'm blown away by this fish!"

"You boys are just downright cruel," says Westerly, drooling over our plates, sipping coconut water through a straw.

After dinner we walk to the main boulevard to hail a taxi. Along the way we pass a shoe store advertising "Pimp Daddy Exotic Animal Shoes." The window display is a mixture of boots and shoes, along with a taxidermy snake, lizard and stingray.

"Can we have a quick peep?" asks Westerly.

Inside we marvel at the garish loafers and cowboy boots, one pair of which blends about five colors and four different animal skins. The salesmen wear suits, look straight out of a Jackie Chan movie.

"Peter would have loved these," says Westerly, pointing to a pair of shiny black ostrich-skin ankle boots.

We continue on. The boulevard whirls with taxis and cars and puttering vans and swarms of motorcycles that jostle between lanes and occasionally veer onto the footpath to get ahead. Lights flash. Horns honk venomously. Chaotic Bangkok is even more chaotic than usual. And of course it is. It's rush hour in the heart of downtown.

We have no luck hailing a taxi so we settle on a tuk-tuk—a three-wheeled motorized taxi. According to my guidebook, we are to hang on tightly to our possessions. Thieves prey on tuk-tuks. They slink up on motorcycles, snatch purses, duffel bags and cameras from unsuspecting tourists, then disappear into the traffic.

We pass shopping malls, trinket and T-shirt vendors, nondescript apartment complexes. Electrical wires crisscross the night sky. On a wide street beneath an expressway, which forms a concrete canopy overhead, traffic lets up, and we actually start moving. Hot pink taxis speed past. Wind whips through our hair.

Our tuk-tuk is bedecked with powder-blue vinyl seats, a dark blue ceiling, and chrome bars and poles to keep us from spilling out onto the street. A row of five interior lights flashes different colors, creating a cocktail-lounge effect. I smile at Westerly, her face turning from purple to orange to blue. She smiles back. Nick pulls out his camera, aims it at her. Backlit by headlights, her Marilyn hair looks angelically gossamer, like peroxide cotton candy. Her visage is wistful. She shuts her eyes, places a hand on her heart. Breathily, forcing Nick and me to lean in close to hear, she sings:

> *If you listen you can hear it call*
> *Wail-a-ree*
> *There is a river called The River of No Return*
> *Sometimes it's peaceful and sometimes wild and free!*
> *Love is a trav'ler on the river of no return*
> *Swept on forever to be lost in the stormy sea*

·

I wake on surgery morning to an email from Som. Dr. Chettawut, who we've been trying to pin down for an interview since we arrived in Bangkok, has agreed to see us an hour before Westerly's surgery.

Nick and I grab a taxi, race over to Westerly's hotel. We find her sitting at one of the ancient computers in the lobby.

"Ready for your close-up, Ms. Windina?" I joke.

She gives me a nervous smile, goes back to her screen.

"So we're going to have to leave a bit earlier, Westerly. Chettawut's going to give us an interview. We need to get there at eleven."

"I need to talk to you both," she says.

"Can we do it in the taxi?"

"No. Let's go up to my room."

Westerly stands. Behind her I catch a glimpse of the computer screen. It's open to a page on *The Guardian*'s website: Patient tells hearing she regrets sex change. We take the elevator up to her room. It's bright, spacious, almost a suite. A pair of Westerly's lace panties is draped over a chair.

"Sit down," she says. "What I have to tell you is, I think, going to have a big impact on the film."

I take a seat at a small table against the window. Nick unloads his backpack and tripod, sits on the bed. Westerly sits across from me. Her floral dress is bold and summery, but her face is demure, makeup-less. She has yet to do up her hair and the bald crown of her head is untypically exposed. She clears her throat, begins.

"Listen, fellas, I have a strategy for the Westerly showcase finale. I would go to the Surfing Awards. If I was called up, I would sing 'Happy Birthday,' which you'd obviously film. You would obviously film the clapping and the roaring and all the rest of it. Okay. If Peter was not invited onto the stage, and not included, Westerly Windina immediately walks out. But the showcase finale still goes on. You know, Stuff you all, here she is. I think the people who are disappointed that Peter wasn't in that top ten won't be disappointed when they see her showcase finale, you know? They'll say, 'Good, she got the last laugh.' So given that scenario, that scenario takes place whether or not I go ahead with the operation. No one will ever know. And the idea is, Has she had it? Or has she not had it? Right, as far as the movie's concerned we should keep it quiet. Because there's a big ending, a twist like nothing ever." She pauses. Inhales. "If in the event that I didn't have this operation, Peter will reappear. You see? He reappears in the end. The twist is: Westerly goes back to being Peter. And Peter just walks from the ocean with his board."

Westerly proceeds to tell Nick and me that she wonders if she's just kidding herself. She says that seeing those "other apes" (referring to her fellow transgender hotel guests) makes her wonder if she's not just like them, if at age sixty-three it might be too late in life to become a woman. I've never seen her so vulnerable.

"What would you do if you were in my shoes?" she asks me.

I tell her that there are two choices. One is totally irreversible; the other is not. "If you're having doubts, why not put the surgery on hold for now? We support you with whatever you want to do."

Nick seconds the motion.

Westerly rants her doubts about the surgery, about "those apes who are just kidding themselves." She says something that is downright homophobic. Westerly insists that Peter was never homosexual, vehemently denies that he ever had any homosexual urges. Yet she's told me more than once that, post-surgery, she hopes to have a relationship with a man. I wonder how much thought she's given to the realities of this, wrapping her arms around a hairy, muscled body, razor stubble, a hard penis.

"Have you ever thought that you might just be gay, but you're sort of trying to leapfrog your way over to the other gender to get out of it?" I ask.

Westerly grimaces. "No straight man ever likes to be called gay."

"I've had people wonder if I'm gay for most of my adult life and it's never bothered me."

"Oh, Jamie. That's just nonsense."

At that moment the phone rings. It's Som, Dr. Chettawut's assistant, wondering why we haven't shown up for the interview. Westerly tells her that we're still at the hotel, that she's having doubts about the surgery, and that we're on our way.

We taxi it over to Dr. Chettawut's. Som greets us at the door. Westerly sits down with her at her desk while Nick and I wait on the couch. Westerly wears a frown that covers much more than just her face. Her shoulders slump. She grasps nervously at her handbag. Even her comb-over takes on a new hue of desperation, her shiny scalp poking through her diaphanous hair.

I pick up snippets—*"I just have so many doubts." "I'm not sure this is the right time." "I woke up with this voice in my head telling me to pull back."*

Som speaks quietly, confidentially. "We ask that our patients be not one hundred percent but two hundred percent sure. If there's even one per cent of doubt, we suggest they hold off."

Westerly follows Som down the hall and through the double doors to talk with Dr. Chettawut. They return about fifteen minutes later and sit back down at the desk. Som produces a document. Westerly signs it. It's the formal cancellation of her surgery.

We exit Dr. Chettawut's with a relieved and giddy Westerly.

She wants first a coconut water, as soon as possible, then lunch. We get her coconut water from a vendor across the street and catch a taxi back to the Bangkok Rama. Westerly drops her gear in her room, returns. We walk to the same café we ate at a couple of days earlier. The gap-toothed waitress recognizes us. So does the sweating, hacking chef. We take a seat. Next to us a family eats big plates of chicken and steaming vegetables over rice, the smell of ginger and lemongrass floating into our faces. When our waitress arrives Nick and I point to their dishes. She laughs, writes on her notepad. A group of young businessmen walk past. Westerly lights up.

"Oh, those boys were looking at me with such loving looks. I must stay Westerly, there's no doubt about that." She orders noodles and iced tea from our waitress and continues. "You know, that's just what I mean, that boy gave me a lovely look. He was looking at me like. . ." She nods her head in the affirmative. "So, I know I look all right. That's fine, everything's fine, it's just that, no operation just yet."

I ask what aside from the trans folk in the hotel prompted her to pull out.

"Just before I woke up this morning I had this dream, and at the end of it someone yelled out, *'We need good men. We need good men.'* I woke up and I thought about that, *We need good men*, and I thought, *Yeah, the world certainly needs some good men.*"

She interprets this dream not as a sign to stay male but for "Westerly to promote good men." She says she wants to "wait to become completely feminized." She'll see how the showcase finale goes. If it's a success then she'll go ahead with the surgery.

This last part turns my stomach. From the get-go we filmmakers have agreed that we'd approach this project in a fly-on-the-wall manner, following Westerly through her metamorphosis, whatever that entails. Her pushing us into filming her showcase finale turns the movie inside out. We entered into this believing that Westerly had suffered gender dysphoria her entire life, that her "completion" was essential. Now it hinges on audience response?

Lunch arrives and Westerly takes her first bite of solid food in five days. "Mmmm." She shuts her eyes. "This is heaven food." With Nick's camera trained on her she eats in showy fashion, giggling between bites, moaning as she chews.

"I'm glad the decision went right to the last second possible before the surgery," she says. "It's meaningful, very meaningful, that I was not sure right to the very last. It would have been different if I'd made up my mind three or four or five days before. That would have been too easy.

"It's a bit like a sniper, dare I make this analogy, where the sniper holds up the rifle, just about to shoot, then drops the rifle, not certain about it. And then sees a clear vision and puts the rifle up again." Westerly enacts this: one eye closed, the other aimed at some imaginary target across the room, hand gripping barrel, trigger finger cocked, dropping the rifle with furrowed brow, raising it with resolve. "And then he's just about to shoot the rifle and, 'Not now. Not now. Maybe tomorrow.'"

She turns to Nick's camera. "That's exactly how it happened with me. So it means I'm not finished as a sniper. I'm not finished as a hunter. This transition still goes forward. It still goes on. It's just going to take a bit longer."

.

There's Westerly pretending to be Marilyn at a press conference, a pack of journalists hanging on her every word. Then there's the person sitting across the table from me—scared, vulnerable, trying to convince herself of this newly arrived-at truth. Most of the time there's a clear distinction between these two Westerlys, but in this case she drifts between both—her artifice not strong enough to veil her real feelings, her real feelings needing a sheen, a luster, some kind of coating.

I too drift between roles: sometimes the director/interviewer, other times a genuine friend and support. We've gotten to know each other dangerously well, WW and me.

"What does Westerly want?" I ask.

"Westerly wants to showcase all those abilities that Peter couldn't, such as in the entertainment field, performing arts. In the same way Peter rode his surfboard, the only way he could express his skills was by the balance of a wizard. He was able to put a little bit of show business into his surfing. I suppose you could call him a showbiz-type surfer, a very powerful one. 'Cause even in showbiz you've got to be powerful, you can't be a wussy. So he did use part of the skills he possessed, skills that perhaps a little girl in him possessed before that. So I'm going to expose those skills at last. And I've preserved—Peter preserved himself for years waiting for something to happen, and now it's happened, and we've got our first opportunity coming up at the showcase finale, where Peter can finally showcase all those beautiful skills without fear and panic attacks. See, I don't have any of those. So we're all systems go. We're going to show the world what we can do. Not just ride a surfboard; that's a fraction of what we can do."

I ask what she is doing to make these dreams come true and she says that she's training, practicing her singing and playing keyboards. She says her "producers"—us—have agreed to her showcase finale and that this has been a source of relief.

"I can relax more, I can evolve as a female more naturally without stress. I'd like to have everything done at once. That's what I'm thinking about right now, I'm thinking about how I'm going to look when I have the money to do everything I want to do, and have a career in entertainment, and include my son in that, too. Because he's a creative guy. He loves movies and music, just like typical Drouyns. I'm preparing myself mentally and physically for the showcase."

I have to ask: "What if the showcase is not the giant success you hope it will be?"

"Well, we tried, didn't we?"

"Really?"

"If I'm given the support that I hope I'll get I don't think there is going to be any problem in getting managers or agents. I mean, all one has to do is to ring a manager or an agent and they'll take you on. I'm looking for someone who can see in me the kinds of skills that can grow into something that audiences really want to see, you know? So I'm not even thinking about people going, *No, no, no, you're not for us;* I'm not even thinking about that. And I think that's a very negative approach anyway. That's never been Peter's style or my style. And Peter did prove that he was a good actor, too, at several stages. Because Peter tried to launch his entertainment career but his persona prevented him, his mind. Imagine if he could have exposed his musical song and dance skills. And now it's Westerly who's going to expose those skills. But give me a chance, for god's sake. That's all I'm asking. If my producers give me a decent chance and support me and have belief in me, there's not a problem about the future, and that's when we will have the operation. And that's when everything will just be roses. Yellow roses."

.

As the afternoon progresses she becomes less and less Westerly and more and more Peter. Not Peter the surf star. That bursting confidence he felt, that sense of boundless possibility, is perhaps the seed, the vestigial seed, that gave birth to Westerly. I'm referring to has-been Peter, the Peter who felt kicked to the curb, the Peter who'd lost all hope.

It starts when we pick her up to go to dinner. She meets us in the hotel lobby with a defeated posture, hugless. The girly clothes she'd been sporting the entire trip are replaced by the jeans and T-shirt outfit she favors on the days she sees her son, Zac—"so I don't blow him out." She's a hurler of complaints: about the construction work going on in her hotel, about the credit card she's maxed out or her bank has frozen or whatever.

It gets worse when the taxi driver drops us off a few blocks away from the restaurant we're looking for. *"My feet hurt." "You guys are walking too fast." "You haven't even complimented me on my new barrette."* She begins walking even slower, complaining even more. The little infrastructure we'd created—Westerly diva one minute, damsel in distress the next; Nick and I her steadfast appeasers—has crumbled.

I feel a sense of failure. I'd never thought of gender reassignment surgery as a put-your-money-where-your-mouth-is thing, a proof of one's sincerity, but given the hundreds of times she'd talked about her need for "completion," given that this was the center around which my entire relationship with Westerly revolved, I couldn't help but feel I'd invested years and money and mental energy on a fraud.

.

Dinner starts with a succulent green papaya salad followed by a saltcrusted baked fish with sprigs of lemongrass and other herbs I can't quite identify poking out of it. It's buttery, melts in the mouth, each stab of the fork releasing a kiss of delicious scents. The restaurant is on a busy corner. Old bowlegged ladies pushing carts waddle past. Uniformed school kids point and giggle at the display case full of live fish. It's a glorious Bangkok night, the air balmy, the sky clear and happy.

Westerly moans and bellyaches her way through all of it. *"My bank card's not working." "You guys are barely paying attention to me." "Smells like a friggin' toilet."* Her hands turn ungainly. Her elbows clunk the table. Her head becomes a burden to her slouching back and shoulders. A scowl consumes her face. Her voice takes on a husk and bitterness. It's as if she no longer has the energy to play Westerly.

I lose my patience. If she'd just been honest with herself I'd have wrapped my arms around her and done all I could to make her feel less alone. But the blaming and lashing out is comically childish. To give her an ounce of commiseration would be contributing to the self-deception that, to me, is the root of her disenchantment. I do not open the door for her when Nick hails a taxi to take us home. That she has to reach out and do it herself elicits a silent treatment that hangs thick on the ten-minute drive back to the Bangkok Rama. Cars whir past. Motorcycles whine by. We are on the opposite side of the street from Westerly's hotel, and to turn around and pull into the driveway means going another half-mile down the busy street, and another half-mile back. Our driver pulls over. "Bangkok Rama," he says, nodding towards the hotel.

Just up the footpath from us, clad in lingerie and slutty dresses, about a half-dozen go-go girls sprawl across a row of benches in front of a bar. They resemble a streak of leopards lazing under neon lights, limbs curled and stretched, paws adorned with stilettos and shiny nail polish. I'd never seen Westerly get catty. In fact she was always the first to praise striking femininity. But in this mood she's worked herself into, the scene to our left is abhorrent. It's nothing she says, just her refusal to so much as glance in their direction. Nick, up front, hops out, opens her door, and escorts her across the street and into her hotel.

He returns with an exasperated shake of the head. He whips open the door, almost roaring, "I need a fuckin' beer, mate!"

.

Patpong feels less like a red-light district than a theme park version of a red-light district. Girls in skimpy dresses make kissy faces from a shadowy doorway. A spiky-haired guy in a silver suit tries to drag us into a club called Gold Fingers—"My bar, big bar, young girls, I show you." The road is lined with go-go bars advertising sex shows. Right down the center of it is a long row of souvenir shops, adding tourists to this otherwise X-rated scene. Honeymooners amble alongside packs of blood-gorged frat boys with faux-hawks. Families complete with kids clutching stuffed animals sip Cokes no more than ten feet from a sign that reads:

PUSSY PLAY PING-PONG
PUSSY SMOKE CIGARETTE

PUSSY SING HAPPY BIRTHDAY
PUSSY EAT WITH CHOPSTICK
PUSSY SIGN AUTOGRAPH

We find a corner bar thumping with music and flashing neon lights. A waft of thick air—body odor, stale beer, a sudden flash of all my worst hangovers—punches us in the face. Nick and I grab a couple of frothy Singhas and find a booth in the back.

On small, circular tables with poles poking up from the center, bikini-clad girls with heavily made-up faces dance. Some are all spread-eagles and inversions. Others just shuffle, as if bored or suffering stage fright. In their nosebleed heels they somehow manage not to kick over the drinks. More working girls, these ones less overt in denim shorts and tank tops, move from lap to lap. Joan Jett's "I Love Rock 'n' Roll" blares. A Hong Kong mafioso-looking guy—sunglasses, pinstripe suit and tie, chunky gold rings and wristwatch—holds court at a table of three girls, one under each arm, the third refilling his whisky glass.

Then, just as we're getting comfortable, just after a full-lipped woman at the bar blows Nick a kiss, the music stops, the house lights come on, and the go-go girls all disappear down a dark hallway. A trio of husky men in red polo shirts comes out and quickly, like they've done this a hundred times before, removes a bunch of tables and chairs at the center of the room. In their place they bring out rubber poles and ropes. A pair of muay Thai fighters in shiny shorts emerges from the hallway, dancing, shadowboxing, throwing kicks. In a matter of minutes the ring is set up and the fighters are going at it with heaving grunts and sweat flying off their foreheads.

I'm reminded of something one of my surfer pals once said to me: "We men are simple creatures. We want to either fuck or fight."

.

"I've made the biggest mistake of my life."

These are Westerly's first words when we greet her in the lobby of the Bangkok Rama. She wears jeans and a white blouse. Dark sunglasses hide her eyes. A scowl mars her face. Her voice bristles with determination. "I've rung Som. I've told her I need to talk to Dr. Chettawut. They're sending over a car."

It's a bright, hot morning. The cacophony of honking horns and food vendors pushing carts down the slow lane take on a Groundhog Day tinge. Sitting bolt upright in the backseat, Westerly is uncharacteristically taciturn. Her orange cardigan—"Just like Marilyn's!"— is bunched in her lap along with her black handbag. She stares pensively out the window.

As we near Chettawut's she tells Nick and me that she wants us to wait outside. "I'm just going to walk in there, hat in hand, and explain that I was anxious, and distressed, and that I want to go ahead with the operation."

She's in there for a good half hour. As we wait out front, a barefoot monk in saffron robes walks past. He smiles at us with a serenity that seems 10,000 miles away from the rollercoaster we've been riding.

Westerly exits with a broken look.

"How did it go?" I ask.

"I don't think it's that good."

"What did they say?"

"They said you've made a decision and it's cancelled. Som's going to talk to Dr. Chettawut and they're going to let me know at the hotel."

In the taxi Westerly relapses into last night's vitriol—all of it aimed at Dr. Chettawut. At the lunch buffet at the Bangkok Rama, she reaches a point of absurdity. Giggling, she says, "It's a tragic irony. It just follows my whole life. That's what's happened to me for years and years. I've got a monkey on my back. I can't get it off. It always ends in disaster."

"What do you think would change that?" I ask.

"Money. Just money. Money buys anything. Well, if you don't have the money you don't have gender reassignment surgery, it's as simple as that."

Her arms are folded, her lips press tightly together.

"I'm going into a black hole that I thought I was just about out of." She raises her hands to her ears as if trying to muffle a noise only she can hear. "Right now I feel like getting a knife and just cutting it off. I mean, to me it's totally separate from me but it's attached. I don't even like looking at it. I don't like looking at it. I don't like looking at it—not for a long time."

.

Westerly gets the news from Som: Dr. Chettawut will not be doing her surgery. But there's a seed of hope. Years ago, when Westerly was first exploring gender reassignment surgery, she'd corresponded over email with a surgeon at Yanhee Hospital here in Bangkok. She'd mentioned this in the taxi and over lunch. Now that Chettawut has officially turned her down, all she can think about is Yanhee Hospital.

"I think we should go straight there," she says.

"Don't you want to call first?" I ask.

"No."

She heads up to her room, returns a few minutes later.

"I've rung Som and told her that I'll be stopping by to pick up all my documents. We'll go there then straight on to Yanhee Hospital. Let's go!"

If the Westerly of last night was a glimpse of the embittered and hopeless Peter Drouyn, then the Westerly that springs to life here is a glimpse of Peter the 1970 Surfer of the Year, Peter the founder of method surfing, Peter the visionary who would change competitive surfing forever. She walks with resolve, a determined glint in her eyes. Rather than wait for Nick and me to hail a taxi, as she's done the entire trip, she steps off the curb and does it herself.

A hot pink taxi pulls over. "Welcome to my taxi," says the driver through the open window. "My name is Chan."

We climb in. Chan is a slight, round-faced man with slicked-back black hair. He smells of Old Spice or Brylcreem or a combination of the two.

Westerly hands him a couple of crumpled pieces of paper—one with Dr. Chettawut's address, the other with Yanhee Hospital's. Chan points to the Yanhee piece of paper. "Famous hospital," he says.

There's not a lot of talk in the car. Westerly exudes faith and dignity. She holds her chin about an inch higher than she did on the last couple of taxi rides. I am wondering if Som and Dr. Chettawut suspect why we so urgently need this paperwork. Do the surgeons talk among themselves? I imagine an online chat room for SRS doctors in Bangkok, the name "Westerly Drouyn aka Westerly Windina aka Peter Drouyn" flashing in red.

Chan is a savvy driver, darting from lane to lane, snatching every little open space, nearly rear-ending the car in front of us in order to make it through yellow lights. When we arrive at Dr. Chettawut's, Westerly hops out, marches through the door. She returns two minutes later, a stack of documents in her hand, a hopeful smile on her face.

She gets into the car, slams the door behind her. "Yanhee Hospital," she says. "And step on it."

Bangkok's streets are choked with traffic at all hours of the day and night. The alternative is the expressway—expensive tolls, but much quicker. We take that option, Westerly and Nick in the back, me riding shotgun. The expressway is elevated. To our left, a cluster of high-rises reaches towards the muted sky; to our right, a sprawl of residential buildings. Tableaus of Bangkok daily life: a team of uniformed school kids chases a soccer ball down a sun-scorched field, an elderly man in a singlet smokes a cigarette on a balcony, a crew of workers spreads wet concrete around the third floor of a skeletal building-in-progress.

Westerly holds her purse against her chest. She stares out the window anxiously, longingly, the light emphasizing her every crease and wrinkle. She starts with a barely audible hum, then softly sings the lyrics:

BECOMING WESTERLY

I lost my love on the river and for ever my heart will yearn
Gone, gone for ever down The River of No Return

ME AND PETER,
WESTERLY AND ME

THOUGH I'M ON SPARRING TERMS WITH WESTERLY Windina, I never actually met Peter Drouyn. He was before my time. I started surfing in the late seventies, when the sport was just beginning to shed its dropout, drug-addled reputation and step into an era of staunch professionalism. Aussies dominated. My heroes were Cheyne Horan from Bondi, Wayne "Rabbit" Bartholomew from the Gold Coast, and Barton Lynch from Manly. My best friend, Jeff Novak, three years my senior, had spent a few months surfing his way up and down the New South Wales and Queensland coasts. Hyperbolically, with a bad Aussie accent and hip and hand flourishes that looked more porn than surf, he described a dream world of perfect spiraling waves and wild larrikins who "love to get on the piss and take off their clothes." At the awards presentation for Bondi's ITN (In the Nude) club contest, freckle-faced "Spot" Anderson hopped on stage naked and crash-tackled event winner Steve "Blackie" Jones. At the Newport Plus Boardriders Fancy Dress party, Jeff told me, Brad "Boomie" Stubbs "climbed on top of a Kombi and pulled a spit the winkle over an entire parking lot full of people."

"What's a spit the winkle?" I asked.

"Spit the winkle," he said in a tone that suggested I should know these things. "Garden hose to the ass. Turn it on. Fill up the tank. Blow the whole thing out."

"Wait. *What?*"

"Your ass can hold like a gallon of water. You fill up with a garden hose, put your pants back on, then, when the timing's right, pull 'em down, bend over, and blow it out like a giant fire hose. Funniest shit you've ever seen."

Novak's Australia tales came right around the time I started entering contests. In 1980 the National Scholastic Surfing Association (NSSA) was taken over by a pair of Aussies. Peter Townend was the 1976 world champion. Ian Cairns had a masochistic big-wave streak. Townend and Cairns were nothing like the Aussies Novak described. In fact, they were railing against those very types. Their mission was to clean up surfing's dubious image and make it as big as tennis or golf. "Their whole trip," as one of my unruly surf bros put it, "is to get surfing on a Wheaties box."

And so the NSSA national team was comprised of the most goody-two-shoes surfers in the sport's history. They brushed, flossed and showed up to contests promptly at 6.30 am, hair perfectly combed, matching red, white and blue tracksuits tucked neatly into their Ugg boots. They got high marks in school. Their mothers cut the crusts off their sandwiches. They were the antithesis of what had drawn me to surfing in the first place.

In flagrant, unpatriotic rebellion, Jeff Novak, my brother Steven and I celebrated "Aussie nights." Armed with cans of Foster's, Midnight Oil blaring on the stereo, we pored over *Tracks, Surfing World* and *Line Up.* These Australian magazines were far more perverse than their American counterparts. Topless women, purple-haired bud, four-letter words and aquamarine, tubing waves splashed their pages, creating a fantasy land into which I wanted to swan dive. It was on one of these nights that my future became clear: I would be a pro surfer.

It was also on one of these nights that I first encountered Peter Drouyn. He wore nothing but underwear, ripped torso slathered in ketchup, fists raised King Kongishly in the air. He glared ferociously from the page. "I'm going to kill or be killed!" read the caption. He was calling out four-time world champion Mark Richards. They were going to duke it out in a one-on-one specialty event called The Superchallenge.

I turned pro in 1986. For five years I traveled on the world tour, always reaching for the big results, but more often getting KO'd by the round of forty-eight and surrendering to whatever mischief my fellow middling pros got up to.

When my career abruptly ended in 1991 I started writing for surf magazines. I did Q&As, profiles, contest reports, travel pieces. It was around 1994, driving away from an interview with yet another myopic, white-bread twenty-year-old whiz kid, that it hit me: These guys' gift to the world is what they do in the water. But they have absolutely nothing to say. If I was going to sleep on couches and subsist on downwards of $20,000 a year, I at least wanted to feel like I was growing and learning something new. I shifted my focus to more mature surfers. But I found that equally unfulfilling. Ex-pros typically live in the past. Surfing is all-consuming. It sucks up the university years; it makes it impossible to be away from the ocean for even just a few days. It drops its brightest stars off a cliff at age thirty-five. So they trade on their "legend" status—doing appearances, competing in masters events, milking their sponsors for $2,000 a month. And often the more "legendary" the surfer, the more shackled to his persona.

It's ironic, really. The 101s of surfing—fighting stance, bent knees, fluidity, improvisation—are rarely applied to even the greatest surfers' terrestrial lives. They calcify. They grow bitter. They grimace under dark sunglasses. Of course my disappointment with my fellow ex-pros was a mirroring thing. As a surf writer, I too was trading on my former glory. I vowed to expand myself beyond the blue curtain. I got philosophical: Surfing is dress rehearsal. Waves are metaphors. Like tadpoles turning into frogs, the evolved surfer must be able to leave the beach and walk through life with bent knees, fighting stance, fluidity and an innate sense that there are no right edges or hard ground, that all is in flux.

I moved to New York.

When I heard about Peter Drouyn metamorphosing into Westerly Windina I was instantly fascinated. When I phoned to ask if I could write a profile of her for *The Surfer's Journal* she was suspicious.

"The surf media has tried to make me into a laughingstock," she said.

It was true. The surf magazines and websites seemed more interested in witty headlines ("The Greatest Switchfoot of the Century," "Dickless") than getting to the heart of the story. They painted her as a freak and a narcissist.

Westerly agreed to the profile. We met at an Italian trattoria near her home on the Gold Coast. She sashayed through the door in white blouse, red bolero jacket and black slit skirt. Her ruby-red lipstick glimmered in the track lights; her ballerina flats clacked on the tiled floor. From a distance she looked like a blonde bombshell. From up close, someone's grandma. She offered a limp-wristed hand. "I'm Westerly," she said, in a breathy, put-on voice.

Before we ordered drinks, before the waiter had even brought us water, she folded her hands together, cleared her throat and delivered her speech.

"This is the unfolding of someone experiencing a new existence. I've been plucked and put into a new dimension. This is actually something that has come and hit me and said, 'You're ready. You're ready to enter this new space and time and there's a mission for you in all this.' It sounds weird, I know. I keep saying to people, 'It's not intentional.' This girl is just—wow! She's out there, but she's real. And I don't want to get out of it. And I can't get out of it."

Westerly took a breath and collected herself. She sat with her back straight, elbows off the table. From her sequined clutch purse she pulled out a vintage hand mirror. Pawing her hair and pursing her lips, she said, "How do I look?"

"You look great."

"It's not easy around here," she said, nodding to the room. Our fellow diners were a mixture of white-collar businessmen, manicured housewives and old ladies sipping coffee. "Australia is such an insensitive, backwards-thinking culture. If you're ambitious, if you have big ideas, if you're out of the ordinary, they just want to chop you down." She shook her head despondently. "Peter was an awkward misfit. He had to do it all himself when he wasn't really a fighter or a swearer or a beer drinker. His life was a lie."

I tactlessly asked if she'd had the surgery.

Westerly shrugged, gave me a look that said, *You poor vanilla man trapped in your black-and-white thinking.* "Let's just say that you're getting around as a girl who was a boy. You're dressing up as a girl because you know genuinely that you're a girl. So it really doesn't matter if you're walking around with testicles and a penis. It's tantamount to the testicles and penis being foreign to you. *They shouldn't have been there! It shouldn't be there!* And you've got to get them off as soon as possible. It's like a leech that has gone into your body and you're trying to rip it out but half of it's stuck. You don't want it there. It's foreign." She took a sip of water. "So if you take that thought through, it really doesn't even matter if you're walking around as a girl with penis and testicles. If you know you're a girl, and you've got the operation coming, so what? Yeah, you're a girl anyway."

Westerly's emotions were right on the surface. It was like watching clouds gather and pass. I asked her when the transformation happened. She launched into an elaborate story about a wipeout in the surf that left Peter with a concussion. "It was just bursting out of me. It was as if the suffering just couldn't continue. And the moment I started believing I was a girl my body started to change. I went from a square gorilla to long-legged, slender. The hips are higher, the bum has lifted right up. The doctors can't believe it!"

"Could you ever imagine yourself going back to Peter?"

"I think about it sometimes. No, absolutely not. It would be a fall back into a very deep hole. Peter was meant to be a girl." A smile trembled across her face. "Peter was a caterpillar who turned into a butterfly named Westerly Windina."

"Who is Westerly Windina?"

"Westerly Windina is a person who has been placed inside Peter Drouyn. She's taken over his body. Westerly has left behind Peter's fears. Westerly—she's a comedian, she's a singer. Westerly has a new life. I've been resurrected!"

"You keep speaking of Peter Drouyn in the past tense. Is he gone for good?"

"He's gone. He's actually ..." She pointed a finger heavenwards. "I think he's up there with Mum and Dad."

·

Our meeting concluded with Westerly showing me her walk. Across the street, in a grassy park with a winding concrete footpath, she strutted as if on a catwalk, *clack clack clack.* "One more," she insisted, as I checked my digital photos. I had the sense that she was rehearsing for something, that this was only the beginning. I drove away with more questions than I'd arrived with.

My post-interview research only confused things. "It's bullshit," said Hawaiian Randy Rarick, who has known Peter for over thirty years. "I remember when he showed up at the Stubbies reunion in high heels and lipstick. I asked him straight out, 'What's this about?' He basically admitted it was all an act."

"When you turn sixty you become invisible to the opposite sex," said Westerly's lifelong friend Mal Chalmers. "Peter always did well in that department. He was a full-on Casanova. He craved the attention. 'Westerly' is a way to keep feeding that beast."

"Peter was a showman par excellence," said surf writer Nick Carroll. "Westerly might be his greatest performance ever."

EN WAS THE LAST TIME
U GOT GOOSE BUMPS?

BELONG

- AG
- HEI
- WA
- SHO

PART TWO

THE EXPLORER

SURFING ARRIVED IN AUSTRALIA BY WAY OF A gentlemanly act. In 1912, Manly surf lifesaver Cecil Healy was invited to the Stockholm Olympics. Hailed as Australia's fastest swimmer, Healy looked forward to a showdown with Hawaiian Duke Kahanamoku, who held the world record in the 100-yard freestyle. But when Healy stepped on the blocks his rival was nowhere to be found. Duke, it turned out, had been given the wrong race time. Officials were about to disqualify him but Healy spoke up, suggesting they wait for him to arrive. Duke won the gold; Healy won the silver. So began a lifelong friendship.

Two years later Duke was invited to Australia by the New South Wales Swimming Association. By the time he arrived in Sydney the First World War had started, and Healy was setting off to France to do his duty. Staying at the Boomerang Camp at Freshwater Beach, Duke carved himself a board at a nearby sawmill and paddled out for the first time on Christmas Eve. A crowd gathered on the beach. They were astonished by this walk-on-water style of surfing. News of Duke's demonstration made the papers. He was asked for an encore.

On January 10, 1915 the surf was bigger, and so was his audience. The surf lifesavers offered to take him out to the waves via boat. Duke found this funny. He paddled out and, dazzling the crowd with his statuesque style, rode all the way to the sand. After an hour or so he asked for a volunteer. Fifteen-year-old Isabel Letham of Chatswood raised her hand. First prone, then on her knees, then standing, then riding gloriously on Duke's shoulders,

Letham became Australia's first surfer.

"Like going over a cliff," she said of dropping into a wave.

Duke spent three months on the east coast of Australia. From Coolangatta to Melbourne he gave surf demonstrations. When he went back to Hawaii he left behind boards. A surf culture was born.

•

Westerly's earliest memories are of Peter at the beach—building sandcastles as a toddler, dodging the shore break as a kindergartener, training with the nippers at the Broadbeach Surf Life Saving Club as a young boy. One day during Christmas holidays in 1958, nine-year-old Peter saw a couple, tanned and towheaded, in the parking lot. From their caravan the guy pulled out a longboard. He trotted past Peter on the squeaky sand. He exuded something cool, something that felt almost dangerous. Peter followed him. He dashed out into the glassy waves, paddled out to the break, and proceeded to ride waves.

Peter was familiar with the lifesaving boards from the SLSC, typically paddled prone, occasionally on knees, but he'd never seen proper stand up surfing, and he'd never seen it gliding across the green face of a wave, arms outstretched, a kind of flying. Watching from the shallows, he cheered the surfer on as he rode regally to shore.

Westerly giggles as she remembers little Peter's instant connection. "He asked him for a go on it. Pete was right upfront, cheeky, and would ask anybody anything."

The surfer started to give him a verbal tutorial, but before he could finish Peter was on his belly, stroking, stroking, peering over his shoulder at the rising mound, stroking. The wave lifted him up from behind and dropped him down a whooshing slope of water. The board teetered from side to side as Peter used his hands to crawl up to his feet. He stood with arms outstretched, just as he'd seen the surfer do, legs in a bent-knee side stance, not unlike a boxer's. Iridescent water—turquoise, emerald—streaked past. Spray tickled his ankles. A yelp of giddy joy hung in his stomach, the kind you get when you drive at high speed over a rise in the road. He heard whoops of approval from the surfer. He soared and soared and soared, time suspended, until the white wash ramped him onto shore, the board's fin digging into the softness. He stepped off onto the sand. He resisted the urge to bow.

For the next half hour or so he surfed, each ride better than the one before, his sense of confidence and command growing. He was a natural, the older surfer told him so.

That night he lay in bed, buzzing, his rides replaying in his head. His arms were sore, his hips felt stretched and sated, his legs felt longer. His skin was baked warm from the sun. He saw the nose of the hardwood board mowing through the iridescence, water spattering off it. He felt like a great explorer captaining a ship, a Cook or a Magellan or a Columbus.

.

Born June 30, 1949, the younger of two boys, Peter grew up in the sleepy little beach town of Surfers Paradise. There were no high-rises back then, just small cottages, a corner pub, a zoo, a penny arcade on Cavill Avenue, a Chiefies hamburger shop and a neighborly vibe.

"Everyone knew each other," remembers Westerly.

Peter's father, Victor, owned His/Hers, a clothing store. He was boat captain of the Southport Surf Life Saving Club. Before the kids were born he played saxophone in a big band, and at night he blew standards in the family living room. Mum, Gwendolyn, a singer and pianist, often joined in. So did brother Tony, who'd taken up guitar at a young age. The Drouyns were a middle-class family with Catholicism and creativity at its center.

Victor was an avid bodysurfer. He'd wake Tony and Peter at sunrise. With Booby, their black and white kelpie, they'd head down to the beach, drop their towels on the cool sand, and dive into the gold-streaked water. Victor would swim to the outside, lost in the sun's reflection. Tony and Peter would splash in the shore break, riding waves with an extended front arm, like Superman.

.

"Peter was meant to be a girl," insists Westerly, with a trembling voice and pleading eyes. She has told me this several times, and every time her mien turns wistful. She shakes her head as if trying to erase the past. "He was meant to be a girl," she repeats.

Before Peter was born the doctor told Gwendolyn that she was pregnant with a girl. She and Victor planned accordingly. Peter's room was painted pale pink. His baby clothes were girly.

In Peter's earliest memories he sits in the family's back garden. He feels the breeze acutely, hears the rustle of leaves as if the volume's been turned up loud. He caresses the orange gerberas and the creamy pink roses and the spotted stargazer lilies with their purple, powdery tendrils. He smells them, rubs them on his face.

Playing in the sandbox at the local park, he loved getting rubdowns and back scratches, feeling other people's hands on his body. He'd take a matchbox and pretend it was a razor, get his little mates to shave him. He was a jealous child. He wanted all the attention on himself, and when it wasn't, when it shifted to other kids, he felt it in his belly.

"When I—when Peter was a little boy he used to watch the cowboy and Indian movies," remembers Westerly. "He'd come home and instead of playing John Wayne he'd play the Indian princess and he'd hide in the flower garden where no one could see him and he wore lipstick and a little skirt. He was always a little kid who wanted to be different and wear colors and wear skimpy things. Even though he looked like a boy, all his emotions and sensitivities were like a girl."

Peter was in the wrong place for this kind of stuff. Surf writer Nick Carroll explains, "When Peter was growing up on the Gold

Coast, the framework of society in southern Queensland was at its most aggressive, at its most ignorant, and at its absolute pinnacle as far as rejecting youth and rejecting vulnerability in general."

On the inside Peter was hypersensitive. Westerly tells the story of teenage Peter going to see a surf movie with Gwendolyn and Tony. "I actually hid behind the seat. My nerves! It was just affecting my nerves and I couldn't believe it. I was scared. I was excited. I knew at that point that I'd be riding those waves one day." Westerly takes a deep inhalation. Her eyes go glassy. "There were two people, like a coin. There was the little boy who was watching everything and thinking everything, and on the other side was the little girl, watching the little boy, saying, 'What are you looking at now? Describe it.' The intensity of observation was heightened, compounded, superimposed. The senses were razor-sharp, from the age of four or five or six."

.

One afternoon in her kitchen, Westerly was leafing through snapshots of Peter's life. So numerous were his press clippings and photo albums that they consumed most of the floor space and tabletops in her kitchen and living room. Westerly wore a black Spandex top that complemented her effeminate collarbone. Her gold hoop earrings twinkled. She was jovial, somewhat in awe of her former self's accomplishments, shaking her head and giggling at the many shots of Peter with beautiful girls. But when she came across a group shot of Peter as an altar boy she frowned.

"That Irish priest," she said, holding the crinkled black-and-white photo up, a red-nailed index finger tapping the jowly, frocked man. "He did all sorts of things to tear the demon, the devil demon, from Peter's mind."

She went on to tell me about Peter's first "cross-wiring." He was eleven or twelve, puberty just kicking in. "This girl he liked, Phoebe, they just wanted to have sex. Because all these surf club men from Brisbane were always talking about sex, they were kind of the evil messengers, if you like, and they would just fill our young minds with all this sex stuff. So Peter and this girl, they went down to the bushes by the river one afternoon, where they pretended to smoke cigarettes with the straw lying around the river shore. That's how we'd do it. We'd wrap newspaper around it. Because everyone smoked cigarettes, so we pretended and then we coughed our heads off and threw that away.

"I think Peter had a bit of a grapple with her. They went down, all clothes, you know, fully clothed, and then Peter kissed her and they started doing the action of sexual intercourse and part of him went into this Neverland trance, what have you, and Peter . . . I think the locomotive blew up. And then Peter thought, *Oh my god, what have I done? I've given you a baby!* It seems funny now, but it was horribly serious then. Peter thought he'd given this poor girl a baby and so he never saw her again. He went home and stayed at home for months. He didn't go out; he just went to the beach with his dog and back. He lost all his confidence and he was waiting for the phone to ring and for some irate parent to ring up saying, 'Your son has given my daughter a baby. What are you going to do about it?'"

Westerly said that after this incident, Peter couldn't concentrate at school, and his grades went downhill. His parents sent him to a psychiatrist. "Suddenly Peter's life went all pear-shaped. All that lovely confidence and all that happiness and ad-libbing and wisecracking and spontaneity, it all just went to pieces."

Peter pulled away from his mates, withdrew from Tony. Booby became his best friend. For a while he stopped going to school. On the sofa, Booby curled at his feet, he watched television— *Gunsmoke, I Love Lucy, The Twilight Zone, The Judy Garland Show*. In the afternoon, honeyed light flooding his bedroom, shutters rustling in the onshore wind, he and Booby strolled down Wharf Road to the beach. They found a quiet patch along a little earthen cliff and sat. Peter could stare at the ocean for hours at a time. The briny smell; the roaring, hissing sounds; the seabirds that glided majestically just inches above the surface; the gleaming waves on which he imagined himself riding high, bent knees, winged arms, spray tickling calves—these things lulled him into serenity. His mates, or rather his former mates, couldn't figure him out. They teased him, threw rocks.

THE DARK HORSE

IN 1960, WHEN PETER WAS TEN, HIS PARENTS bought him a secondhand balsa board from a shaper who'd moved up to the Gold Coast from Sydney. Peter lugged it down to the beach every day, before and after school. The waves at Broadbeach were by no means great, but his enthusiasm made up for it. He danced up and down the board, hanging five, hanging ten, cross-stepping back to the tail, stomping cutbacks, dropping into a low crouch and dipping his head into the curl. On his bedroom wall hung a poster of Juan Belmonte, the famous bullfighter from Spain. Peter's flourishes—the sweeping hands, the jaunty ducking and weaving, the triumphant soul arches—were not unlike Belmonte's.

He surfed his first contest in 1965: the Cadillac Classic at Greenmount Beach. Suffering from a bad case of nerves, he finished fourth in the four-man final. Later that year he won the Juniors division of the Queensland Titles, which earned him a round-trip plane ticket to Sydney for the Australian Championships, then the most prestigious event in the country.

In the weeks leading up to the event Peter trained hard, surfing twice, sometimes three times a day with a newfound rigor and intensity. He flew down to Sydney with his Queensland teammates. They checked into a cheap hotel on Manly's Corso. That night they went to a competitors' meeting at the Manly Pacific, a pub across the street from the beach. If it were today, you'd easily confuse this pre-contest gathering with the final blowout that happens at the end of events. The bar was five deep with singlet-clad, broad-shouldered blokes. Big fists passed pint glasses and jugs over heads, spume dripping into salt-matted blond hair. The din of hyperbolic surf chatter. The Easybeats on the jukebox. The smell of beer, cigarettes, sweat.

The competitors were aged fifteen to twenty-two, bodies tanned and chiseled, confidence bursting. There was Robert "Nat" Young, strapping, movie-star handsome, chatting up a pair of "Miss International Airline Hostess" contestants. There was Midget Farrelly, blond hair parted neatly to the side, face like a yelping coyote's. There was Kevin "The Head" Brennan, pugnacious eyes, his bronzed cranium too big for his jockey-sized body. The Head had recently won both the Juniors and the Open division of the NSW Titles; he would be Peter's greatest challenge. It was exciting to be in the company of Australia's surfing elite, faces he and Tony knew from the magazines they pored over at night. Midget in particular; Westerly can still remember watching him win the 1962 Makaha Invitational in Hawaii on the news and thinking, *I want to do that!*

Peter grabbed a beer, listened to a couple of barely audible speeches from contest officials, and felt a heady rush that was a mixture of kinship and having much to prove. Queensland was still a backwater, and though he was state champion, Peter was still a dark horse, a rumor. A second beer found its way into his hands. In the sway of bodies he spoke first to a brown-skinned local girl whose boobs kept poking him in the arm, and then to a trio of aggressive locals who told Peter he didn't stand a chance, their words delivered in beer spray, their back pats a little too hard.

At 10 pm the pub closed, spilling the raucous crowd out to the footpath. Peter crossed the street to check the waves. Under the iconic Norfolk pines that line the promenade he saw the contest scaffold on the sand, banners flapping in the sea breeze. The moon was near full, reflecting a stripe of silver on the inky water. Waves bobbed and gasped. He imagined himself on them, sweeping a big bottom turn, cross-stepping to the nose. Then he heard footsteps, voices, and when he turned around, there were the three guys from the bar. One grabbed his arms and held them behind his back.

Another—"a redhead with freckles, I can still see him"—punched him repeatedly in the face, the stomach, the ribs. Peter saw a blur of red, tasted hot metallic blood. The blows kept coming. When they finally let go he fell like a rag doll, his face slamming the brick footpath.

Heads, faces, all out of focus, hovered above him. He recognized Bob Evans, the filmmaker and editor of *Surfing World*. Bob picked Peter up in his arms, blood everywhere. "Am I gonna die, Bob?" asked Peter. Bob assured him he wasn't. He took Peter up the hill to Manly Hospital. A doctor stitched him up—gashes on his forehead, in his mouth, on his chin. Bob phoned Peter's dad. Peter spent the night in the hospital. When he woke in the morning Victor was at his bedside. Peter broke into tears. He was sure that it was all over, that he wouldn't be able to compete.

"Dad said, 'Look, we won't give up on this. We'll find a way,'" says Westerly.

The first eleven doctors they spoke to insisted there was no way Peter could compete, that he risked a blood clot. The twelfth doctor, a quirky Scot, opened his cabinet and pulled out a new plastic spray bandage.

"The doctor sprayed his entire head and face, covered it with bandages, sprayed it some more—it looked like a nappy," remembers Westerly.

Peter showed up at the contest the following morning with something like steam coming out of his nostrils. The sky was bright and blue, the waves small and docile. The double takes—from spectators, fellow competitors, judges—only fueled him. Peter paddled out to his first heat and won easily. Same with the next round, and the next, and the one after that.

Westerly has told me this story more than once and every time her voice starts to crack right about here. In this instance, she's sitting in the dining room of the Bangkok Rama. Her gossamer hair cascades down the left side of her face, her makeup is freshly done. She wears a lacy little black dress.

"He was always a late starter, like a racehorse. Always at the back of the field." She clasps her hands together under her chin, shuts her eyes. She looks like she's praying. "He was probably coming last. So he paddles in and he starts catching these inside waves, and he just went berserk! He was a wizard, the little kid! Turning, changing foot, hanging ten, big roundhouse cutback, gorgeous style, perfect trim line. Right on the beach he'd walk off the front of his board. And he won it easily, the final. That was the beginning of his whole career."

A photo from the day, in *Surfing World*, shows Peter clutching a trophy in each hand. On one side of him stands Midget Farrelly; on the other fellow Queenslander Phyllis O'Donnell. Peter wears white shorts and a black V-neck sweater over a polo shirt. His hair is cut short and neat. The right side of his forehead and the left side of his chin are covered in bandages. He does not look triumphant. He looks bashful, reluctant. His eyes are cast downwards.

"That was incredible. My superhero, Midget, was right next to me, in person, holding a trophy, looking at me. And I'm almost in panic attack mode."

I ask Westerly why Peter was assaulted.

"They were jealous of him," she says. "They knew he was a threat to Kevin Brennan."

This is a very different account from the one I got from Peter's peers.

"He got a little bit fresh with one of the judges' wives or something. And that judge was from Manly, and he didn't take too kindly to Peter," remembered fellow Queensland team member Andrew McKinnon.

"Somehow he loudmouthed and upset a lot of girls. Someone jumped on him and started to punch him out. He wouldn't have been drunk. The other guys would have been," said another of his fellow Queenslanders, Bob McTavish.

"I have it on good authority that he was trying to chase one of the Freshy guys' girlfriends, and he got the shits about it and clocked him," said Bruce Channon, former editor of *Surfing World*. "At that stage Peter was just a brash kid from Queensland that got beat up, and everyone on the beach knew about it, and I think Peter suffered mentally because he knew everyone knew what really happened, and he had to eat humble pie, and I think that was a problem for Peter right from the start."

.

Peter returned to something of a hero's welcome on the Gold Coast. His beaming face—a "Colgate smile" they called it—was plastered all over the papers. Mates who'd sensed his fragile, introspective side now saw only the exultant Aussie champ. And it was more than just a personal victory.

"The moment Peter won that, all the New South Wales surfers started trickling up to Queensland. From now on people respected Queensland surfing," says Westerly.

But Peter's inner demons were by no means exorcised. He continued to struggle with what Westerly says today would be an obsessive–compulsive disorder, though back then there was no such diagnosis.

"It was like martyrdom. It was like suicide. Peter went to this doctor who was the first one in Surfers Paradise to prescribe Valium. Peter was the first [one on it]."

.

In 1964 Peter struck up a close relationship with the board shaper Peter "Hono" Hohnesee. Hono gave Peter a job at his factory in Mermaid Beach. Caked in foam dust, the toxic smell of resin seeping through his dust mask, Peter would watch closely as Hono mowed the planer up and down the blank, curved the rails with a surform, carved a vee in the tail with a sanding block. Peter was a quick study. Not only did he start shaping himself, but with his ace skills in the water he was a dream test pilot, taking the boards where few surfers could. Peter found himself wanting more looseness, maneuverability. In his head were all these lightning slashes and screaming cutbacks that the boards were too clunky to do.

Peter begged Hono to make the boards shorter and lighter. At first the board shaper resisted. Peter was insisting on chopping a foot or more off the length and glassing the board with just the thinnest layer of fiberglass. Hono reckoned they'd crumble in the hand. Peter was unrelenting. In the end he got what he wanted: an eight foot eleven that weighed twenty-four pounds. It went brilliantly, a Porsche to the prevailing Cadillacs.

Westerly tells me how Nat Young and Peter struck up a friendship. One day the two of them were out surfing Byron Bay together. Nat saw the sharper turns Peter was doing on his new design and asked to try it. "Nat rode it for three hours!" says Westerly. A couple of weeks later Nat came up to the Gold Coast to get a closer look at Peter and Hono's new boards. He rode one at Burleigh and, as Westerly describes it, was "stealing Peter's moves."

Not long after, a mixture of chemicals led to an explosion in Hono's factory. Hono was literally blown out of the window. The entire place burned to the ground, destroying evidence of the great design leaps they'd been making. Hono suffered third-degree burns. It would be a while before he'd shape again.

Peter headed up to Noosa, saw fellow Queensland team member Bob McTavish, a sprite of a twenty-two-year-old. Bob was an excellent surfer/shaper. Peter told him about the designs he and Hono had been working on, how he was pushing for "shorter, lighter." Bob, it turns out, was on a similar tack. He made Peter a nine-foot board that weighed fifteen pounds.

"In those days that was considered a feather," remembers Westerly.

•

The 1966 Australian Titles were held in choppy, shapeless waves at Greenmount Point on the Gold Coast. Peter had hit a particular groove with his surfing. He was piercing the lip, slashing back, trotting up to the nose and riding absurdly high in the trim line, his board barely connected to the wave, his matador arms a study in grace and poise. He surfed his heats as if he was competing solely against himself, pushing for some private ideal, his head dizzy at the end of his rides.

"Pete didn't win it by streaks," laughs Westerly. "He won it by a country mile."

Two consecutive Australian junior titles was a monster feat, though to hear Westerly tell it, one that was never properly acknowledged by the surf media. She says that a prominent surf journalist of the time did not photograph Peter, essentially blackballing him. That journalist did, however, photograph everyone else.

"They made it look like they [Nat Young, Bob McTavish, Keith Paul] had innovated those maneuvers. Peter was just shattered. He just couldn't believe what they were trying to do to him. They were trying to destroy his confidence. All they'd ever put in the surf magazines was Pete smiling, as if it was a Hollywood magazine not a surf magazine. And then saying horrible things about him, saying he's got a big ego."

.

The 1966 World Championships in San Diego marked a milestone for surfing, in particular mainstream interest in the sport. President Lyndon Johnson sent competitors a letter of welcome. *Life*, *Newsweek* and *The New York Times* reported from the beach. From *Newsweek*: "Five or six years ago, the World Surfing Championships would have been about as welcome in a U.S. city as the Pot Smoking Olympics."

Of course a Pot Smoking Olympics of sorts did take place, just not within whiffing distance of the contest site. I've talked to several surfers who competed in the event. They describe scenes straight out of the movie *Animal House*—all-night ragers, trashed hotel rooms, stoned, patchouli-scented longhairs doing donuts on the sand in their rented ragtops at 2 am.

Peter's win in the 1966 Australian Titles earned him an invite to the Worlds. With a band of merry teammates that included Nat Young, Midget Farrelly and Bob McTavish, among others, he flew to California in late September.

I've tried to imagine what a heady trip this must have been for Peter. He's seventeen. He's been in the contest game for only two years and he's got two Aussie Titles under his belt. His heroes, the very surfers who got him started on this odyssey, are sitting next to him on the flight over. They have tremendous respect for Peter's surfing; they consider him a threat, a potential crown-snatcher. In *Surfabout* magazine's coverage of the 1966 Australian Titles, Peter is featured in two prominent action shots, both poised in a stately hang five. From the article:

> Peter Drouyen [sic] emerged as a clear cut winner from Cavanagh and Spence, and it seems that when Peter reaches the seniors he will be the boy to watch. As a matter of fact the day after the finals, Nat and Peter had an unofficial contest at Burleigh Heads where the surf was breaking perfectly between 10 and 12 feet, the water was clear, conditions were absolutely unreal and it seemed that Peter almost had the edge on Nat that day.

I imagine Peter at the World Championships, held at Mission Beach Jetty and Ocean Beach, reveling in the excitement of sharing waves with surfers from the USA, Peru, France, South Africa, England and New Zealand. I see him making about fifty new friends, exuberant conversations over beers about waves and girls and board design, invites to crash on couches in Malibu, Biarritz, Newquay, a whole new world opening up. I see curious Pete digging the California surfers' style: the deck shoes, the rolled khakis, the canvas team jackets, the Wayfarers. I hear him throwing a "bitchin" here, a "boss" there, a Yank "gremmie" rather than an Aussie "grommet."

When I ask Westerly about it she frowns.

"It was a horror trip for Peter."

She explains that it was supposed to be an Australian team thing, that Peter expected camaraderie and support. But instead there were all sorts of dramas. Nat and Midget were in the early stages of a bitter rivalry that exists to this day. *Tracks* editor John Witzig and Bob Evans rallied around Nat.

"His teammates ditched Peter. Peter was alone. A lost seventeen-year-old. He was having an extended panic attack, he didn't even know where his surfboard was, he was being held together just enough so that an ambulance didn't show up and take him away."

I tell Westerly how I had imagined the trip.

"It should have been. It could have been had Bob Evans, who was supposed to be president of the Australian National Association, looked after him and chaperoned a seventeen-year-old."

She claims that Bob Evans just exploited whichever surfer was the flavor of the day—at that time Nat—and adds that his surf movies were terrible: "He wouldn't be taken seriously in Hollywood."

Westerly tells me how Peter's super-short, super-light board snapped in half just before he left for California. He was forced to compete on a more traditional design, which limited his performance. He finished a respectable eleventh in the Open Men's division (there was no Juniors).

Nat Young, meanwhile, arrived in San Diego with "Magic Sam," a nine foot four square tail with a swept-back fin designed by Californian George Greenough. The favorite to win the event was Californian David Nuuhiwa, who cross-stepped and hung ten and surfed in the traditional longboarding style. With Magic Sam like an appendage, Nat planted one foot at the center, the other at the tail, and heaved up and down the face with brutal aggression. The judges had no problem determining which was the more progressive style of surfing.

Nat Young's victory in the 1966 World Championships sparked what would become the "shortboard revolution."

•

If ever there was a good time in history to be purging inner demons on a wave, it was the latter half of the sixties. In Hawaii, in California, up and down the coast of Australia, all around the world, surfers sawed a foot, sometimes two feet, off the tails of their boards. Wave riding went from a passive, hood-ornament style to aggressive, dynamic, pyrotechnic. It was a shift that left many old guard surfers in the lurch.

Peter thrived. He told surf journalist Tim Baker in a 1997 issue of *Deep*:

> I was just able to manage on the land, but excelled in the water, and I think that created the power surfing that you've heard of. That's where the power surfing started. It was a rebellion thing. It was based upon a personality, and the closer I could get to the wave, the quicker I could relax, the quicker I could get confidence. Because I had a lot of those problems, I powered. It was the rebel. I had to get it out of me. I'd punch the wave, just in there, hang in close, up the nose, bang!

I ask Westerly about power surfing and she is all bobbing head and flickering hands in her description. But her irritation quickly turns to despondency and then sheer bitterness when she tells me about what Peter for years referred to as "Surfgate," a conspiracy to write him out of surfing history. In a 1967 issue of *Surfer*, an article titled "We're Tops Now" heralded both the shortboard revolution and new Australian ascendency. Nat Young featured prominently. So did Bob McTavish, and an eccentric Californian named George Greenough. Peter was scarcely mentioned.

Westerly's lips curl sharply down at the corners when she tells me about the hurt Peter felt. I see frown lines in her face that might trace directly back to this piece.

"Politics and injustice worked against poor Peter," she says. "He was devastated by how they sidelined him. They forced him into exile."

THE OUTSIDER

RANDY RARICK IS A TALL, FIT, SIXTY-FOUR-YEAR-old man who lives a few houses in from the beach at Sunset, one of the North Shore of Oahu's finest waves, where he surfs nearly every day. As one of the founders of the IPS (International Professional Surfers) in 1976, and the executive director of the Triple Crown of Surfing from its 1983 inception until 2012, he has calmed many a pro surfer enraged by some perceived injustice. His reasonable, sympathetic tone is of the sort found in suicide interventionists.

We met in his home office. The walls were covered with surf shots from his far-flung travels. The shelves were stacked with books about surfing. The screen saver on his computer was an image of a wave. Randy wore a blue Aloha shirt, shorts, no shoes. About the only non-surfing element to the scene was his extensive collection of palm-sized model army tanks, displayed in a glass case.

Randy met Peter Drouyn on his first trip to Australia in 1968. Randy was staying with renowned surfer Keith Paul, a mutual friend, in Narrabeen. Peter was in Sydney in May for the 1968 Australian Titles. The pair, both eighteen, hit it off. After the contest Randy went up to the Gold Coast and stayed with the Drouyn family.

"We were kind of opposites," said Randy. "I was low-key and Peter was very flamboyant, very outgoing, always had a smile on his face, but very dramatic. He always wanted to make a statement."

Randy said it was hard to get a read on the family dynamics, but he sensed that Peter's mother and father wanted him to be more than just a surfer.

He remembered hanging out with Peter in the "playroom" above the garage. The song "Hey Jude" had just come out, and Peter pulled out the 45. "He goes, 'This is amazing, listen to this!' and he put it on, and he started getting wound up, and as the music got going he started screaming and getting more excited. As it reached the crescendo he just started taking the furniture and busting it and breaking the place and doing a full demolish, and I was sitting there going, *We're not on drugs, we're not drunk, we're not anything, it's just Peter coming out.* By the end of the crescendo the whole room was destroyed. It really seemed odd to me that you'd do that at your parents' house."

After a stint on the Gold Coast, Peter and Randy drove the 700 kilometers down to Newcastle for a contest. Along the way they stopped for surf, food, beer and a naked run through the sand dunes of Taree (Peter's idea). They arrived in Newcastle on a Friday morning. The waves had already blown out, the contest didn't start till the next day, they were restless.

"Peter goes, 'Okay, let's go get some girls. Here's what we're going to do: we're going to go to downtown Newcastle, we'll go at lunch hour, they all get out of their offices at lunch hour, and we can score a couple of girls then.'"

"I go, 'That sounds like a plan.'

"So we went into Newcastle and sure enough, all these young secretaries come out of their offices, and we see two, and he goes, 'Okay, let's go for these ones, and we'll line it up to meet at such-and-such place at eight o'clock.' So we go up to 'em and we chat 'em up, and of course Peter's his charming self, and I'm speaking with my American accent—there weren't many American surfers around back then. We go, 'Okay, we'll meet you girls here at eight o'clock.'

"So then I go, 'Okay, great, we got a couple girls,' and Peter goes, 'No, that's not good enough.' He says, 'We gotta get a couple more.' I go, 'What do you mean a couple more, what are we going to do with 'em?' He goes, 'No, no, no, trust me on this one.'

"So we look around. 'Okay, there's a couple of hot ones!' So he goes over, does the same thing, he chats 'em up, he goes, 'Girls, how'd you like to go out tonight?' 'Oh, yeah, that'd be great.' 'Okay, we'll meet you at eight fifteen,' and he names this other spot, close by.

"I go, 'Okay, we've got four of 'em.' He goes, 'No, no, we gotta get a couple more.' I go, 'Peter, we've already got four girls lined up, we can only take two at a time.' He goes, 'No, no.'

"So we go and he finds two more that have come out of their offices and are eating lunch. We go and we chat 'em up again, and same thing, 'Would you girls like to go out tonight?' 'Oh yeah, okay, Friday night, let's do it.' 'We'll meet you at eight-thirty.'

"By this time I'm going, 'What are we going to do with these six girls?' Peter goes, 'Well, the eight o'clock ones weren't that good so let's forget about them. We've got the eight-fifteen ones and if they don't show we've got the eight-thirty ones for backup.'

"So we go and meet the eight-fifteen ones, and he goes, 'Oh, they're not that good-looking, forget about them,' so we ditched those two, met the eight-thirty ones, and sure enough we went out for the night."

Randy told me how the four of them bought some wine and went back to the five-dollar-a-night caravan park where Peter and Randy were staying. The girls were no older than eighteen.

"I'll never forget, I'm in one side of the caravan, and there's a little partition, and Peter's in the other, and Peter's just really try-ing to make the most of the evening, let's just put it that way. And all of a sudden coming out of this room are all these noises, kind of defensive, 'No, no.' And the girl with me goes, 'What's he doing to her? What's he doing to her? What's he doing to her?' Finally we had to stop and say, 'Peter, everything cool in there?' And the girl says, 'No, no, we can't do this.' And by this time, unfortunately, the girls were a bit inebriated, and the one with Peter, she's had a little too much to drink, and she passes out. We go, 'Let's take her back to her house.' So we throw her in the back of my van and we take her to her house, and we're being really quiet, and we walk up to her house, and we slide the window up, and the girl's passed out, and we just took her and pushed her through the window (laughs), and just *whoom*, this bag of laundry falls in, and we go, 'That's it, she's in, let's go.'"

Randy showed me a photo from when they met up the following day. The bare-chested, tanned surfers stand with their arms around the innocent, sweet-faced girls. Randy poses earnestly; Peter holds something up in his left hand—a Popsicle? The freedom of youth is palpable. Randy and Peter look easy, lighthearted, in no hurry to get anywhere, save for their heats, perhaps.

"All that next day the catchphrase was, 'What's he doing to her? What's he doing to her?'" laughed Randy. "But I got to say that the two girls were really cute, and it was a lot of fun, we had a good time, but 'What's he doing to her?' kind of sums up Peter. 'What exactly *is* he doing to her?'"

I asked Randy if he knew of Peter ever having a serious girlfriend. He said no, but pointed out that they were closest from age eighteen to twenty-two, footloose years.

"Peter was a ladies' man, a charmer. He was always striving for that attention, and really striving for somebody to really want him, but as soon as he went for somebody I think he put up a defensive wall. It was always about the chase, winning her over. It was like a contest to him. Once he got the girl it didn't matter anymore."

Randy told me how Peter would blatantly go after friends' wives. "It was about pursuing the unattainable." Later, in the mid-eighties, he'd run into Peter after a long time of not seeing him, and Peter tried to hit on Randy's wife, too. It wasn't the first time I'd heard stories of this sort.

In October 1968 Peter and Randy took a P&O liner to Hawaii. Peter stayed at Randy's place, one of those classic North Shore houses of the era—boards and beds strewn about every corner, a village of empty beer bottles on the kitchen counter, a week's worth of dishes stacked in the sink, a piss-splattered toilet, a mildewy and sandy shower. Peter slept on a mattress in the corner of the living room. "One day he jumped out of bed and goes, 'Oh my god, they're in here! The girl I was with, I've got crabs from her! There's crabs in my bed!'" Randy tells how they burned the sheets, doused the mattress in Brasso cleaner.

They went to an orgy. "It was at some rich guy's house in Manoa Valley. This guy took a five-gallon can of Wesson oil, and he had this room with a tiled floor, and he went *galoop, galoop, galoop* [Randy mimics tipping out drops of oil]. There was like twenty of us there, and everybody took all their clothes off and we just dived in and we were rolling around with guys and chicks—a total orgy. And Peter was totally into it. He was loving it."

I asked Randy what he thought about Peter's feeling hard done by. He said that he'd definitely seen Peter get the bad end of the stick, that in the late sixties New South Welshmen always got the nod over Queenslanders. He also said that part of the problem was Peter himself.

"He was never satisfied. It was never enough. Peter never felt he got the accolades or recognition he deserved."

•

In the 1968 Bob Evans film *High On a Cool Wave*, an eighteen-year-old Peter Drouyn trots out from between the iconic beach-front homes on the North Shore. He surveys the surf melodramatically, a board-toting Charlie Chaplin. His brawny chest glistens in the Hawaiian sun; his Hollywood smile twinkles. He paddles out to big, dangerous waves at Pipeline. He gets some decent rides. But it's one wave in particular that shows his genius.

A triple overhead bomb stands up, its teal blue face burnished by strong trade winds. Peter strokes, pops to feet, falls down the vertical wall. Hanging by his toenails, he manages a bottom turn, sets a jittery line, tucks into a sort of survival crouch, both hands gripping the rails of his board. His line, though, is just a touch too high, the upwards-surging water on the brink of taking Peter with it, barrel-rolling him over the falls. But his fin releases, and in a brisk, gravitational swat, Peter's board sideslips down the face a couple of notches. It's a vicariously weightless moment; you feel Peter's heart leap to his throat. His fin gains traction, he careens forward, and disappears into a deep, cavernous pit of a Pipeline barrel. The wave gasps and heaves and ejects him in a cloud of spit. If this ride were today, during, say, the Pipeline Masters, one of the biggest contests in the world, the entire beach would erupt in hoots. This ride happened forty-six years ago. On a board that did Peter no favors.

Which is to say that Peter surfed magnificently in Hawaii. Today the North Shore is a mecca for surfers worldwide, but back then it was still being discovered. The waves were big and powerful, the lifestyle was rough and spartan, the locals didn't take kindly to haoles (white people). It was a true test of a surfer's mettle to do well in Hawaii, both in and out of the surf. Peter's surfing on the North Shore speaks for itself. I asked Randy Rarick how he got along with the Hawaiians.

"Peter had a hard time on the North Shore," he said. "He was a bit too brash for the locals."

•

In November 1968 Peter flew from Hawaii to Puerto Rico for the World Championships. On the flight over, passing through the Bermuda Triangle, the plane hit heavy turbulence. Emergency lights flashed. Oxygen masks fell out of the overhead consoles. The plane dropped thousands of feet, bouncing people out of their seats. Pandemonium erupted throughout the cabin. Everyone, especially Peter, was sure the plane was going down.

Peter had a window seat. He'd boarded the flight wearing only a T-shirt. It was icy cold. He shivered so hard he thought he might have a seizure. By the time they arrived in San Juan he was coughing up blood. Airline staff had to help him off the plane.

Westerly says that Peter's Aussie teammates did nothing to help him, neither during the flight nor after he'd seen the doctor the following day and been diagnosed with pleurisy, an inflammation of the lining surrounding the lungs. It was the Hawaiians who took Peter in and looked after him, specifically event-winner Fred Hemmings and David Nuuhiwa. From his edge-of-death position, says Westerly, Peter felt the true spirit of *aloha* and *ohana* (family). "The Australians never once came over to check up on him," she adds.

Westerly tells this story over lunch one day, her eyes drifting back to 1968, to Puerto Rico, as if it were unfolding in real time. Her face is raw with vulnerability, her arms are goosepimpled, she wilts in her chair. Her coffee has gone cold. She hasn't touched her sandwich for fifteen minutes.

Peter was way too sick to compete; in fact, he was bedridden for a week. "Finally Fred Hemmings said, 'You're coming with me. We're going to go up to the bar, and we're going to drink this shit out of your system!' We started with rums on fire, down the hatch, and then there were competitions between me and Fred and this guy from Florida, Dick Catri. Then we did a fake mass, like a church mass, to thank the lord for his blessings in saving him, with Freddy Hemmings as the priest."

Westerly laughs as she describes Peter, blind drunk, lying flat on the ground, covered in a white sheet, flowers, candles, and Fred and Dick on either side of him.

"Those guys saved me! Then they took me to this dance, and they got me, they got Peter, a senorita. And they said, 'Peter, all you've got to say to her is, *Tu eres muy bonita*—You're a very beautiful girl!'"

Westerly chokes on her glass of water. She shifts in her chair. Her voice changes. "Do you know by this time the Hawaiians already knew Peter had a problem? They are very aware people, those Hawaiians. They've been through that discrimination."

.

Surfer magazine's coverage of the 1969 Australian Championships depicts a wonderful event: hefty, well-shaped lefthanders at Margaret River, excellent performances by the Lucky Country's best, riveting carves up and down the face by Nat Young. Nat actually wrote about it. Not the surfing part but the awards presentation that followed:

> The things I remember after dinner are vague. Everyone consuming literally gallons of anything alcoholic and the party had really started to move. Some guy executed a perfect "ham bone," dropping his pants, and the food and beer started to flow freely from one room to another through the air. Ted Spencer was suspended across one end of the room, while beer and food of all descriptions were hurled at him. Drouyn splattered tomato sauce all over everyone. The Queensland judge never managed to get down his glass of wine, because every time he lifted glass to his lips, he would see someone who would look better wearing it, so he immediately would throw the lot over them with just enough time to fill it up and repeat. The record player ground to a stop in the middle of "Cheap Thrills"—further inspection revealed the needle clogged in tomato sauce. Woody urinated all over some girl that had been asking for it all night. Now the party was in full swing, everybody was drunk and covered in food . . . Mass hysteria broke out among the women as Drouyn opened the door and emptied the rubbish can into the atmosphere . . .
>
> You may very well be disgusted by all this, or you may be amused, but it really doesn't matter, because it was fun. Everyone was in the same state, and I am quite sure I have never experienced an "animal out" like the close of the 1969 Australian Championships.

Westerly remembers a very different 1969 Australian Championships. She describes the board design Peter had been working on in preparation for the event—a round pintail based on a board he'd brought back from Hawaii. She explains the four rounds of competition in which Nat and Peter were tied.

"The rules stated that if the points were even you bring it to a grand final to decide the winners—whoever wins that wins the Aussie Title. Pete picks up his board and goes out and annihilates Nat Young, goes out and makes him look like a swimmer. I say that with all humility. Peter just wanted to kick 'em all in the butt, just kick the whole friggin' dishonesty, the whole rotten, corrupt friggin' system."

Westerly lets loose a giggle that belongs to a death row inmate. She tells me how they announced Peter the winner, how the Queensland team cheered for him and slapped him on the back and lifted him up on their shoulders, how Peter felt triumphant, ecstatic.

"Then the captain of the Queensland team comes up, he's ashen grey, he's shaking his head, and everyone's just, 'What's wrong?' He says, 'They've taken it off Peter. They're giving it to Nat Young.' Of course we were in shock! 'Why? Peter just won it!' 'Oh, they say that Nat was more consistent than Peter the whole way through.'"

Westerly holds my gaze, her face smeared with hurt. "*More consistent? That's bullshit! They were neck and neck, finished on the same points, and Peter annihilates him in the grand final. That's against the rules!* But it seems they've changed the rules."

Westerly's power of recollection is incredible; it's as if these memories are riding across the glaze of her eye.

"Can you imagine the damage? It set him back. His panic attacks, his confidence. His sense of justice and fairness . . ." Westerly's voice cracks. Her hands plead. Forty-five years later the disappointment is still palpable.

I spoke to one of the judges of the 1969 Australian Titles, and despite all the years that have passed, he asked that I not mention his name. He confirmed that Peter was outright robbed.

"He lost a couple of contests because he was discriminated against. I know that for a fact. Peter was discriminated against because he was an asshole. By that I mean he was very arrogant."

He went on to say that Peter exited the water knowing he'd

won it, and so did everyone else. He described the period between the news that Nat had actually won and the awards banquet.

"Peter went off that he didn't win it. He was going to go up onstage and give it to 'em. The banquet was held at this pub. A bunch of us were walking up there through the bush. It was pitch black. Peter's telling everyone how he's going to go off. He got onstage and instead of going off he sang *Moon River*, then he gave a professional speech."

•

The disparity between Nat Young's account of the 1969 Aussie Titles awards ceremony debauchery, Peter at the tomato sauce-splattering center of it, and Westerly's account of a distraught Peter reminds me of that unforgettable assertion Westerly made during our first meeting: *"Peter was an awkward misfit. He had to do it all himself when he wasn't really a fighter or a swearer or a beer drinker. His life was a lie."*

I've done enough of my own inner searching to be aware of our many masks, of the way in which one friend or social milieu will extract one side of ourselves, while another will extract an entirely different one. But the idea that a person could live for over fifty years so totally untrue to themselves was painful to think about.

When I was researching my Westerly profile I spoke with many of Peter's colleagues, and in the midst of my questions, every one of them asked if I'd spoken to Mal.

"Mal who?"

"Mal Chalmers. Peter's best mate. If anyone's going to give you insights into Peter it'll be Mal."

I got Mal's phone number and called him. A well-respected lawyer on the Gold Coast, he spoke thoughtfully, compassionately. It was obvious that he cared a great deal about Westerly. In fact, he was the first of the blokes to actually refer to her as "Westerly."

I asked if he'd seen any signs that Westerly might emerge. Like everyone else I spoke to, he did not think about it for a second.

"No, not at all," he said. "Look, Peter was never a happy man, he feels like a victim, he's always been difficult to reason with, he's always had a hard time of it, but definitely no signs of a girl inside him."

Mal said that he and Westerly remain close, that he makes it a point to see her about once a week. He described a sad scene of Westerly in her depressing little council housing flat, spending way too much time alone.

That explained the pictures.

In the beginning of my fact-checking phone calls to Westerly, we observed a professional decorum. About seventy percent of our conversation was devoted to the business of my profile, and thirty percent to whatever digressions. This soon got flopped. And then the fact-checking was done and the calls were simply casual chats—*What have you been up to? Did you see such-and-such movie?*—probably the sort of phone calls Westerly and Mal had.

Then came an email with a self-portrait attached. Shot in the mirror, Westerly poses pin-up style in a silver high-cut dress, silver heels, hair and makeup to the nines, lips pursed, sassy hand on hip, the camera's flashbulb like a stalking paparazzo on the footpath in front of Chasen's. *Silver girl star Westerly is M.... M.....! Dec 29th 2008* was the caption.

I might have replied with a *Cool!* or *Nice shot!*

Then came another self-portrait shot in the mirror, in a different outfit, similar sassy pose, flashbulb. Then another. Then another. Then five in a single attachment, each image almost the same as the one next to it. They were daily. They were sometimes two or three times a day.

If I wrote, *Nice shots!* she came back asking, *Which is your favorite? Why? Do you see it? Do you see the great miracle taking place? I tell you everyone is just in total shock!*

Some were close-up shots of her face. Others had a campy, burlesque vibe. Eventually there were topless shots. She typically sent them in the wee hours, Queensland time. I felt her insomnia, her loneliness.

•

I met Mal Chalmers in person in late November 2012, on the eve of my trip to Bangkok with Westerly. A sturdy, deeply tanned man in his early sixties, he wore a striped T-shirt and the sort of higher-cut boardshorts favored by surfers in their twenties. He was the same guy in person as he was on the phone: honest, genuine, warm, compassionate. After twenty minutes of talking to him I had the sense that I could trust him with my life.

There was one surprise. Mal has only one hand. The other, his right hand, he lost in an accident in a sawmill where he worked when he was twenty-three. It's something you hardly notice when you spend time with him (he's a keen, rock-solid surfer), but when you first meet him and go to shake hands . . .

One night over a beer at a bar in Nobby Beach, where Mal lives with his wife (his two kids are grown up), he told me about the North Shore winter in the late sixties when he and Peter lived together in a caravan. They were in their late teens, able to drink beers all night and rise at dawn and not feel a thing. The surf pumped. There were countless sessions in which they hooted each other over the ledges of massive, heavy-water waves. They were conquering fear, discovering what they were made of. A bond of a very particular sort was forged.

"His race calls were legendary," said Mal.

Everyone I spoke to mentioned Peter's race calls. And he didn't give them up easily. At awards banquets or other random piss-ups that popped up around the contests, someone might shout, "Eh, Drouyn, give us a race call!" That would set off another request, and another, and another, until the entire pub or party was chanting: *Race call! Race call! Race call!*

Finally Peter would take center stage, someone would hand him a beer jug, and using it like a bullhorn, he'd go right around the room, improvising a kind of surf contest/horse race in which *Nat Young's up the center, bashes lip, cuts back, rebounds off the foam, but there's Wayne Lynch on a late takeoff, he ducks into the tube, he disappears, he disappears, he's in, he's in, he's OUT! Oh wait, outside, ladies and gentlemen, the wave of the day! And there's Peter Drouyn, right in the slot. He drops in late, he hooks off the bottom, he clocks the lip like it's George Foreman's chin, he hooks off the bottom again, he carves into a big, what, a 360! Did he just do that?*

I never got to hear Peter's race calls, but I heard several impersonations.

I told Westerly how much Peter's peers loved them.

Her eyes lit up. "Oh, Peter was so talented," she said like a doting grandmother.

"Would you do one for me?"

She shook her head. "That was Peter's thing."

"Come on, Westerly!"

She held up her palm as if refusing a second glass of wine. "That was a Peter thing."

•

Mal said that for as long as he's known Peter he's always been all or nothing.

"He was a real visionary. He had it in his mind that he wanted to win, and if he didn't win, he didn't have a backup plan."

Mal often played the "realist," tapering Peter back in his grandiosity, or helping him to start anew after a combustible ending.

I asked if the surf world had done Peter wrong. Mal said that he believed it did, citing the example of the 1969 Australian Titles. He also said that Peter took his defeats especially hard. For instance, the North Shore, 1970.

I can't overstate how important it was for a surfer to prove himself in Hawaii. Beyond surfing skills, it was manhood, courage, ocean knowledge, character. True colors were shown in the face of a twenty-five-foot wall of vertical water. And like a gold rush, it was all there for the taking. An unknown could distinguish himself, rise to the top of the heap, in the course of a single northwest swell.

Peter did this in 1970—at Sunset, Pipeline, Waimea Bay.

That would prove to be his best competitive year. He placed fourth in the Smirnoff Pro-Am at Sunset Beach. Then he went out and won the Makaha International, a massive feat. Since its inception in 1954, the Makaha event was hailed as the most prestigious in the world. Peter's victory came at a time when the focus was shifting over to the Duke Kahanamoku Invitational, held at Sunset Beach. Not to worry. Peter could do Sunset.

He surfed like a superman right through to the final. He was riding a momentum that seemed divine. The best waves fell into his lap. He stabbed his board into all the right places. The judges smiled at him.

ABC's *Wide World of Sports* was on hand for the final day. So were a heap of bikini girls from Honolulu. There were six surfers in the final, but really there were only two: Peter Drouyn and Hawaiian Jeff Hakman. Jeff would disappear behind a blue curtain, come out, weave a big hooking cutback. Peter would follow suit on the wave behind. It was as neck and neck as those horse races Peter parodied. When the buzzer blew Pete was sure he was in the lead. He exited the water all smiles and fist pumps.

Mal remembers watching the scoreboard with Peter, waiting for the final scores to drop. Peter beamed as they called out the results. *"And winning the 1970 Duke Kahanamoku Invitational, Jeff—"*

"That just devastated Peter. He was just finished! He wasn't going to surf again. It just took the wind right out of his sails."

Surf contests are subjective. Even from the beach it's often tough to call a winner. When you're in the water, competing, unable to watch your opponents' rides it's even more so. That said, you do get hunches. And when the hunches come, but the call continuously swings the other way . . .

Did Mal ever watch Peter self-sabotage?

"I think when he had the surf shop in Surfers [Paradise]," he said. "This was '71, '72. It could have been a great thing but he sabotaged it. You know, when girls were getting changed he'd want to look at the bikinis."

I spoke to some other peers of Westerly's about his surf shop and they gave similar reports. Peter was always messing around, Peter would disappear the moment the surf came up, Peter was too arrogant to handle customers.

"It was a golden opportunity to set up his life," continues Mal, "and I think it was shortly after that—when the shop failed to succeed and he didn't know where he was going with his life—he had a sort of breakdown."

Mal explains that it was right around this time that he lost his hand. "I didn't think Peter was there for me at the time. But now in hindsight I can understand why he wasn't, because he had his own demons to deal with. So we had a bit of a cold period there. From my point of view I think it was a different mental thing. And I can say, 'Well, look, he really wasn't the hero I thought he was.' It was a turning point for me. I always thought he was a strong character, but underneath it was that fractured soul. It was sad, tragic, because he had the world at his feet, you know? And a lot of it was self-sabotage. He couldn't blame anyone else."

Nostalgia washes over Mal as he reflects on his and Peter's travels together in the seventies. Back then, to be a globetrotting surfer was to be an explorer, a pioneer. There was London, France, a long drive across the U.S. There were those six-foot Hossegor A-frames, topless girls on the beach, the water bathtub warm, just the two of them out. There was that crazy night in Waikiki.

"Because we've had such good times together," says Mal, "it's not something you forget easily."

THE ACTOR

THERE WAS SNOW ON THE GROUND, THE temperature two or three degrees, the tiny, musty, claustrophobic hotel room, the creaky bed that killed his back, the dog-eared scripts that he'd gone over and gone over ad nauseam, and of course there were those demons, they took his breath away, they were like pinpricks to the heart.

It was the winter of 1971. Peter was in London. He'd come over to audition for the Royal Academy of Dramatic Art (RADA), one of the most respected drama schools in the world. Since he'd arrived a few days earlier he'd been doing everything right—practice, practice, practice—but now the fear and self-doubt set in. Had there been a surfable wave nearby he'd have run to it, but there wasn't, so he did the next best thing.

He hit the pub, ordered a pint, brooded over its frothy lip, ordered a second, felt the fear abate slightly, ordered a third, and somewhere near the bottom of it found levity and even clarity.

And so it went for the days leading up to what Peter felt was his destiny. On the afternoon of the audition he had just a couple of beers. He caught the tube over to RADA, following the elaborate directions that the Orson Welles-looking hotel receptionist had scrawled on a sheet of stationery and handed over with a "Godspeed to you, dear lad!" and a "Break a leg!"

And he did. With just enough beer in him to silence the demons and draw out the pluck and focus and whatever that stuff is that gets us out of our own way, he delivered his *Henry V* and *Tom Jones* monologues on the mark. Not long after he got the good news: he'd been accepted into RADA. He also got the bad news: the next term didn't start for nearly a year!

With the excitement of the audition behind him, and nothing but the sad hotel room and dreary London streets and no friends to speak of in front of him, Peter fell into a depression. He knew deep in his bones that there was no way he'd be hanging out in London till the RADA term started. Depression turned to panic attacks. It was a hell he was all too familiar with, and it seemed unnecessary, regional. So he thought, *Bugger this.*

He caught the train down to Cornwall, hurled himself into the great elixir that is the ocean, found solace and a much happier version of himself on the steel-grey waves of Newquay. He got a job in a surf shop, shaped a bunch of boards, and took them over to the southwest of France. He sold the boards at a healthy profit, crashed on friends' couches, assumed the guise of flâneur, albeit with a surfy bent, slashed up and down the meaty waves of Gué-thary, drank obscenely cheap bottles of good Bordeaux, dazzled and was dazzled by a seemingly endless array of Martines and Brigittes and Aurélies, and found his center, or as close to a center as he was capable of.

After a couple of weeks he headed back to England, this time to Devon, where he stayed with a family he'd met who lived in a farmhouse amid rolling hills and livestock. The family bought and sold antiques for a living, traveling often to Holland. Peter went along on one of the trips, worked for them. It was fun to be so far from the competitive surf scene that had wronged him.

In Devon he learned of another world-renowned acting academy, the London Academy of Music and Dramatic Art (LAMDA). LAMDA was having open auditions for the upcoming term, starting in less than a month. Peter decided he'd give it a go.

For the audition you had to do two pieces: one from Shakespeare, the other modern. Peter chose the ones he knew: *Henry V* and *Tom Jones.*

Peter's hosts went to Holland, leaving him alone to sink deep into his rehearsals. The weather was nasty cold. Snow covered the grassy hills. Peter carved himself a sword from a piece of wood. In the afternoons he'd rug up in wellies, a wool coat, scarf and cap, and head outside. He'd find the cattle, usually at the crest of a hill overlooking a valley, and perform for them.

"Snow falling on their heads and their ears, and their noses were just running, avalanches of snot, it was so friggin' cold!" laughs Westerly at the memory.

Peter reasoned that the cows had heightened sensitivity, that in their simplistic cow brains they knew the difference between a true delivery and a false one.

"One of the cattle would move its head towards Pete and he'd think, *Thank god for that, someone appreciates me.*"

After earning the bovine equivalent of a standing ovation, he'd move onto the next hilltop, take up with a fresh herd of cattle, and experiment with a louder, more forceful delivery.

"The Shakespeare scene was 'Harfleur,' where they're losing this particular battle, so he rallies the men for one more attack. It needs to be roaring, then quiet, then roaring, then quiet, and it finishes with a roar. Well, Pete's voice was never deep 'cause inside was a little girl."

Westerly transports herself back to the rehearsal. She draws a vivid image of Peter knee-deep in snow, snow powdering his head and shoulders, vast whiteness, his audience—the snow-covered cows—huddled around him, standing so still Peter wondered if they were dead, their eyes empty and unblinking.

Peter channels a massive, Laurence Olivier-inspired Henry, roaring so loud it echoes across the entire valley, his sword raised above his head like Excalibur.

"Lo and behold, two cows, then three turned their heads and looked at him. He thought, *Right, I'm going to the audition tomorrow!*"

Peter catches the train to London, takes a double-decker bus to Hammersmith, checks into a little hotel. His room is small and moldy; he slips into a funk. Sure enough, his demons emerge.

"It was almost like, *They're here! Stop, stop, stop! No, it's all right, just hang in there."*

He figured a couple of beers would do him good. He went downstairs to the dingy pub, ordered a beer, got talking to the tweedy, bearded fellow on the bar stool next to him, a Dubliner with a brogue so thick Peter had to ask him to repeat everything.

"He had Peter in stitches. And Peter probably had ten or fifteen of these big beers." Westerly measures a giant pint glass with her hands. "He got totally wiped out."

Neither Westerly nor Peter can remember how he made it up to his room that night, but Westerly clearly recalls the bolt of panic Peter felt when he woke in his clothes, looked at the clock, and saw that the audition was less than two hours away. The room spun. His head thumped. Worse than a hangover, he was still drunk. He got up, went to the toilet and tried to make himself throw up, but it wouldn't come. A belch as rancid as a fart stole from his mouth. He grimaced in disgust, changed into boardshorts and sneakers and nothing else, and hit the street.

It was viciously cold out. The sky was low and grey. The buildings looked sad. Patches of snow huddled in shadows. London workers trotted down footpaths in heavy wool and gloves, each breath a puff of smoke. And there's Peter, half naked, sprinting through it all like he's training for the Olympics, only his head's so blurry he can hardly see straight, his lips mumbling his line from *Henry V*, "Now set the teeth and stretch the nostril wide." He ran for the better part of an hour, hoping to shake off the fuzz.

He went back to the hotel, showered, dressed, raced to catch the bus, and showed up at LAMDA about fifteen minutes early. When he sat, when he finally stopped, he was so nervous he was shaking.

"It would have been perfect if he'd auditioned as the Hunchback of Notre Dame," laughs Westerly.

He entered the theater, met the three dour-faced teachers. "They looked like parole officers in the Alabama State Prison," says Westerly. "Peter thought, *Have I come to court or something? Is this the right place?"*

Peter took the stage, realized he'd forgotten his sword, stuttered and flubbed his way through the *Tom Jones* piece. There was a long pause when he finished.

"May we have your Shakespeare piece, please?" asked one of the three teachers.

Quivering, Peter launched into it. As the lines started coming out of his mouth he found himself taking them up, way up, so ginormous and roaring that, as Westerly puts it, "If you'd have heard it you'd have called the fire brigade right away! You should have seen their faces. Well, their mouths were so wide open that you could have stuck some ten-pin bowls in them quite comfortably."

Westerly chuckles. "The mouths stayed open for a long while. When they finally closed them it was like the end of World War II. They stared at Peter for about three minutes. Finally the guy on the left says, "That'll be all now. We'll be in touch. Goodbye now.""

•

Peter went back to Devon, gathered up his things, and headed over to the southwest of France, where a friend had lent him a cottage to stay at in Arcachon. The winter swells pumped, and he made plenty of new friends amid the rifling tubes of La Piste and Hossegor. Between sessions they lit fires on the beach, sipped wine and ate sandwiches. Peter was lavishly complimented for his freakish surfing skills.

But this wasn't why he'd come to Europe.

"Pete thought, *Well, I'm back. It's not great to be back, but at least I feel safe, I feel secure, no more panic attacks.*"

After two weeks in Arcachon Peter flew back to the Gold Coast. He moved in with his parents, withdrew from friends, and slipped into a heavy depression. He saw doctors, was prescribed medication. On one of his more crestfallen days a letter arrived from LAMDA. The news was exactly as Peter had expected.

"That was the final straw. That was the last time Peter attempted to become the thing that he was meant for."

The telling of this story takes place over two breakfasts, a leisurely drive through Southport, a visit to some op shops and a long dinner at CSi Club Southport, a workman's restaurant that Westerly and Zac frequent—three days in total. I'd asked Westerly to tell me about Peter's stint at the prestigious NIDA (National Institute of Dramatic Art) in Sydney, and instead of starting in 1972, the year he was admitted, she took it back to Surfers Paradise in the late fifties, when Gwendolyn would take little Pete and Tony to the cinema every Sunday. Westerly's descriptions had all the fairy tale qualities of *Cinema Paradiso*, a movie about a boy who falls in love with movies. There was Marilyn and Judy and Montgomery and Marlon, towering twenty-five-feet tall in black and white, there was the quoting of lines from *A Star Is Born* and *Judgment At Nuremberg* and *The Wild One*, there were the vivid details: the marquee with its lights and letters, the ruddy, tubercular man in the ticket booth, the scuffed seats and velvet curtain, the crunch of popcorn, the butter and salt-slicked fingers. It was beautiful watching Westerly inhabit these days of wonder and imagination.

She remembers Gwendolyn taking Peter to the TAB when he was in his teens. They'd make small bets, cheer loudly for their horses. Peter loved the race calls, their urgent tempo, the fact that they were happening in real time.

Peter went on auditions for talent shows. They rarely ended well. He had this huge theatrical side that surfaced of its own accord, but try to draw it out on command and it failed him.

"Mum would take Peter up to Brisbane, they'd go into the studio for the audition, fill out the form, go right up to the edge of when it was Peter's go and then he would wilt, the panic attacks overwhelming." Westerly shakes her head in awe. "He'd say, 'No, Mum, I can't.' She'd say, 'Okay,' and they'd walk out. This insecurity was so powerful inside of him. It was like all his bones were riddled with insecurity the moment he stepped on land."

Peter had a hero who bridged his two loves. His name was Miki Dora. In the mid-fifties Dora was Malibu's finest surfer. Known as "Da Cat" for his nimble footwork and jittery flourishes, he rode with elegance and attitude. But his legend was built on much more than just his surfing.

In his car he kept a bottle of champagne and two flutes. At VIP parties in Hollywood Dora and a friend would fill their glasses and walk backwards past security. He was a petty thief—supposedly he once stole a famous actor's Oscar. Surf contests came to the fore in the late fifties. Dora took part for a while, albeit reluctantly. In one event he rode a twelve-foot tandem board in the final (the surfing equivalent to running a ten-kilometer race in ski boots). In another he went up to collect his first-place trophy and, in front of fans, judges, media and fellow surfers, hurled it straight into the sand. His coup de grâce came in the 1967 Malibu Invitational. In the semifinals, with thousands of spectators watching from the beach, he took off on a wave, dropped his shorts, and flashed his bare ass while riding the length of First Point.

Dora is the most quoted surfer in history:

No problem is so big or so complicated that it can't be run away from.

My whole life is this wave. I drop in, set the thing up and, behind me, all this stuff goes over my back; the screaming parents, teachers, police, priests, politicians—they're all going over the falls headfirst into the reef. And when it starts to close out, I pull out the back, pick up another wave, and do the same goddamn thing.

Waves are the ultimate illusion. They come out of nowhere, instantaneously materialize, and just as quickly they break and vanish. Chasing after such fleeting mirages is a complete waste of time. That is what I choose to do with my life.

Dora's repartee had an urban edge to it, but his aesthetic was pure and simple and even transcendentalist. He despised the commercialization of surfing. When *Gidget* hit—first the book, then the movie and TV series, Malibu Barbie, Chevy Malibu, the Beach Boys, Jan and Dean, Frankie and Annette, the whole hideous surf craze—Dora felt as if his beloved Malibu had been ripped out from under him. He knew it was time to hit the road.

Funded primarily through bogus credit cards, forged checks and the kindness of bewitched, often deep-pocketed friends, Dora gallivanted around the world riding the best waves, drinking the finest wines and living life on his own terms, all the while avoiding any semblance of "work." His surfboard was his magic carpet and his wits were his wings, and from the late sixties up until his death in 2002, except for a couple of brief prison stints, Dora lived the *Endless Summer* lifestyle, defining what it means to be a surfer.

He traveled with great panache. In Argentina he played tennis and dined in the finest restaurants with the president's daughter. In Romania he lived with gypsies in a paisley caravan. In Morocco he wore a turban and got around by camel. It's hard to say how many of these accounts are true, and probably a lot aren't, but no matter. Dora lived by the creed: "Never let the truth get in the way of a good story."

His legend grew to such absurd proportions that even unpleasant brushes with Dora carried big street cred. You have Miki over for dinner, you invite your wife's best-looking friend, you bust out your finest wines and favorite albums, you serve up a four-course meal, and at the end of it, you hope that he's pocketed the Montblanc pen or ivory shoehorn you planted in the bathroom, just so you can brag about it to your friends.

Drew Kampion wrote about the time Dora showed up at the *Surfer* magazine offices in his typically mysterious and high-strung manner. He sat in his van in the parking lot for a long while, let news of his arrival spread throughout the building. John Severson, the publisher of *Surfer*, went out to greet him, brought him into his office, invited editor Kampion to join them. Dora talked about his recent trip to South America, how he'd brought back "certain compact, highly portable natural resources from their rich native soils." After more cryptic preamble, after stating that "opportunity only knocks once," he opened his briefcase, took out another smaller case, opened it, pulled out a velvet pouch, and produced from it a constellation of "rare Brazilian topaz." Miki poked at it with jeweler's tweezers, took great delight in Severson and Kampion's wondrous faces. "Only once in a lifetime," said Dora.

"How much?" the publisher asked.

"How much?" exclaimed Miki, stiffening.

"For one of . . . For this one," said Severson, pointing gingerly at one glorious gemstone.

"I should have known," huffed Miki, snapping the case closed so briskly it almost caught John's indicative digit. "These are highly personal . . . precious family keepsakes . . . very important to me . . . heirlooms I could never bear to part with . . . How could you be so presumptuous as to think I'd ever sell them?"

The jeweler's case went into the briefcase and, all in the same motion, Dora rose and fled the room. John called after him, trying to explain that he hadn't understood, had just made a mistake, it had seemed Miki wanted to . . .

But Miki Dora was gone. A car door slammed, the little fourbanger chugged to life, and the van wheezed out of the lot.

•

"Peter loved Miki," Westerly tells me. "He loved his style and his showmanship. He was always larger than life." In old surf movies of Dora you see him clowning on the beach, holding court, suffering fools nastily. In dark sunglasses and with a snaggletoothed grin he hams for the camera, but also hates the camera—he smiles sardonically, raises his middle finger.

"Peter Drouyn had that Dora thing," the filmmaker Jack McCoy told me. "Look at me, look at me, look at me. *Don't look at me!*"

•

"So what about NIDA?" I ask Westerly over plates of Kung Pao chicken and sticky rice.

Westerly leaps back to 1968. At the height of his surfing powers, Peter got word of an audition for the play *Tom Jones*, to be staged at the Gold Coast Theatre. Salt-crusted from the morning surf, Peter tumbled in, read for the leading role, nailed it, and plunged into rehearsals with acclaimed director John Trevor. *Tom Jones* had a four-night run, its 1,000 seats sold out every night.

"So Pete had given up on acting. But he'd heard about NIDA, and in 1971 he rang John Trevor. And John was actually the chairman of the Shakespearean Theatre Trust, a huge thing in Sydney then. Pete called John, asked if he could help him get an audition."

Westerly goes into a long impersonation of Trevor, with his cane and his cigars and his elegant English accent.

"John said, 'You get yourself down here and we'll talk about it.'"

Peter caught a bus to Sydney. John picked him up at Central Station in his old MG. Westerly describes the rattle of the car, John's round spectacles, his ascot, the cigar dangling from his mouth, his cream-colored blazer and pressed cream-colored trousers and polished brown leather shoes, "shiny like a mirror."

"John saw the potential inside Peter when he did *Tom Jones*. Although John nearly slapped Peter over the face many times and stuck him behind a curtain: *Drouyn, I'm going to strangle you if you don't learn your lines! You stand there in that circle and you just say those bloody words!* He was like a sergeant major in the Zulu War!"

Westerly does a funny impersonation, bouncing from aristocratic/militant John to her studied Marilyn giggle, smile, crumpled shoulders.

John took Peter to his home. After catching up on all that had transpired in London, he called NIDA. It turned out that they'd just had their auditions for the upcoming term. John convinced them to give Peter a shot.

"John saw the potential in Peter, and I think he saw right through to Westerly. This man was extraordinary, unique, quirky, all the Einstein things. Peter got along well with those sorts of people—the wise mentor, the Merlin if you like. He pulled out a sword and said, 'Put this sword in your hand, Drouyn. It's the Excalibur!'"

Westerly describes the sword in great detail, the jewels, the sharp blade, the heavy weight of it. I thought she was speaking metaphorically, but no.

"So John hands Peter this sword. 'You're going to use the sword and it's going to become part of you, and we're going to instill you with the spirit of St. George and Henry V, and we're going to turn this into an epic feat.'"

For the next four or five days John worked with Peter on the two scenes, breaking down every line, every intonation of every word.

On the day of the audition Peter was hit with a bad case of nerves. But he thought, *I can't let John down.* He went to a corner pub and had just two beers. He entered the theatre at NIDA, met the panel of five who would be auditioning him. Pleasantries about John V. Trevor, director of the Shakespearean Theatre Trust, were exchanged.

Peter took the stage, did the *Tom Jones* bit, and everything fell right into place. Then he did the Shakespeare piece, using John's Excalibur, and "annihilated it." The members of the panel said little but smiled approvingly.

Peter went back to John's. The next day came the phone call: he was in.

"They usually took fourteen out of about 10,000 people who audition. Pete got a fifteenth place. They made an extra spot for him."

•

In January 1972, Peter moved into a flat in Coogee with three fellow NIDA students. He started his first term a few days later.

"But as soon as Peter walked through those gates he found a world that was alien, it wasn't what he expected. Peter picked up on a falseness in the people. It was like those saloons in western movies, they're not real saloons, they're just facades held up by two-by-fours. They were all acting like little gods and goddesses. They found out Pete was a champion surfer and ostracized him."

The irony of this is glaring, and while I resist getting psychoanalytical, I can't help but see a pattern: ostracized by the surfers for being too theatrical; ostracized by the thespians for being a great surfer.

Westerly tells me that about a month into the term, Peter was browsing in the library when he found *The Life of Constantin Stanislavski*, the biography that describes method acting. He was fascinated. The idea of full immersion in a character struck a chord that he knew intuitively as a surfer. He devoured the book, found more like it, filled his head with the "Method."

"Peter wanted to be like Brando or Montgomery Clift or Clark Gable. He was interested in the Method but his teachers discouraged this," says Westerly.

That first year was full of strife. Of his fourteen fellow students, "Peter didn't get along with at least eleven of them." His teachers were promoting a troupe/Shakespeare approach while Peter wanted the Method and all its room for exploration.

"They called him everything from a selfish actor to someone who's not a team player to someone who's lazy to someone who acts like there's no one else in the room to someone with limited acting ability in the theatre."

There were a couple of teachers whom Peter got along well with. According to Westerly, both told Peter that they saw things in him that they'd never seen before in an actor. But that wasn't enough. At the end of his first term Peter was called in for a meeting with some of the NIDA faculty.

"They're all sitting there like Knights of the Round Table," remembers Westerly, her eyes fixed on her half-eaten meal, her mouth pinched, her head shaking in revulsion. "They say, 'We've come to a decision that you're not suited to this institution, and we're of the opinion that we can't accept you for a second year. So, um, pack your things and go.'"

THE MOVIE STAR

THE DECEMBER 1973 ISSUE OF *TRACKS* FEATURES Evo's dispatch from the first leg of the trip. Titled "High Adventures with Bob Evans," he lays down a mission statement, explaining that he has been making surf movies for fourteen years, that they have featured the best Aussie surfers and that he hopes his films have helped them achieve the goal they were after:

> "This new picture will reflect what I believe is a more complete picture of what the surfers of the world have attained in finding out for themselves, what surfing has done in broadening their style of life... Sure, I know plenty of guys are happy in being surrounded by waves and this is all they need but, I think for more people surfing has opened up fresh fields of interest—travel, adventure, new friends, new attitudes—all of it opened up by the magic that surfing has introduced."

He lists the sponsors: Australian Film Development Corporation, AMCO & Bonds, Qantas. He introduces the team he's assembled: Peter Drouyn "because he will have a go at damn near anything on land or sea," Bruce Channon, Gaylene Grayson (one of the sponsor's girlfriends), and his son, Brett Evans "so I can keep an eye on him." He lays down their ambitious itinerary— a six-month odyssey that goes Mauritius, South Africa, Angola, Canary Islands, Morocco, Portugal, Spain, France, England, Central America, Japan, and Indonesia. He tells how they boarded their flight out of Sydney all fired-up and stoked only to realized he'd left behind 10,000 feet of Ektachrome (all the film, in other words) in the trunk of his car. That's OK. They order champagne, lots of it, and slip right into what would become the spirit of the trip (the film arrived a couple days later).

Seated on the sofa in Bruce's living room, I ask what it was like traveling with Peter Drouyn.

"Peter from the start had figured the movie was going to be about him. Whether Evo had figured that out at the start or not, I don't know. But Peter had certainly figured it out. So every time we arrived in a new country, Peter would deck himself out in the clothing of that place. In South Africa he bought an Afrikaner safari suit and hat. In France he bought a beret and a baguette. It was part of this acting thing that he was moving into, or wanted to be a part of. He'd seen *Last Tango in Paris*, and so he'd put on a little scene about that in various restaurants that we'd get to."

The trip followed the model laid down by *The Endless Summer*. They were on the search for the perfect wave, or at least some really great waves. There were, of course, digressions. In the Transkei they visit a leper colony. In Mauritius they climb the highest peak on the island, the 2,700-foot Piton de la Petite Rivière Noire. From Jeffreys Bay they loop around Capetown and up the west coast to the fabled Elands Bay, where they score double-overhead, oily-glass lefthanders strewn with bull kelp, their heads so big and vines so long they look like giant squid.

There's a whole lot of Peter charming women throughout the film. On the beach in Japan he holds a cute, bashful, bikini-clad girl's head in his hands and kisses and smiles at her. In an al fresco café in what looks like France, he and a willowy brunette rise from the table. Peter takes her hand and slinks James Bondishly off with her, presumably to some elegant honeymoon suite. You get the sense that he essentially fucked his way around the world. There's a lot of hamming for the cameras: Peter fist-pumping like King Kong atop a Mauritius peak; Peter swaggering naked on a French beach; Peter, jowls stuffed with tissue, impersonating Brando in *The Godfather* on some sailboat on a tropical sea.

Was Peter just constantly *on*?

"We fought over it, it almost came to fisticuffs," says Bruce. "To his credit, he was the catalyst that got things going. But on the other side, I was helping Evo to make a film and Peter would have used up all our film before we got out of J-Bay. The little scene at the start in Mauritius where he's firing guns and things, that went on for hours, we shot so much film of that and it was always just going to be thrown out. I was a surfer, I wanted a good surf movie, I didn't care about that other stuff, whereas Peter, he was on that 'I want to be a movie star' thing."

I ask Bruce if there were ever quiet moments with Peter. "Aw, yeah," he says without hesitation. "He was good company."

Was there any serious conflict?

"Evo and Peter would get into heated arguments. They had a father–son relationship. They'd lock each other in the toilets and bash each other. They'd come out with no blood, with arms around each other, the problem resolved."

Bruce says that Evo was brilliant but terribly disorganized. "We were dead broke in France. We got to France with no money. Evo was hassling his brother to bail him out, or the sponsors to send him money. We got to England and borrowed enough money to get us to Japan. And in Japan he convinced Cathay Pacific to give us air tickets down through Jakarta to Perth, which got us back home again.

"Evo had bowel cancer very young in life. He had a colostomy bag. It shaped his life, I feel. He spent a long period in hospital, had an operation. The hole he had was gross. It was like a Balinese toilet, it was always dirty. He had to clean it constantly. But from that moment on I reckon Evo lived every day like it was his last. So he had this wonderful outlook on life. Every day was a bonus. He'd sing Italian arias in this big voice; he was a larger-than-life character. That's why you'd go on a trip like that; you'd have no money but you'd have a three-course meal that night, you'd have the best wines, devil may care, sort it out in the morning. He borrowed money, but didn't always deliver on his promise. It would end where you'd never deal with him again, but the passion and charisma he brought were almost worth it."

•

Peter Drouyn surfs magnificently throughout the film, and gets better and better with each destination. In Mauritius, at the fabled Tamarind Bay, he's all twitching bottom turns and beefy off the tops. In South Africa, at Jeffreys Bay and Cape St. Francis, he's tensed and angry, a rhinoceros horn of a front arm telegraphing his dizzying zigs and zags. In Japan, surfing a small beach break in Speedos, he bashes the crystalline lips with a vengeance.

The climax comes in Bali at Uluwatu, a world-class lefthander that breaks at the base of dark, craggy cliffs topped with a Hindu temple. Peter exudes something feral, possessed. It's not something that happens solely on the wave, it's in the paddle out, the way he straddles his board and cranes his neck up to create a watchtower from which to see rising swells. The water is a velvety emerald green, the offshore wind sends needles of spray over the backs of waves, a sort of acupuncture that, when it showers Peter as he duck dives under pitching lips, charges every cell in his body.

A three-times overhead wave looms, Peter wheels around, strokes, feels lifted, raised up by some hand of god, pops to his feet and whooshes with great speed down the face. While the offshore wind grooms and organizes the lineup, it also dimples the surface, and finding the edge, setting the rail into precisely the right wink of water, is key. It's here where Peter goes into his transcendental state. That hyper-awareness—a combination of watching, reading, intuiting—quiets the senses, so while he's heaving his board up and down the face, his body nearly upside down in some of his top turns, he's actually deeply relaxed. His rail work is masterful. Big, freight train waves such as these require marathon pacing, as opposed to the sprint that is small-wave surfing. It's something like navigating a maze—pick the wrong line and you end up in a dead end, not making the wave. Peter literally sits back into his bottom turns, his ass caressing the surface of the water, his hands part Bruce Lee, part Merlin the spellcaster.

It doesn't take an erudite surfer to get that this is an athlete extending beyond himself. He is without a leash, Uluwatu's shoreline is not a sandy beach but a jagged cliff that eats surfboards, yet Drouyn insists on attempting a figure-eight cutback in which he carves back into the tube and spears the lip. In the seventies, surf movies often had animated parts that depicted the surfing you did in your mind, probably on acid—barrel rolls, loop-the-loops, corkscrewing aerials in which you boardslide across the sun. Peter's move is of this ilk. He's so profoundly in his groove it's as if he just wants to finger tap untouched reaches of the wave. The bodysurfing, the long swim against currents, the crawling over shallow coral reef to retrieve his boards—well, that's just what sea creatures do.

I've always believed that great surfers need not be doing anything highly advanced for us to sense their genius. Peter supports this in a slow-motion bit where rather than zig and zag he simply stands tall, arms casually at his sides, and enjoys all that Indian Ocean energy running beneath his feet. His stance is narrow, his torso is Herculean, his golden locks flutter like a cape.

"I adapted Method acting to surfing," Peter told surf writer Tim Baker in *Deep* twenty-plus years later:

> You focus, like the ninja. You focus completely and clear the mind and do the exercises before you go out and develop the power, the energy, and your mind is so clear that the only thing coming at you is the reality of life and the mobility of time. That is, wherever you walk or in surfing, there is bound to be something coming at you. In this case, it was waves, but I didn't call them waves. I could clear my mind so much that they were just things. There was no names to them . . . it was all just instinct. I grew a beard, I never shaved and I never wore any colors, because that's all against the natural—that's self-possession. I unleashed all the self, material things around you, shaving. I became the complete one with

nature . . . so the body movement is all completely natural . . . The incredible thing was this enhanced your ability to stay on the board so I really couldn't fall off. I was glued to the board, so you were one with this painting, this picture, that was moving.

I ask Westerly about this session. She tells me much the same thing she told Tim, but adds a few more details: a dugong that swam up to Peter, keeled sideways, looked into his eyes with a sort of aquatic familiarity; an albatross that played follow-the-leader with Peter as he glided across a lustrous wall. "It was never captured on film," she says, "but I promise it happened just as I've told you."

•

The poster for *Drouyn and Friends* featured an exaggerated, superhero-like Peter Drouyn floating in the sky, fully nude with a big dick. Two-time world champion Tom Carroll was a thirteen-year-old, freckle-faced grommet when he saw it hanging in a local shop in Newport, Sydney. "Drouyn floating through the air, nude . . . I thought, *Where's the surfing in that?* As a kid I was looking for the surfing. I thought it detracted from that. But it was a strong image. I'll never forget it." Adding even more weirdness, to help promote the film, Peter appeared in a nude pictorial in *Cleo*.

•

Drouyn and Friends premiered at a wine cellar in Sydney. Phil Jarratt wrote about the night in a 1977 issue of *Surfer*:

> The star presented himself for the occasion in a yachtsman's navy blazer and flared white slacks and when the lights came back on he let forth with a stream-of-consciousness rave that incorporated every nuance of manic brilliance that he'd

picked up in bars around the world, the National Institute of Dramatic Art, and a decade in the jetstream of international surfing. With a bevy of hand movements that fell somewhere between those of a punch-drunk fighter and those of an effete politician he enacted Evo's dream. These days, whenever I think about Drouyn and the fine line that separates genius from madman, I recall that performance and I am reassured.

Sadly, *Drouyn and Friends* flopped. Reviews were mixed—mostly poor—in the surf mags. It didn't get nearly the run in theatres that Evo and company had hoped for. It may have been upstaged by the zeitgeist-changing *Morning of the Earth*, which featured Nat Young and friends living free and easy on the northern New South Wales coast. It may have been that the travelogue form was on the out. It may have been Peter Drouyn overkill.

Bruce Channon regards the film warmly. "*Drouyn and Friends* was a fulcrum point. It showed me where I wanted to go. Not long after I went to work at *Surfing World*, and that whole path."

Westerly is still disappointed: "No one understood. No one got it."

In 1976, while touring *Drouyn and Friends* in Florida, Bob Evans died suddenly of a brain hemorrhage. He was forty-seven.

•

I love the film because it encompasses much of what had attracted me to surfing in the first place. There's the great, iconoclastic, mercurial Big Personality, delivered in spades by Peter Drouyn; there's travel to far-flung places; there are epic, dreamy waves; there are gorgeous, foreign girls who likely speak not a word of English. When I add that up in my Peter/Westerly-mining state I come up with a repeated theme: escape.

A few legs into my pro tour life, probably half-drunk at a bar or scribbling in my journals on a long flight, I had the realization that travel was like severing ties to your own personal history. In a new country, amid the white noise of a foreign language, not only can you reinvent yourself, but you can access new sides of yourself that might never surface otherwise. This was something very different to the "finding out what you're made of" that happened on the competitive surfing front. This was a very singular inner journey. It was the person who came out when I was laid over for three days in Rio, alone in a mosquito-infested hotel, or on the twenty-plus hours and four flights it took to get from LA to Cape Town, or in the deepest, darkest corners of a heavy jetlag trip. It was a heightened kinship with the fictional characters I was spending time with via Norman Mailer, Paul Theroux, Jack Kerouac, F. Scott Fitzgerald, Tom Robbins, Jean-Paul Sartre, Dostoyevsky. It was a self-erasure of sorts, at least I imagined it to be, and it was intoxicating.

Later, when my pro surfing career ended, I continued to travel frequently, this time under the guise of journalist/writer. Now I realize it was surfing that cracked that open for me. It's actually built into the deal: you start at your local break, you venture up and down the coast, you do a trip to some good-wave destination, and if surfing gets its claws into you, you spend your days dreaming of Jeffreys Bay in South Africa, or Uluwatu in Bali, or the North Shore of Oahu. You spend your twenties and thirties and possibly the rest of your life chasing waves around the world.

This has been my path and the path of most of the people in this book. For a long while I patted myself on the back for being intellectually curious, for throwing myself at new cultures, new experiences. I saw only the romance. But well into my thirties I started to think about the flipside. What was I running from? Why couldn't I stay in one place and be happy? Why did I feel so rootless? The same way decades-long substance abuse can rewire your chemisty, render you dissatisfied with everyday joys, so can too much of this wave- and adventure-chasing. You find yourself forever on the outside of things. You know that you've always got a ticket out.

This seemed to be the plight of Miki Dora, in the very literal sense. And though there's much more to it, this no doubt contributes to the saga of Peter Drouyn/Westerly Windina.

·

After that year on the road shooting *Drouyn and Friends*, Peter fell into a deep depression. It was as if the Gold Coast could no longer fulfill him. His parents admitted him to a mental hospital.

"It was a horrible place," says Westerly. "Peter was fearing for his sanity. After two weeks he departed through a window in the middle of the night and went home."

THE VISIONARY

IN MANY WAYS PETER WAS THE LAST MAN standing, though he didn't see it that way. It was 1976. The radical design experimentation that spawned from the shortboard revolution had subsided, and boards were becoming more conventional. There was a new generation at the fore—Mark Richards, Wayne "Rabbit" Bartholomew, Peter Townend, Ian Cairns, Shaun Tomson—who saw great potential for competitive surfing.

"We were nearly trying to will a sport into existence," remembers 1978 world champion Rabbit Bartholomew. "We felt we had to transcend ourselves to bring attention to the fact that we regarded ourselves as professional sportsmen. It was against the grain internally, because there were a lot of surfers who didn't see themselves like that, who still just wanted to be wild child surfers."

Peter had come from the longboard/wild child era. The surfers he'd grown up competing against had nearly all been put out to pasture. Peter, though, had seamlessly made the jump from longboard to shortboard. He was still hailed as one of the best surfers in the world.

But Peter saw only the failures. He saw the 1966 Aussie Titles where they made it look like Nat and Bob and Keith were inventing all those power moves. He saw the "We're Tops Now" article, and that whole friggin' Sydney mafia conspiring against him. He saw the '69 Aussies when they took it off him—and felt something like knives in his heart. And those were just the obvious ones. There was also the Aussie Titles in 1970, when they tried to change the format on him. There was the cover shot that was never a cover shot. There was . . .

These were the things that flitted across Peter's mind on, say, a long solo drive up the coast, or yet another sleepless night. These were the things that brought on the demons. Left alone for too long, they'd spiral and snowball and sabotage.

•

In 1976 the IPS was formed, corralling together a ragtag bunch of contests to create the original international pro circuit. When Peter got word of this he felt like the train was moving on without him. *They're doing it again!*

And then the phone rang.

Brian Kelvin, general manager of Stubbies clothing, a friend of Peter's father, introduced himself, explained that Stubbies was hoping to break into the burgeoning surf market, and wondered if Peter might like to direct a contest.

"Direct" was what Brian had said, but "mastermind" was what Peter heard.

"I thought of all the bad points of surfing: the judging, the judging criteria, the competitive style, the infrastructure of contests was wrong, the number of surfers in the water, the types of judges, everything was just on the nose," Peter told Tim Baker in 1997:

> And I think one of the reasons, if not the greatest reason for the demise of surfing competition; it had quite simply run its term and it needed a big change, it needed a complete revolution, you know, much like any other historical revolution, for it to get going again, so I came up with that idea . . .
>
> Funnily enough, I knew it would work the moment I got off the phone. There was never any doubt in my mind that it would work, and that's something that still to this day I find quite remarkable, that I never, ever once flinched, never doubted that it would work, and I never doubted that we'd

get good surf. And it was like the perfect, like St. Peter and the fishes, like walking on water.

Up until that point, heats were comprised of four or six competitors, a blur of surfers in colored jerseys, making it impossible for the spectator to get a sense of who was winning. Drawing from boxing, tennis and the Roman gladiators he'd seen in movies, Peter came up with man-on-man surfing.

"We want something concrete, some physical and mental contact where we can vibrate off each other," he told Phil Jarratt over a few schooners at the Surfers Beer Garden floorshow in the summer of 1976 (as recounted in Jarratt's book *The Wave Game*). "Like in boxing, we want to be able to touch the other guy. Let him look at me and say, 'Well fuck you' or 'I love you' or 'Let's fight it out to the end.' Let's have some contact going."

"You want the surfers in this contest to be human," said Phil.

"Yeah, exactly. Until we have some sort of contact in surfing contests it's going to be the same thing year after year. It's stagnated even though the prize money is bigger these days. Sponsors don't really see the value in surfing contests. They just see the value in selling their goods to young people. Tennis sponsors like tennis. In surfing the sponsors think surfing contests are ridiculous, they don't understand. A guy can actually whip a guy off the wave, beat him up, come onto the beach and have a fight if you like. That's okay. We won't give any bonus points for it but the important thing is that they can beat each other up. This is the sort of contact that can be done along rhythmic lines."

"Like Ali dancing round his opponent for the entire first round or Arthur Ashe throwing his racquet over the net," said Phil.

"Yeah. Ali might dance around the ring for the first two minutes but there must eventually be physical contact for a win. There's got to be a blow thrown. Now if they wanted to those boxers could dance for fifteen rounds without throwing a punch and who's gonna win?"

"But surely you're not suggesting that surfing is a real contact sport?"

Peter took a sip of his beer. "Phil, it can be. I feel it's the only way surfing is going to reach into big money in competition. Contact both physically and mentally. A blow must be thrown. Surfing's the same. I mean I could dance around a ring showing my style and my aggression and what's the judge going to say? Oh, he's got a lot of style. He would have done well if there'd been a fight. There must be contact in surfing."

•

It was more than just the man-on-man format; Peter let his imagination run wild as he conceived of every last detail of the Stubbies Pro. Since its inauguration in 1962 the annual Bells Beach Easter contest in Victoria had been Australia's biggest surf tournament, drawing contestants from around the world. But Bells was often blustery cold—surfers in full suits, spectators in woollen sweaters and heavy jackets. Wasn't it high time Queensland laid claim to this title, what with Michael Peterson and Rabbit and Peter Townend hailing from there? Peter wanted sunshine. Peter wanted flesh. Peter wanted Burleigh Heads!

Nailing down the right time slot was key. Peter had it etched into his nervous system. For as long as he'd been surfing, March was the month of crystalline cyclone swells wrapping themselves around the Gold Coast points. He declared the dates: March 12–20. The contest needed less than half this many days to run, but the waiting period would ensure they got the best-quality surf. Press releases were sent out: the Stubbies Pro would introduce a revolutionary new format, the prize purse would be a whopping $12,300, with the winner receiving $5,000, the biggest first-place check ever.

•

While Peter was imagining punch-ups in the Stubbies Pro, punchups were actually happening on the North Shore of Oahu. Rabbit Bartholomew had written "Bustin' Down the Door." Published in *Surfer*, his treatise announced in no uncertain terms how the emerging rookies from Australia and South Africa meant to achieve revolution on the North Shore. Hawaiian culture is built on respect, humility. Surfers in particular observed a let-your-surfing-do-the-talking ethos. Rabbit's bold claims pushed them over the edge.

There were some serious beat-downs meted out on Rabbit, his fellow Aussies, and a South African or two. Death threats followed. It got so bad that more than one surfer lived in a state of siege at the nearby Kuilima resort.

With a briefcase full of invitations, Peter flew over to the North Shore, his first trip there in six years. Within a couple of days of his arrival he got into a biff with a local out in the surf. "There's a bit of aggro out there," he told Rabbit, who was holed up at the Kuilima.

Rabbit laid it out for him. "Look man, this, this is like real," he said. "But I don't think you're in the firing line, so yeah, just be careful."

Rabbit is remembering this twenty-five years later from his Tweed Heads living room. He breaks into laughter. "So he arrived, and he just disappeared. He absolutely just disappeared [back to Australia]. Then he arrived back on the North Shore, I'm talking about six weeks later. And he came and saw me again, and I'm still holed up, and he told me that he'd left me that night, and he was staying at Randy Rarick's place, and he went back and they had got his surfboard and attacked it with a knife or something, or an axe or a machete. And he got all paranoid, very quickly, and then he heard some rustling next to him, and he's turned around and he's just punched . . . *he's punched out a telegraph pole!* And broken his hand. And then, classic Drouyn style, just packed up and left that night for Australia."

While Peter was back in Australia, the press got wind of the tension. "Aussie Surf Champs Threatened" went one of the headlines. The articles teemed with quotes from Peter Drouyn. Word of this got back to the Hawaiians, fanning flames. Drouyn returned to the North Shore with none of the jitters of the first trip. He was all P.T. Barnum braggadocio. In a packed conference room in the Kuilima, an IPS conference was underway. The Hawaiians had only recently settled their score with the Bustin' Down the Door crew, but it was still eggshells, one false move and it could slip back to full-blown war.

Randy Rarick was at the podium, talking about next year's tour. "And now I'd like to bring up Peter Drouyn," he said.

Peter's entrance was full of the very cockiness that had got the Aussies into trouble in the first place. Clad in head-to-toe white, he swaggered through the parting crowd like a rock god taking the stage. He grabbed the mic, raised a pledging hand. "In March 1977 we're going to have man-on-man surfing," he announced. *"There's gonna be blood on the rocks at Burleigh!"*

Rabbit, Randy Rarick, Peter Townend, Shaun Tomson, everyone I talked to laughed when they remembered how bad Peter's timing was, how poor his choice of words.

•

Burleigh Heads is a long, sand-bottom point break that produces super-fast, super-hollow righthanders. Black boulders line the water. Behind it is a grassy knoll that stretches up to a headland. Save for the apartment blocks, it is the sort of idyllic scene you might have seen airbrushed on the side of a decked-out van in the mid-seventies. Peter saw it as a natural amphitheatre, with the waves as center stage.

A couple of days before the start of the Stubbies Pro, a team of workers pulled up to the Burleigh parking lot in trucks and pickups and began constructing what would become a small village of stages and towers and kiosks. At the Gold Coast airport, surfers dragged their cumbersome board boxes from the baggage claim out to the bright Queensland sun. They raced for Burleigh, checked into their hotels, and beelined for the water. Cars fought for parking spots, out of their doors poured surf fans and groupies from up and down the east coast. In the four-foot, sapphire blue waves, the typical pre-contest, psych-out-your-opponents session took place. Rabbit wrapped a blisteringly hard roundhouse cutback. PT stomped his tail and pulled into the tube as if parking a Porsche 911 in a singlecar garage. Michael Ho flew so fast across the rifling inside section he got speed wobbles and actually had to slow himself down.

The pre-contest reception was far more of an event than any pre-contest reception that had come before it. Held at the Burleigh pub, the forty-four invitees were first greeted by the Gold Coast mayor, then let loose at the open bar, where there was a huge smorgasbord of food, complete with a butter sculpture of a tubing Burleigh wave and a miniature surfer ducking beneath the yellow curtain. Lord Tally-ho Blears, a wrestling champion with a booming, baritone voice, had been flown over from Hawaii to MC the event.

"We'd like to extend a big welcome," he said, "to what's shaping up to be *the greatest surf contest on earth!*" He listed off the countries represented—Australia, Hawaii, South Africa, USA, Brazil, Bali, Great Britain—then handed over to Peter.

Peter was deep in character. With sweeps of the hands and juts of the hips he revved up the competitors with an explanation of how he'd developed the man-on-man format, how they'd be implementing a new judging criteria that favored individuality and free expression on the wave, how it was perfectly fine to drop in on your opponent—in fact, extra points would be given for destroying his ride. He delivered a state-of-the-union speech about professional surfing, its leaps and bounds forward, the poetic nature of dancing across water and getting paid for it. He funneled it all back to the Stubbies Pro, snapped his heels together, made parentheses with his hands: "We want to see Nadia Comaneci Olympic perfection: ten out of ten!"

.

The wave gods clearly liked what they saw in the Stubbies Pro because they delivered gorgeous, spiralling tubes for the six days of competition. Competitors played hide-and-seek with judges and spectators as they slipped behind blue curtain after blue curtain. The sky was cloudless. The sun blazed. The grassy lawns and headland were packed with spectators, creating the very natural amphitheatre effect that Peter had envisioned. And they were all in shorts and bikinis, tons of flesh, tie-dyed girls on quilt blankets as if it was Woodstock, flocks of blokes in cut-offs perusing the numerous tents selling surf gear, hot dogs, beer. It was well and truly the biggest sporting event the Gold Coast had ever seen.

One of Peter's beefs with surf contests was biased judging—typically the judges sat shoulder to shoulder. Peter remedied this by stationing them in towers twenty feet apart from each other so that they could neither see nor discuss each other's scores. A giant Marlboro scoreboard flashed the scores. Concert speakers blasted Lord Tally-ho's witty commentary.

For five consecutive days competitors delighted in the excellent waves, in the rock concert vibe, in the revelation that was man-on-man surfing. And on the sixth day, exactly as Peter had predicted, the swell jumped up. Double-overhead waves screamed down the point, producing below-sea-level tubes that, in their trough, refracted the sandy bottom and turned a dazzling mother-of-pearl. As contests go, it was an aligning of the stars. The surfers couldn't have dreamed up better conditions. The crowd—20,000 strong—was spellbound.

In the finals Michael Peterson and Mark Richards one-upped each other. For the first time in surfing history a kind of jousting took place. The sheer drama of a single ride resonated with all in attendence, even the non-surfers. Competitive surfing was elevated to a more pure, highbrow form. It didn't hurt that in the dying minutes local boy MP took off on one of the waves of the day, ducked behind the curtain, had all of Burleigh Heads holding its collective breath, and emerged halfway down the beach to thunderous applause.

"Man-on-man changed the face of surfing," said Peter Townend. "It made professional surfing what it is today."

"Man-on-man surfing is still the benchmark today, it is still the system of choice, and Peter Drouyn introduced that to the world," said Rabbit Bartholomew.

"Peter Drouyn was a genius," said Phil Jarratt. "He created history with the first man-on-man surfing event and he'll always be remembered for that."

THE VICTIM

THE 1977 STUBBIES PRO WAS THE FIRST EVENT OF the IPS season. To avoid accusations of bias, Peter did not compete in it. He did feel the buzz and promise of professional surfing. He watched the so-called greatest surfers in the world duke it out on his home turf and, truth be told, he felt he could have kept up with them. Easily.

So at age twenty-seven—ancient back in those days—Peter joined the pro tour. He'd missed the first event, but so what? He was a racehorse whose game was to come from behind. He competed in Australia, Japan, South Africa, USA and Hawaii. He was drawing from a wave-riding vocabulary that had been expanded on by his younger competitors. It wasn't that they were doing things Peter couldn't do, but they were quicker, zappier, lighter. Where Peter's torso struggled to keep up with his slashing surfboard, the torsos of MR, Shaun and Rabbit led. But his resolve was mighty.

"When he finds his target Peter Drouyn is unstoppable," the surf writer Mike Perry told me. "There are very few humans, perhaps no human, in my experience that have as much fierceness of character to achieve as Drouyn does."

"Peter was one of *the* greatest competitors," former pro Cheyne Horan said, and launched into a story about the time he competed against Peter during his rookie year, how Peter screamed at him, gave him psychotic looks, threatened to kill him.

And he was fun. "We would pull up to Cave Rock," remembered Rabbit Bartholomew, Peter's travel partner for much of that season, "and he would go into a recital, like something straight out of a movie. It was like Humphrey Bogart. And then it was Brando. And he'd make up these characters, and we'd all have names. We'd be just reeling with laughter!"

Peter performed well in the dozen or so events. By the time the tour landed in Hawaii for the final leg, he was ranked number four in the world. He was in solid contention for the 1978 world title. There was just one hitch. The prestigious Duke Kahanamoku event—the same Duke in which Peter placed second in 1970—was by invitation only. Because of Peter's sabbatical from competitive surfing, he was not part of the twenty-four invitees list. Here was an IPS World Tour that purported to be reaching towards tennis and golf as far as professionalism goes, and yet a world title contender was not even able to compete in one of its points-rated events?

Another injustice!

Peter was enraged. He tried to rally his fellow competitors to boycott the event if they wouldn't let him in, but he got nowhere.

There was a competitors' meeting at the Royal Hawaiian hotel. Peter's tour mates were gathered on foldout chairs, as were the Hawaiians who'd had beefs with the cocky Australians the previous winter. In the middle of a speech by one of the sponsors, Peter stands, announces that the system's flawed.

"You've got to let me in," he pleads. "I can win the world title!"

He looks around the room at his fellow competitors. They twiddle thumbs, stir nervously, look away.

Peter raises an electric hand in the air, fingers outstretched. "They crucified Jesus Christ," he bellows. "But you're not going to crucify me!"

He storms out of there.

•

Cheyne Horan told me that story one day while I was on the Gold Coast. The following day I saw him out in the surf at Currumbin Alley. The waves were overhead and relentless. The crowd was thick. Amid the spume and flying fins he shouted out to me, "Really important stuff about Drouyn, Jamie. He never got his due, and that's just wrong. That thing about the Duke, the next year they made a rule that if it was an IPS World Tour event, it couldn't be invite only. Drouyn was the guy who showed this flaw in the system, but only after it was too late. Wrong, mate. Just wrong."

.

Even more wrong, especially in the eyes of Peter Drouyn, was the fact that for the 1978 Stubbies Pro, the sponsors decided to hire not Peter, but Bill Bolman, a used-car salesman who'd worked as beach marshal that first year, to direct the event.

"He was probably a good car salesman, but he had no business running a contest of that magnitude and importance and evolution," Peter told Tim Baker.

> I entered as a competitor and they changed the rules in the heat. I won't go through it, but I was screwed in the heat completely and there was no protest. They wouldn't take my protest. I went and they just shut the door on me and I knew it was pointless in me proceeding with my previous fourth-place entitlements, invitations to all the contest, because I could see that they were going to do that to me time and time again.

.

By the end of the decade Peter's conflicted relationship with surfing was at an all-time low. Surfing, the literal act, had been the greatest comfort he'd ever known, it had saved his life. But surfing, the business, the industry, the establishment, had delivered the cruelest blows.

In a 1980 issue of *Surfer*, Peter Townend interviews Peter Drouyn. Their conversation takes place in Sydney days before the start of the 2SM/Coca-Cola Surfabout. This conversation is nothing like the one they had in 1971, when Peter was on top of the world. At thirty, Peter is ten years older than most of his opponents, and he is the only surfer from the longboard era still competing at the pro level. The photo of Peter that kicks off the piece is a far cry from the ones a decade earlier—swagger gone, hairline receding. He leans against a windowsill, left arm wrapped around his selfshaped board. In his right hand he holds what looks like a slice of lemon. His expression is bewildered, with puckered lips and creased forehead, as if he's just sucked the lemon.

> PT: In 1971 *Surfing* magazine did a classic interview with you called "Drinks at the Bar in '79," and you said some things that were futuristic at the time. Do you think far too futuristic, seeing '79 has come and gone?
>
> PD: Maybe I was prophesizing something that I would do in the late '70s, but not knowing really what I would do. When I did "Drinks at the Bar," I was thinking if nobody else did anything, maybe Drouyn would, and it happened in '77 [the Stubbies Pro]. I thought if it happens in '77, in two years if they keep on the right track, in '79 we'll all be drinking at the bar, our own clubs, our own social places. We'll all have heaps of bread; we'll have copyrights over ourselves; we'll be protected from the media and the public and from ourselves. After the first Stubbies, it didn't go on the right track. The wrong people got hold of it; they raped it; they're using it. It's such a shame—we've gone back to 1970.

Their conversation bounces from surfboard design to contests to *Drouyn and Friends*. Peter has shown up in Sydney with a radical asymmetrical board design that seems less functional than a declaration of his individuality. He's soured on contests, still maintains that "there's got to be contact in surfing for it to work as a competitive sport," refers to the judges as "those five idiots on the beach."

PD: I think surfing contests were a mistake for me originally. When I was about ten or eleven (as a kid I was given a strict Catholic upbringing), I went to a heavy school and got involved with Surf Life Saving Clubs and their establishment ways and their nightlife. I'm talking about in the dormitories and things, it was very heavy then. I got this crossfire thing. All my morals were mixed up and I needed an escape. It wasn't school—I got claustrophobia in school, and surfing was the only thing for me. I do believe that if that hadn't happened, I may not have gone past my first contest. I'd be doing my acting now, from then, from that age. I think I'm a mistake. I don't think I was meant to go this far. It was only because of a freak accident, and it happened fair enough, and that's a development of my personality.

PT: Are you disappointed with your career in surfing?

PD: No, I'm not. I've got a lot out of it. In fact, I've got an education out of it from traveling, and I think this is one of the reasons I don't have anything in the bank now, because I knew I had to have an education, and money in itself isn't whereas traveling and keeping your eyes open and concentrating and having fun and taking some dares everywhere you go is. Like me and Evo [Bob Evans] dared a lot. It just taught me about the world, and these days people say traveling is as good an education as any. So in fact, I've got an ace up my sleeve. I'm a psychologist as a result!

PT: How do you see utilizing that education now, that streetwise education you develop from being a surfer?

PD: Through my acting. I'm positive I would have been an actor from the start had I not gone and freaked out and got lost in the ocean to escape. I've always been an actor. I'd reenact films after school—I'd sing, dance, have parties, be a disc jockey, and act Clark Gable and John Wayne. I was full-on into that scene.

PT recalls Peter's Brando-in-*The Godfather* impersonations, asks about his acting heroes:

PD: Brando is my total hero. Clark Gable—I love his manly type of style, he's straight, but cheeky. William Holden and Errol Flynn. On another level, Michael Caine, Pacino, and Hoffman. The level of performance I like is being a gentleman first, cheeky second, and mix the two. I think Brando is number one forever for me.

PT: Have your heroes been important to your life?

PD: Totally, because I'm an emotional sort of person. I'm pretty sensitive and I need people to look up to, to follow, to get ideas off, to help me sustain a happy state.

PT: Were there any people in surfing that you would have considered heroes?

PD: Mickey [sic] Dora, Phil Edwards, Johnny Fain, Midget, and there's another one in there somewhere, Kemp Aaberg. There're others, but those guys mainly, especially Dora, Edwards, and Joey Cabell. Those three, they were my heroes, but in a different way. They were my heroes because they were rebels and because—partly to do with my escapism—I became a rebel, an outcast on my own. I wanted to kill the world; I wanted to get on top of it, get on top of myself. I found that Dora had the kind of rebellion I needed to follow, Cabell had the aggro and the killer instinct, while Edwards had the style and the beauty and the couldn't-give-a-damn attitude in contests. I combined those three and it really helped me.

PT: I know you're not going to give up surfing today. You might retire from the scene, but you'll continue to surf. Guys like us never do lose that stoke. But what were the memories for you of being part of the surfing scene?

PD: Let's go through them: winning the Queensland, winning all those titles I talked about. I suppose screwing all those beautiful girls from here to Brazil, Angola and back, risking VD, risking everything. My mental state and playing the Flynn, the Gable, there is a bit of it in me. All those places I saw. Piss-up parties with Evo. The night we screwed in bed together. We had a chick. Here's poor Evo with an injury in his stomach; he's screaming and in pain and I had stitches in the head and the chick had some disease. We were all in there, and we all had our health problems and our mental states, and there we were in the middle of Angola with mines on the road, troops ready, the UFLO, the FLUO, and the COUI [all liberation armies] all around us. The hotel we stayed in was bombed six months later! Things like that, getting lost in the desert. Peru. Puerto Rico when I caught pneumonia. I was in bed—it wasn't a bed; I was on the concrete floor. I nearly died. Beverly Farrelly brought me a big capsule one day—the capsule blew me out; I didn't know what it was. Brothels and so many other incredible things. Put it this way—that was the kind of deviate side. While on the other side, we went to London. I stood in an English museum all day looking at one painting. I was into art; I was into shape, form. That stint at NIDA was incredible for me. I was into everything.

PT: You said it'd take $50,000 a year to get you to surf full-on competitively again.

PD: It'd cost them more than that. It'd cost them a million dollars. A contract to get me into the water again would be under different circumstances. In other words, I wouldn't be standing around anymore wasting my time, getting sweaty armpits, heavy chest colds, looking to the left and looking to the right and not knowing which way the wind's blowing. I'd be there. They'd drive me in a Mercedes to the show; they'd dress me, clean my fingernails, do my hair, have my best surfboard, have all the inventions I've ever wanted to do. Make a movie of it as well. They'd send me out into the water, and there'd be no judges. It would be an exhibition of style thing, and it would be the people I choose to do it with me. Of course that's impossible, but that's not dreaming—that's reality.

PT: Flipside [of the tape]. Another cup of coffee? I've got to think what else I want to ask you, mate.

PD: It's good we have a break, because this is the last interview I will be doing with *Surfing*, I can assure you that.

PT: You can never see Peter Drouyn in the public eye in *Surfing* again? He's going to be in the public eye in acting?

PD: Right. That's exactly true. Drouyn's going to put his 100% effort now into acting, and he is going to be what he should have been a long time ago. He's twenty lengths behind at the moment, but I've seen racehorses come from there. [laughs] Champions, right? I can do it; I'm going to do it.

The interview ends with PT explaining how Peter Drouyn felt his surfing was going unappreciated in the Surfabout. Though the following day he had a heat in which, win or lose, he'd earn at least $400, Drouyn impulsively took a cab to the airport, disappeared, left the money behind.

"Drouyn is now back on the Gold Coast," writes PT,

pursuing his acting career, while working as a builders laborer, and probably slipping in a few waves every now and then at his favorite break which begins with a B and ends with Heads.

It remains to be seen whether he will divorce himself from the surfing scene. He has been one of Australia's most outstanding talents for close to two decades and I wonder if like Muhammad Ali, Drouyn will once again endeavor to make a comeback.

I hope so. Surfing needs colorful, controversial people like Peter Drouyn. Without them, life would be so boring.

THE HAM

SUSIE STENMARK LIVES WITH HER HUSBAND, Mark, in a three-story modernist home with spectacular views over Sydney's Palm Beach. In the eighties and nineties she was one of Australia's top models, doing campaigns for Chanel and eventually becoming their head of PR. Later she worked as a features editor of *Vogue Entertaining*, and a news anchor for Channel Seven. Now in her fifties, Susie still has the long limbs and angular facial features of a model. When I met with her on a hot February afternoon, her auburn hair was pulled back in a ponytail. She wore a powder blue T-shirt with a seventies graphic on the front, red shorts, and black and white Chanel sandals.

Sitting at a table in her living room, she told me that she first met Peter Drouyn in the late seventies. They'd been cast in an advertising campaign for the State Government Insurance Office (SGIO) in Queensland. It was an ongoing gig that would last several years. Susie played the wife, Peter played the husband, dogs and kids were weaved in.

"Peter was really fun. He was a very natural guy, really good-looking, great skin, lovely coloring, just a sweet guy," she said. "One year we were doing a commercial up in Queensland, on the Gold Coast I think it was. Peter arrived on set, and to the director's amazement, from the time he was cast to the day of the shoot, he'd grown a pencil-thin moustache and he'd slicked his hair back like a matinee idol, channeling Clark Gable or Rudolph Valentino. And the director's like, 'Where did this come from?'"

The director took Peter aside for a little chat. Peter was committed to this new look of his, but the director wasn't having it. They'd cast Peter to play a better-than-average-looking everyman. In the end the director handed Peter a razor and off went the moustache.

In the scene, Peter and Susie walk along a narrow wooden pier, she holding a picnic basket, the two of them discussing something insurance-related. Peter is so absorbed in the conversation that he fails to see the end of the pier. Susie stops right at the edge; Peter steps off and falls into the water. Susie told me that at first Peter resisted the falling in the water part, but after a bit of coaxing he went along with it, and it came off well.

"It was just a simple commercial, just a glance at the script and you got it, but Peter took it really seriously. He went into his Marlon Brando, fingertips to his forehead, furrowed brow, just really angsting. And he says to the director, 'What's my motivation?' And the director, again, you know, raised his eyes, like, This guy's not what I bargained for, and the director said, 'Your motivation, Pete? Your motivation is you're getting paid.'"

We shared a laugh. Susie reiterated that Peter was lovely to work with. The day before I'd sent her a link to our Westerly sizzle reel. She said that she liked it, was fascinated by Westerly. "I have to say, though," she said, "I don't like the way she's separated herself from Peter, speaking of him in the past tense."

•

Slapstick suited Peter. In 1982 he was cast in what would be the most widely viewed piece of his entire career.

Elle Macpherson saunters up the beach, a red bikini accentuating her divine curves, a can of Tab Cola in her right hand.

The shot flashes back and forth between a close-up of Elle's smiling face and 34C breasts, and a close-up of a can of Tab spilling into a glass.

Elle passes a couple on the beach. The girlfriend plays with her hair. The boyfriend, Peter Drouyn, sips from a can of Tab. His eyes glom onto Elle, and as she passes, his head follows her. There's that classically male moment in which his eyes drop from the back of her head to her ass.

Peter's girlfriend, meanwhile, is unimpressed. She grabs a bucket of water. When he turns around, rapt, she dumps it over his head. Elle sees this and laughs, his girlfriend laughs, and Peter laughs. A Tab can appears on screen, and its shape transforms into an hourglass.

This commercial, it turns out, was what rocketed Elle into super-modeldom.

For Peter it was a paycheck, and a good one, but still miles from the serious acting he aspired to.

THE COMEBACK KID

PETER DROUYN LOVED MOVIES AND IT'S HARD
not to imagine him staring up at the giant screen as Rocky Balboa
thrusts a series of knockout punches into Apollo Creed's skull, Peter's hands crushing his popcorn, his shoulders following Rocky's,
the spell of this modern David and Goliath following him out of
the theatre and into the bright Surfers Paradise streets where the
seedlings of the Superchallenge begin to take root.

Thirty-four years old, new kinks in his cutback like faint wrin-
kles on an ageing supermodel's face, the black abyss of oblivion
singing his name, Peter conceives of an idea that would at worst
thrust him back into the limelight, at best crown him heavyweight
surfing champion of the world.

Much had changed in design since Drouyn had started surfing—longboards had gone to short, zip-zapping twin fins had
become popular in the mid-seventies, Simon Anderson famously
introduced the three-finned "thruster" in 1980, some pros were
even riding four fins. *The* real *greatest surfer in the world can ride
all boards*, thinks Peter. *The real greatest surfer has range, he can ride
the nose à la Phil Edwards, and he can bang the shit out of the lip à la,
well, Peter Drouyn.*

He thinks about surfing as art. Like opera, like ballet, like ab-
stract expressionism, one needn't be a singer or a dancer or a paint-
er to appreciate great wave riding. He imagines a judging panel
comprised not of the accredited (brainwashed!) ASP (Association
of Surfing Professionals) judges, but rather a mixture of non-surfers that spans the highbrow and low—say, a drama teacher from

NIDA alongside a bloody cab driver from Brisbane!

A roping Burleigh barrel, much like the ones that kissed the finals of the '77 Stubbies Pro, peels across his mind, and he begins to write his proposal:

Five heats on five different board designs, judges who know nothing about surfing but recognise great flow and style when they see it, a three-day showdown held at Burleigh Heads, bring in all major national media, $5K prize purse—winner take all!

And ready for the best part?

The Superchallenge will pit Peter Drouyn against four-time, reigning world champion Mark Richards.

A lot of tossing and turning that night, a lot of note-scribbling and crossings-out and insertions-in-the-margins, a flash of triumphant Rocky deluged in flashbulbs and fans, a glimmer of the great Ali dancing in the streets of Zaire after taking down Foreman in the "Rumble in the Jungle," a crystal-clear image of a grandiose finish in four- to six-foot Burleigh amid an entire headland full of spectators followed by Peter onstage, a bikini-clad, lotion-slicked girl handing him his giant $5,000 check, a downcast MR dumping a magnum of champagne over his head, the burning eyes, the spume dripping down his bare chest, the crowd chanting "*Drouyn! Drouyn! Drouyn!*," the groupies lining up at the edge of the stage ... He doesn't sleep a wink.

In the morning he phones Mark Richards, presents his idea with bursting enthusiasm, plays up the "perfect Burleigh with just you and me out" part. With little hesitation, MR is in.

•

Peter slips right into promoter mode. He shoots out press releases to the media, gets Channel Nine to promise coverage, sends invites to the judges, applies for a permit to hold the event at Burleigh Heads. He orders up a quiver of boards from Gold Coast shaper Nev Hyman. He trains hard, surfs feverishly, fine-tunes his diet. At night he shadowboxes in the bathroom mirror.

He takes out an ad in *Line Up*, the ad that was my introduction to the mighty Peter Drouyn. Peter in his underpants, arms sprawled as if nailed to a cross, bare torso slathered in ketchup, his own poems wrapping his frame, a kind of run-on, full-body thought bubble: *"I'm going to kill or be killed, I'll kill myself to prove to the world that I am the Super Master of the surfboard." "I will be leading a new second-era revolution that will, with the help of the Almighty, destroy all surfing corruption and clear it out to start again, and reap the million-dollar bracket for all my best friends, the unknown greats of surfing."*

He gets access to an ahead-of-its-time computerized scoring system that will heighten drama, bring race call-style tension to the magnificent Superchallenge.

The first setback comes when the council refuses to give him a permit for Burleigh Heads. A surf contest is only as good as the waves it is held in—no one knows this better than Drouyn. His plan B is Currumbin, but that too gets knocked back. He's forced to settle for Ballina, a hit-or-miss beach break down the coast.

·

On the morning of the Superchallenge Peter shows up in a specially made pink and purple lycra bodysuit, his close-cropped hair dyed peroxide white. He is wiry and fighting fit, not an ounce of fat on his vascular body. The sky is grey, the wind unfavorably onshore, the waves big and messy. They get through a round or two, then comes the rain, and behind it the thunder and lightning, a full-blown cyclone that rips through the contest site, sending everyone fleeing for the parking lot, everyone except for Peter Drouyn, who stands amid the toppled scaffold and drowned computers and banners blowing off into the sky, shaking his fists at the spectators, at the judges, at MR, at the Channel Nine bastards who never even showed, at God. Why this cursed life? Why this trail of disaster? Why never a single fucking break?

"The Superchallenge was the worst thing I ever got involved with in my life. I still kick myself to this day as to why I actually got involved."

This is Mark Richards, thirty years later. He's grey and balding, leathery, but still strong and fit for a fifty-seven-year-old father of two. We're sitting on a fluffy couch in the VIP area of the 2014 Quiksilver Pro at Snapper Rocks on the Gold Coast. Top-ranked pros study the slightly overhead waves with intense concentration. A tanned and blonde surfer girl interviews John John Florence for a camera crew. A cabal of pro surfers' wives, all ridiculously hot in their leggings and black baseball caps and shiny lip gloss, sip coconut waters around a table. The overcast sky is on the verge of rain. In the water, Coolangatta local boy and reigning world champ Mick Fanning streaks across a feathering silvery wall and heaves a giant gouge out of the lip. The crowd roars their support.

Mark explains that it was less about the variety of boards and more about the thought of surfing excellent Burleigh with just one other guy in the water that appealed to him. "It was a great idea that crashed and burned," he remembers. "And one of the reasons I did it was because of what Peter had done with the Stubbies. I had an unbelievable amount of respect for what he'd actually done. For pro surfing it was revolutionary. Everyone came away from that event going, 'Peter Drouyn is a fucking genius. We just saw the future of pro surfing.' That Stubbies, at the time, was possibly the greatest surfing event that had ever happened." Mark sweeps his hands across the break. "We're sitting here at the Quiksilver Pro now, thirty-seven years later, and really the blueprint that Peter laid down for man-on-man pro surfing is still happening right out in front of us right now."

Mark wears sandals, navy-blue cargo shorts, a white Quiksilver T-shirt. He's polite, gentlemanly, one hundred percent present. At the height of his fame he was remarkably humble. He attributes this to his parents and his Newcastle upbringing—"Egomaniacs are not tolerated at all in a working-class town." I ask him if he enjoys hanging out at surf contests. He laughs. "Not really." He says that it's strange being at a contest without a specific purpose. Just then Portuguese pro Tiago Pires trots past, contest singlet on, neatly waxed board under arm, his face clenched with determination. The hooter sounds, the commentator announces Mick Fanning the winner, the crowd cheers and claps.

Mark seems comfortable in his retirement, but over the years I have definitely witnessed former world champions, or former near world champions, looking lost and slightly wounded at surf contests, especially when a swarm of autograph seekers runs in their direction, only to stream past and mob Kelly Slater behind them. *Ex-pro surfers should not hang out at surf contests*, I once wrote in my journal. *It's like living in the cobweb-infested garage of the mansion where your first love resides happily with her new beau.*

I ask Mark about his first encounter with Peter Drouyn. He says that he watched him surf on a trip to the Gold Coast when he was a pre-teen grommet. He remembers his own father, a keen judge of surfing talent, making the comment that Peter was at least as good, probably even better, than Nat Young, Midget Farrelly, Keith Paul and all the rest.

"He had incredible front and charisma and personality, it was nearly like there was an aura around Peter," says Mark. "He was a magnetic personality, people were actually drawn to him. I didn't know him well enough to hang around him, but I got the impression he was a shitload of fun."

I ask about the shift to Westerly.

"I have trouble getting my head around it, but I respect where he's at and what he's doing," he says. "Peter was such a man's man. He was a strong, olive-skinned, really good-looking man with a lot of confidence. The guy was a total chick magnet! The women loved him. It's such an extreme change, and I think that's why people were so shocked."

Of all the former world champions I have interviewed, Mark comes off as the most at peace with himself. He tells me that his original plan was to be a shaper, but pro surfing got in the way. "Even when I was world champion I always knew that this lifestyle is going to stop soon, and the moment it stops I'm back in a garage-sized room with two side lights and a dusty blank, mowing foam for the rest of my life."

Mark says that in recent years his love of surfing has backed off, that in fact it is often a source of frustration—the crowds, his waning physical fitness. "As you age your horizons broaden, your view of life and what's important and the experiences you want to have just take on a much broader spectrum," he says. "I used to dream of spending a month at a great wave, now I dream of a month in the snow, snowboarding with my kids."

THE MISSIONARY

AFTER THE SUPERCHALLENGE DEBACLE PETER got a job selling real estate on the Gold Coast. And while he was a brilliant salesman, he couldn't work his magic with something his heart wasn't in. He figured a way out might be to get a tertiary degree. He enrolled at Brisbane's Griffith University. Taking courses in Asian Studies, he learned China's history, politics and cultural intricacies. He studied the Chinese language, learning to read, write and speak in Mandarin.

"I came to Griffith three years ago with a vague, sketchy idea that this might give me some direction—that it might take me back to Asia, where I'd traveled extensively," he told *Surfing* in 1986.

A year later, "Drouyn's Foray," a *Surfer* article penned by Mike Perry, presented a different take:

Sitting in a smoky real estate office, Drouyn drank a beer and wiggled his toes in his stiff leather shoes. It was summer in Queensland and he was trying to sell someone else's idea of paradise. He could feel himself going soft. The tan was fading. It was all slamming shut around him and he knew it. But by the end of that beer he had plotted out a whole new reality for himself. If the West had decided to screw Peter Drouyn, then Peter Drouyn wasn't going to hand them the Vaseline! He'd take his skill, his knowledge, his competition savvy and his instincts to the biggest population on the planet and he would train a team of communists. He'd transform non-surfers into champions; he'd be the first man to surf in Red China!

In the fall of 1984 Peter wrote a letter to the Chinese Yachting Association proposing that he introduce surfing to the People's Republic of China. "I knew no one had surfed there," he told Tim Baker in *Deep*.

I might be able to revive myself, plug myself back into surfing again. It was dreadful what was going on in my head. And, of course, I honestly felt no one appreciated anything I'd ever done in my life . . . I just wanted to live in China. I wanted to get right away from everything and build a national team and then send it against us [Australia] and Hawaii and piss on them. All I wanted to do was feel like I belonged somewhere and maybe in China they'd let me feel like I belonged.

In January of 1985 Peter received a letter back from the Chinese Yachting Association inviting him to Hainan Island. He approached the trip with the utmost professionalism, shaping a quiver of ten boards for his students, making instructional videos in which he speaks Mandarin, bringing over all the latest surf magazines and movies.

"Peter was like Lawrence of Arabia," remembers Westerly. "They laid out the red carpet for him, escorted him around with a big entourage of government officials and a convoy of brand-new cars."

Peter was given twenty students, aged ten to twenty-one, all trained gymnasts. They'd never so much as seen a surfboard. He eased them into the sport with lectures and movies. They watched his instructional videos, mimicking pop-ups and the side-stance in front of a large screen. For the first week or so Peter got the ego boost he so desperately needed. In one of Westerly's newspaper clippings from the trip, Peter stands on a surfboard set in the sand, his body torqued in a swooping off the top. Behind him, lined up in a row, his twenty students try to follow suit. "Aussie leads first wave on China's beaches" reads the headline.

There are more photos from the trip. In most he's in instructional mode. In a couple he sits at the heads of long tables overflowing with food and drink. He doesn't look particularly happy; in fact, he looks drunk. There's one photo that could almost be a production still from *Lawrence of Arabia*, minus the camel. Flanked by a pair of Chinese officials, Peter wears loose-fitting white linen trousers and a white T-shirt. Sunglasses hang from his neck with Croakies. His face is regal, resolute. His head is wrapped turban-like with a white T-shirt.

But China too went bad. Westerly claims that Peter's hosts plied him with decadent meals and way too much booze. She describes Peter spitting unidentifiable hunks of food into his napkin when no one was looking. After "five weeks that felt like two years," he flew home.

THE COACH

THE GARAGE IN BARTON LYNCH'S AVALON HOME
on Sydney's northern beaches is packed with surfboards, wetsuits,
boardshorts, leashes and fins. Old, spider web-covered trophies fill
a row of shelves, among them his big gold cup for winning the
1988 World Title.

Fifty years old, greying hair, aquiline nose, disarming grin, Barton Lynch has a lighthearted and easygoing demeanor. He laughs
a lot, mostly at himself. He works as a surf coach and an ambassador for the surf label Hurley. He has lived in this two-story home
for twenty years. He has a daughter, Tamarin, eighteen, a model.
When I met with him he'd just returned from a trip to Hawaii
with his new wife, Holly.

The purpose of my visit was to ask Barton about his relationship with Peter Drouyn, but because we've known each other for
thirty years, five of which were spent on the pro tour together,
there was a bit of catching up to do. We remembered the time a
dozen of us dressed up in bad disco polyester and ran amok on
the streets of Tokyo, the time Rod Kerr pulled an all-nighter in
Spain, went straight from the bar to the contest, scrabbled into his
jersey, paddled out into his heat, tore a little left to bits, and on the
inside, riding in a slightly pained stoop, in full view of judges and
spectators, threw up all of last night's beer and chorizo. We asked
after the boys—*Pagey's making surf wax, Kong's got a swim school up
in Brunswick Heads, Ross is chasing eighty-footers in Tassie.* We were
like old war buddies.

I first met Barton in 1983. During a break between legs of the tour he stayed with my friend Jeff Novak in Manhattan Beach. With the exception of his suntan, Barton looked and acted less like a pro surfer than the lead singer of a punk band. He had close-cropped dark hair with a single long strand that he fingered incessantly. Head-to-toe black clothing draped his skinny frame. Anti-booze, anti-yobbo, anti a lot of things, he listened to Crass and Subhumans and fancied himself an anarchist. He slung his strong opinions around freely, and exuded a deep inner confidence, as if he was in on some private joke on the world.

Barton was a rookie on tour that year, and though he'd won a few major tournaments at home, he'd yet to prove himself on the world stage. But you'd never know that watching him surf. On his Aloha thruster with signature black crescent moon on the deck, he never stopped moving. When you're a competitive surfer you're forever projecting yourself into do-or-die moments, imaginary world titles that depend on scoring, say, a 9.0 on your next ride. Barton did this infectiously. For the week he was in Los Angeles, every surf session was elevated, every wave held great stakes.

I went along for the ride when Novak dropped Barton at the airport for his flight to France. Watching him drag his coffin board bag through the Pan Am terminal; the ease with which he checked in with the pretty hostess; the eight-month itinerary on Harvey World Travel stationery that went something like Paris, London, Rio, Tokyo, Honolulu—it was exciting, I got a vicarious hit of the touring life. After shaking hands goodbye at passport control, I knew I'd been in the company of greatness. Sure enough, a couple of weeks later Barton surfed from the trials right through to the final to win his first ASP tournament, the Lacanau Pro. In a snap of the fingers he went from Aussie hopeful to global superstar.

I joined the pro tour in 1986. My first leg was Australia, my first contest the Stubbies Pro at Burleigh Heads. After a twenty-hour trip from LA to Honolulu to Sydney to Brisbane, and less than twenty-four hours in the Lucky Country, I lost in my first round to a loudmouth Californian named John "Bam Bam" Parmenter. Actually, I didn't so much lose to him as not back down when he hassled me for a wave that was rightfully mine, which resulted in a double-interference. Bam Bam was known for his Mr. T persona. He paddled up to me, sat menacingly on his board and puffed out his chest. *"Mess with Bam Bam and you're goin' down, wuss!"* he said in his gruff voice. At the time I was reading *McEnroe: A Rage for Perfection*, a biography of the famous tennis player. I barked a flurry of *fuck offs*, we got in each other's faces. No blows were thrown, but I was proud of myself for holding my ground. There's a kind of prison yard mentality to pro surfing. It fosters hubris and machismo. Later that year I read Norman Mailer's *Armies of the Night*. In it is a scene in which two men are riding on a train. Their eyes lock and they get into a stare down. "The bigger man is the one who averts his eyes first," writes Mailer, or words to this effect. At the time I was sure this was a misprint or a typo. Only years later, when I'd moved on from competitive surfing, did I understand what he was getting at.

At any rate, my early elimination in the 1986 Stubbies Pro gave me ample time to study my favorite surfers. Back then there were very few coaches, but in his campaign for the world title, Barton Lynch had hired Peter Drouyn. Before Barton's heats, the pair would find a quiet spot away from fellow competitors and surreptitiously scan the lineup. By this time Drouyn was showing his thirty-six years—thinning up top, crow's feet, slight belly. But his swagger marked him unmistakably as a big shot. He pointed, swiped his hands, drew plays with his fingers on the grass. While Barton was in the water Drouyn watched with the same burning intensity that manager Ion Tiriac heaped on Boris Becker in the 1985 Wimbledon final. Peter made signals with a red T-shirt, sometimes with his left hand, others with his right. He paced a lot, fist-pumped after a good ride. It was seductive, this private bond they shared.

•

In his open-mouthed garage, with birds tweeting in the trees, I ask Barton why he chose Peter to be his coach. He took me back to 1977, when he was a surf-stoked thirteen-year-old living in Mosman. He'd heard about the Stubbies Pro from a schoolmate, dropped everything, hitchhiked up to the Goldie, and watched in total awe as man-on-man surfing was born.

"I realized that the person who had thought of that, and had the foresight and the imagination to actually take his mind into the future and understand how our sport could be packaged, must have had a pretty good understanding of how it may play itself out and the scenarios involved in man-on-man competition," explains Barton. "I was looking to get some support around me. I had been out there on my own traveling and touring and organizing and negotiating sponsors and doing everything on my own, and I was looking for more a manager than I was a coach. But in Peter Drouyn I saw the opportunity to have a bit of both."

Barton hired Peter in 1985. At the time Barton lived in Manly. Peter moved down from the Gold Coast and rented a place nearby. Much of their training was fairly standard. Barton would go out and surf, and Peter, clipboard in hand, would take notes. After, they'd discuss what might be called the "big picture" stuff: Barton's overall mien on a wave. There were fitness drills to build speed and stamina. There were countless simulated heats in which Barton would set his watch for twenty-five minutes (standard heat time) and try to pick off the best four waves in that time period—a big part of competitive surfing is synchronizing with the ocean. But the interesting stuff came from Peter's training at NIDA.

"I remember at Bells Beach particularly, the conversations around Method acting and the opportunity to absorb yourself in a role to the point where you are no longer you, but you were the role, you know what I mean? You've gotta be able to absorb yourself in the role of being a champion, of being a winner, of being the guy that's going to succeed without any of your own negativity or any of your own thoughts coming through to take away from the amount of concentrated effort there is in the performance.

"There were weeks when he had me crawling around the floor

as a leopard, and I was the leopard, and it would have been a hilarious little scene for someone to have seen, him coaching me to be a world champion surfer, but in the process teaching me to be able to let go of the concepts of who I am and actually be this leopard crawling around on the floor in a little house in sleepy, cold Torquay."

Barton laughs. But he adds that it's all stuck. Many of the drills he learned from Peter he employs today in his own coaching.

The relationship began to sour when Peter lined up a new sponsor for Barton. In the eighties, webbed gloves were a fad. They helped you to paddle faster but they looked hideous. Barton felt something was amiss but he went along with it anyway. "I wasn't into the webbed gloves, mate."

It got worse at the 1986 Stubbies Pro. That coach–athlete relationship that to me looked so harmonious was in fact anything but.

"It was a best-of-three-set final against Tom Curren," remembers Barton. "I come in from the first round and Peter goes, 'There's something wrong with your hands. Your hands aren't right.' And I'm thinking, *I'm not about to be able to change my frickin' hands right now in the middle of the final!*"

Barton sensed that Peter was grabbing at straws. "The concept of me holding my hands differently when I'm riding a wave is not something I've ever thought about and it's not something we've ever discussed, and we're in the middle of a three-set final, I've lost a set and I've got to come back in this next set, and that's the best advice you can give me? I'm a little bit confused. And I went out and I lost the next set. It was over, and I remember thinking to myself, *Jeez, that was weird advice, my hands weren't in the right . . .* Your hands kind of just hang where your hands hang when you're surfing, you know?"

Barton shuffles in his chair.

"I started to lose a little bit of confidence in him. Then there was a night up there where he went out and I stayed in and he came home and he was a little bit strange. I remember thinking to myself, *Is he on drugs? Has he actually gone out and done drugs?* He was getting a bit weird on me. And he actually started to talk some stuff about Tom Curren and Tom Curren's family and saying some things that just didn't gel with me, mate. I didn't say anything that night because I knew it was something . . . it wasn't the normal Peter who I had been spending all my time with. This was Peter, but it was different. And in retrospect, I don't know whether it was drugs, I don't know whether it was alcohol, or I don't know whether it was just a different chemical balance in the head that had brought out a different personality, a different person that I hadn't seen in Peter before. And I remember that night thinking, *Oh, I don't like this. You don't say things like that about someone. You don't say things like that about their spouse and their family and friends.* It almost could have been like an anger response, or a response where you're in the heat of battle and emotion takes over and all of a sudden you are thinking a little differently, you know?"

Shortly after this, about a year into their relationship, Barton severed ties with Peter. It was an amicable split.

I ask if he thinks Peter becoming Westerly is genuine. Barton answers with an emphatic yes. "Peter's always been different, mate. He's never been your normal Aussie bloke and I've never really been that either and I know in my life there have been times where I've had to dumb down to fit in with my community. There's many times I've had to sort of drop who I am and go out and get on the piss and just start to act normal and be normal and fit into the community that I'm a part of. And Peter's never been the sort of person that would do that. He's a showman, he's put himself out there, but there's always been integrity in the development of our sport and our culture in what he's done.

"Without Peter Drouyn our culture would be particularly bland and it would be full of these puppets who really are all there because they want to be accepted and they want to be cool and they want to be a surfer and they want to be a part of this thing. And I think that it's the people like Peter Drouyn and Westerly Windina that bring the character and bring what is real life, what is our world, what is outside of our little microcosm of surfing.

"Our world is full of everything that you could imagine. That's what people forget. Whatever you could imagine, the worst things in the world that you could conjure up in the back of your mind, people are doing it, people are living it. And we're scared of it. We don't like what we see, we don't like what we hear because we wanna stay in our bubble. We're safe in our bubble. And traveling takes you out of your bubble and expands your world. But people like Peter Drouyn slash Westerly Windina, they're the type of people that challenge the way you feel, challenge the way you think, and ultimately help you to grow. You know, the ones that come out and go, 'Hey, this is who I am. I don't care whether you like it or not. This ain't exactly comfortable for me, that's who I am. That's what I want to be. That's where I'm going with my life. I want to grow and be true to myself and my own emotions.' *That's the shit, mate!* That's the real stuff. And surfing doesn't have enough of that. Surfing's full of people who want to be liked and that's why most of us got into it, because we want to be a part of something. And we looked at it and it was so frickin' cool, that's what we want to be a part of. *I want to be cool; I want to fit into that group, that culture.* And consequently we ended up with a lot of puppets in surfing. And 'different' in surfing is actually someone who rides a different board. *Oh, he's different! Oh wow, look, he wears a hat, he's different!*

"It's such a small-minded culture, and it's so self-righteous, and it's so judgmental. And I learned these things about surfing when I was a kid, when I didn't live at the beach and I didn't come from the beach and you'd come from where you live to the beach and you'd see surfers and I never even liked them. There was a long period of my life where I thought surfers were the biggest bunch of wankers on the face of the planet. I thought they had their heads so far up their asses. I thought, *What a pack of wallys! I just don't even want to be a part of this thing.* You know what I mean? But thankfully, surfing's all I really did."

·

Barton's reflections on surf culture echo Peter's. In a 1982 *Surfer* interview:

> Surfers are basically very conservative. They might appear outrageous and look colorful but deep down, I'll tell you, nine out of 10 are not rebellious, they'll accept whatever's going. . . Most definitely surfers are more brainwashed today than they used to be. They are really brainwashed by commercial productivity. Once upon a time you were simply brainwashed by surfing photographs which was a lot more pleasing in those days. It was all innocent stuff. Now it is *sell, sell, sell*. Don't be yourself and you'll get ahead.

I ask Westerly her thoughts on the surf culture today: "Australian surfers are very immature. They get about in packs with their baggy shorts and tattoos, they have a tendency towards violence." She tells me a story about a group of surfers heckling her. This was early on in Westerly's emergence. She says that she felt a mixture of intimidation and rage. Her response was to paddle out and surf beautifully. "That shut them right up," she says. One afternoon I ask if she wants to drive down to Burleigh to check the waves. She turns almost angry. "I want no part of that end of the Gold Coast," she says, referring to Burleigh, Kirra, the Superbank. "They're like wolves. Like friggin' packs of wolves."

THE WIFE SEEKER

IN HIS PRIME, NAT YOUNG WAS A STRAPPING, swaggering, Greek god of a ruggedly handsome regular foot. In the surf, he took any wave he wanted and careened up and down the face with tremendous power. He was demonstrative; Rabbit Bartholomew remembers the time he turned so hard he broke his fin clear out of his board: "He just bellowed so loud, you could hear him down the valley." Nicknamed "The Animal," Nat did not suffer fools gladly, and never shirked a punch out in the water. "He was an overwhelming presence and accorded an almost messianic awe," wrote surf journalist Paul Holmes. *The Encyclopedia of Surfing* calls him "arguably the most influential surfer of the second half of the twentieth century."

In the seventies Nat moved up to Byron Bay, lived in an old farmhouse, grew his own vegetables, smoked a lot of pot, and found something akin to God on the long, winding northern New South Wales point breaks. He had a shaping bay room on his farm and mowed foam in the nude in order to get closer to his boards.

Nat's lived a full life. Married twice, four kids, an author of books and a producer of documentaries about surfing and skiing, he still does both obsessively, splitting his time between Angourie, New South Wales and Sun Valley, Idaho.

I first met him in the late eighties when the ASP added a longboard division to the French leg of the tour. Nat, in his early forties, was far more sophisticated than his knuckle-dragging surf brethren. He'd have just flown in from a *Men's Vogue* shoot with Bruce Webber in Paris, or just arrived back from a surf trip to Italy with his French sponsor, Oxbow. He wore scarves, knew how to order wine. He was the sort of surfer I aspired to be when I was his age.

I spoke with Nat over the phone. He told me that he felt great sympathy for Peter, that he considered him a good friend at one time. Without prompting, he told me how, at the awards presentation for the 1969 Australian Titles, Peter got up in front of the crowd and did one of his race calls.

"It was so fresh and fantastic, and we were all into it, everyone there, hundreds of people. He was this incredible showman. I thought he'd go on to become a great actor."

I told Nat that Peter remembers the 1969 Australian Titles as a heartbreaking experience, that he felt robbed of his title.

"I have no memory of that. I just surfed in that final and did the very best I could. That's how contests are. You come out of the water and someone tells you you either won or you fucking lost. It never really bothered me that much because you've got to win and you've got to lose."

I asked Nat if he could ever remember a side of Peter that seemed depressed or withdrawn.

"Not really. Because he was so good-looking, everywhere we'd go together socially, he could always make up for it by the fact that he was always getting the best-looking girl. And he was charming. He had this incredible aura of 'super cool.' Especially in that era, you'd just never have thought that Peter was a girl. It was just so off our radar."

In the late eighties Nat was living with his family in Angourie, a small coastal village in northern New South Wales with a fabulous right point break. Peter would visit Nat nearly every weekend.

"Peter was having a tough time. He didn't even have a board, so I'd lend him mine. His father, who by then was a friend of mine, used to call me and tell me how frustrated he was with Peter. One weekend Peter told me he was going to get married and have a family. He was single at the time. I didn't think much of it. So the next weekend or so, we were out in the water, and Peter said to me,

'So where do you think the best women in the world are?' And I said, 'I don't know.' And he said, 'I'm gonna tell you: South Africa.' He said, 'I'm going to go over there, I'm going to find the most beautiful woman in all of South Africa, I'm going to marry her and start a family, just like you.' I said, 'That's really great, Peter. But it doesn't really work like that . . .'"

•

In July 1989 Peter flew to Durban for the Gunston 500, an ASP event in which, at age forty, he would likely have been the oldest competitor. The contest, though, was not the real purpose of his trip. He rented a suite in a plush hotel, and took out an ad in a Durban newspaper: SURFING ENTREPRENEUR SEEKS LIFE PARTNER.

Westerly tells me this story during an interview at her house. She's all winks and chuckles. "It was like a big model casting. There were about fifty gorgeous girls—blondes, brunettes, redheads, the whole lot. The bellhop kept winking at me. Peter was like James Bond! So he interviews every girl, none were right, he thought, *It's all hopeless, yet another failure*, when wouldn't you know it, in walks Stephanie, the last girl in the queue. Peter took one look at her and thought, *That's it! She's the one!*"

Peter brought Stephanie back to Australia and married her. A year later they had a son, Zachary. Not long after they divorced. Custody battles ensued for nearly a decade.

"I remember him coming down to visit as it was all falling apart," said Nat. "He was really happy about his son, but from what I could gather, the mum was trying to keep Peter away from him."

•

Nat doesn't remember much about Peter in the early and mid-nineties, and there's very little coverage of him in the surf media. In fact Peter was studying to get a nautical engineering degree, at Griffith

University in Brisbane and at a college in Tasmania. He figured wave stadiums were the next logical step in surfing's evolution.

But Nat definitely remembers a surf contest in Noosa in the late nineties, a legends event that was more a reunion than a fierce competitive thing. At the banquet Peter got up on a table and started calling people out.

"He was just so insulting to everybody, to everybody's wives, and to what everybody stood for. He even started ripping into me, and we were friends!"

Why did it all go bad with Peter?

"Peter always believed that he was the best. And then people, particularly on the Goldie, would tell him that he's the best, and he'd believe it and he'd actually take it to heart. And that was a real problem for him."

Nat explained that for a good decade, when he was in his forties, he was getting paid $1,000 a week by Oxbow essentially just to be Nat Young.

"Peter never had anything like that. He was pissed off that he wasn't given the recognition and the accolades and the money that he deserved for his incredible talent. There's this thing in Australia called the tall poppy syndrome—as soon as you rise above the people you're cut down. Well, Peter never really got to that, he's like the reverse of tall poppy. Because he was never regarded as the best surfer in the country, he never made it to number one, what he had was this whole thing of, *I deserve to be the best 'cause I am the best. The world owes me a living.* And the world didn't fuckin' listen and didn't want to know. And it's a shame, but that's just the way the world is. The world is cruel."

Nat said that when he first heard about Peter becoming Westerly he was sure it was a put-on. "I think we were all guilty of going on the Peter that we knew."

He added that he hoped to run into Westerly soon, so he could let her know that he fully supported her. "It must have been so hard living with that lie within yourself. It must have been unbelievably frustrating. At least he hasn't got that to deal with anymore."

THE DREAMER

WHILE I WAS WRITING MY PROFILE OF WESTERLY in 2009, I emailed 1978 world champion Wayne "Rabbit" Bartholomew and asked if I could interview him. He replied saying that he found the whole thing really strange, that he was completely lost for words, and that he didn't want to be interviewed. At first I was taken slightly aback. But as I continued speaking with Peter's peers I found more people who felt this way. Betrayed. Maybe a little heartbroken. It was sort of the adult version of learning that there's no such thing as Santa Claus, or that Superman is fiction.

I first encountered Rabbit in the pages of *Surfer* in 1978. Clad in an Everlast robe, clenched fists pumped triumphantly overhead, he looked fierce and kingly. And he was. That year he won the world title.

In 1982, when the Op Pro came to Huntington Beach in California, Rabbit's sponsor, Quiksilver, arranged for him to stay with a local team rider, Bobby Knickerbocker, a sixteen-year-old kid who lived with his single mother in an oceanfront home in Newport Beach. Bobby did what good friends do in moments like these: he called my brother and me and told us to get our asses over there immediately. "Just don't tell anyone Rabbit's staying here," he made us promise. In our little world, Rabbit may as well have been Michael Jackson.

My brother and I stayed for a week. I had no memorable conversations with Rabbit—I was reduced to stutters in his presence—but I observed him closely. His diet consisted primarily of what today we call "super foods": brewer's yeast, bee pollen, soy milk, sprouts, avocado. When he wasn't surfing he locked himself away in his room, as if preserving his energy. But when he slipped into his blue, red and white Rip Curl spring suit and made his way to the water, the showman came out. He didn't walk across the hot sand. He trotted, as if being chased by a swarm of screaming groupies. In the water he sprint-paddled and caught four times as many waves as anyone else. He surfed as if he were in the finals of the Op Pro. You could almost see him picturing his fellow surfers as opponents, the wooden lifeguard tower as a grandstand.

Rabbit was never my favorite surfer. He was unbelievably good, but his style didn't caress me in the gut the way others did. But his charisma and flamboyance shaped the way I thought about pro surfing. In the 1977 surf movie *Free Ride* he hops from one pinball machine to another, playing both at once with cool and command (this is how he earned his nickname). In the playground of a Coolangatta park he rides a swing-set as if it's a surfboard, cross-stepping, ducking, weaving, crouching low into an imaginary barrel with a face full of stoke. Rabbit was a spur. He made me want to drop to the popcorn-scattered floor and knock out 200 push-ups right then and there.

By the time I joined the pro tour Rabbit was past his prime. He coached and mentored a couple of boy wonders, a reciprocal arrangement in which Rabbit would share his hard-earned wisdom and in return get a shot of young blood. He continued to compete, but his ranking was falling fast. His belly was dropping. His hair was turning grey. The flesh-colored zinc oxide that he'd used his entire life had created a sort of raccoon tan line; even in nightclubs it looked like he was wearing sunscreen. He started a band—lead singer, of course. At parties and banquets he sang covers, with an emphasis on Jaggeresque stage antics.

One year, 1991 or so, during the Foster's Newquay Surfmasters in Cornwall, England, Rabbit's sponsor, Billabong, hosted an expression session. Unlike a typical contest in which entire rides are scored, expression sessions reward single moves: best cutback, best re-entry, best floater. The Billabong expression session felt like a dream. Held at a neighboring beach a few miles down the coast from the Surfmasters, it was so heavily shrouded in fog that you could barely make out the surfers from shore. No geographical markers—parking lot, trees, rocks, cliffs—were visible. Mist droplets clung to our hair and noses. The little kiosk that served as contest headquarters was Hawaiian-themed, with thatched roof and old pictures of Waikiki beach boys, creating a peculiar Lars von Trier-meets-*Gilligan's Island* vibe.

The surf was small and junky. For a floater I couldn't even remember I won £300, paid in cash. That, along with the frothy pints being slapped in my hand at the post-event celebration, put me in a damn good mood. Rabbit was there, not as a competitor, but as a director/ambassador. He was the one handing out the prize money. The sky turned dark, the mist turned to solid drizzle, crowding about fifty of us damp surfers and officials into the little kiosk. Suddenly a kick drum thumped, an electric guitar twanged, and there was Rabbit at the mic. I recognized the tune instantly, more from Sid Vicious's slurred rendition than Eddie Cochran's.

"Uh look-a there!" shouted Rabbit, pointing somewhere over our heads with such conviction that nearly every one of us looked.

"Here she comes.

"Here comes that girl again . . ."

I hung on his every lyric, every way-over-the-top flourish. The song, "Somethin' Else," is about a guy who dreams big and makes it happen. Rabbit came from humble beginnings. There were times in his youth when he had to steal just to eat. In my beer-awakened state this was Rabbit singing his life story. And it was also every competitive surfer in that room's story, or story-in-progress. This is what you do as an athlete: you reach high and you tell yourself you deserve that thing you're reaching for. You pump yourself up with Rocky narratives. The inner voice that loops repeatedly in your head is a less witty but equally megalomaniacal Muhammad Ali:

I'm so fast that last night I turned off the light switch in my hotel room and was in bed before the room was dark.

If you even dream of beating me you better wake up and apologize.

I'm not the greatest; I'm the double greatest. Not only do I knock them out, I pick the round.

Or, as Rabbit put it (or, rather, Eddie Cochran): *"I keep right on a-dreamin' and a-thinkin' to myself, When it all comes true man, wow! That's somethin' else."*

In that moment Rabbit's performance was a pep rally, but looking back I see it less romantically. When the movie *Boogie Nights* came out and ageing porn stars Dirk Diggler and Reed Rothchild jumped into the studio to record their half-baked songs to launch their delusional careers as rock stars, I was reminded of all the mid- to late-career pro surfers I'd watched try to grab on to some kind of stage, some platform to feed their titanic egos. When *The Wrestler* came out in 2008 I was once again reminded of my pro surfer brethren, albeit the mid-life version. Through both my own shortcomings and those of my peers I have become hyper-aware of how surfing can maroon you.

As Rabbit's contest results declined, his benders increased. He was not an angry drunk, but it was hard to watch someone so charged with inspiration slump and slur. He had a habit of pounding his chest and making grand pronouncements. His tour mates looked after him at 2 am when he needed a couch to sleep on. His was by no means a graceful transition from pro surfing back to the world—but then it never is.

After what Rabbit described as "bottoming out in a nightclub," he reinvented himself as a coach in the early nineties, and led the Australian National Team to several victories. From 1999 to 2008 he was the president of the ASP. Among his many great contributions to the sport was the Dream Tour. Throughout the eighties surf contests were held at popular beaches with dubious surf.

The Dream Tour's motto was "the world's greatest surfers in the world's greatest waves."

One night around 2007 or so I ran into him at Lei Lei's restaurant, a popular surfer hangout on the North Shore. He shouted my name, wrapped his arm chummily around my neck, burrowed the crown of his head into mine. The word "Aloha" is an Hawaiian symbol. Also means "head to head." "Ha" means "breath." Rabbit's head rubbed so hard against mine I wondered whether I'd done something to piss him off. But his Jack Daniel's breath assured me I was in the hands of a playful bear. We reminisced, asked after mutual friends, ordered more drinks. When the restaurant closed a group of us agreed we weren't done yet, and headed to the bar next door. Crossing the parking lot in that ambling, shouting-over-each-other's-heads way that you do, Rabbit walked up, put his arm around me, and launched into stories of how he hung out at the very same bar we were headed to back in the seventies, how he'd score weeks and weeks of epic waves at Sunset, how the sand was perfect at Off the Wall, how the tubes would peel all the way to Rockpile. His descriptions were vivid, his right hand almost painting the scenes he described. He wrapped his arm so tight around me it was more like a headlock. He banged his chest so hard it thudded. His face flushed with emotion.

"See, that's it, Jamie! I'm still there! You gotta understand this, I'm still there!" He double-banged his chest, extended his arm, and slowly opened his fist as if releasing a hundred doves. *That's where I live, man!"*

•

In 2011, when my co-director Alan White and I went to visit Rabbit, he was living in Terranora, a town of rolling hills on the northern boundary of New South Wales. To get there from Westerly's house we took the Pacific Highway south. Along the way we went under a bridge that I was later told is actually the driveway that leads to Billabong CEO Gordon Merchant's multimillion-dollar home. We were running ahead of schedule so we drove down to Duranbah, one of Rabbit's favorite surf spots, to check the waves. On the headland, with sweeping views over the sea, was the apartment building owned by nineties pro surfer Luke Egan. Luke lived in the penthouse with his wife. Not far away were the million-dollar homes belonging to 2007/2009 world champion Mick Fanning and soon-to-be world champ Joel Parkinson.

All of which made Rabbit's nice two-bedroom brick home appear modest by comparison. Which seems terribly amiss given Rabbit's giant contribution to professional surfing.

Rabbit was his typical animated, energetic self. In turquoise long-sleeved Hurley T-shirt and boardshorts, white hair slicked back, he introduced Alan and me to his sons, Jagger, nine, and Keo, seven. They were sitting on the couch, watching surf videos.

"The boys did well today," said Rabbit, and explained how they'd just returned from a father-and-sons dawn patrol at Duranbah.

Alan and I joined Rabbit in his office. A quiver of boards stood at the ready in the corner. A *Bustin' Down the Door* movie poster hung on the wall. It took almost no prompting to get Rabbit talking; in fact, it seemed like there was a lot he wanted to get off his chest.

"You know, Jamie, when this whole thing came out about Westerly, and the *Today Tonight* program rang me and said they wanted to get me on camera, I said, 'Well, what do you want me to say?' and they said, 'Well, just wish him good luck!' I said, 'But you don't understand, this is my boyhood hero, this is like a superhero to me, and he became a good friend of mine, you know, we went out on the world tour, we chased women, we had fun!' And I said, 'I find this really difficult.' I do. I just find it really difficult. It is very surreal, and very difficult for me to come to grips with."

Rabbit said that when he first heard about it he was sure it was yet another piece of Peter Drouyn theatre. This was confirmed by their mutual friend Randy Rarick, who told Rabbit the same story he'd told me, how Peter admitted that it was essentially a desperate grab for attention.

"I get that, I totally get that," said Rabbit. "Driving cabs in Surfers Paradise definitely isn't where he should have ended up. He should have ended up in some exalted place. But he just couldn't work with other people, and all his projects went to dust, and he ended up broke."

Rabbit speaks with tremendous passion, drawing out vowels, hands slashing and karate-chopping the air. So dramatic are his sweeping arms that if we were in a restaurant, he wouldn't knock over the waiter's tray of drinks, he'd send it flying across the room. Rabbit reminds me of a realization I had a few years back: great surfers become great storytellers. What once emanated from their feet later emanates from their mouths.

Rabbit remembers one of the first times he saw Peter in person, at the 1968 Australian Titles. Rabbit was thirteen at the time. He sat up on the hill with one of his young mates, rapt, inspired.

"Peter Drouyn was just magnificent. He had this aura about him. It was the early stages of him going into the Brando persona. He was walking around Greenmount like a king, with a caddy who used to carry his surfboard. He had these really classic hats, and really stylish clothes, and I'd go, *Wow!* He just had the swagger. And it was the best swagger there was." He takes a breath, looks off wistfully. "He really was an actor. He was an actor's actor. And surfing was his stage. But it wasn't enough it seemed.

"These guys were larger than life. It was like when I first went to Hawaii and saw my larger-than-life heroes. You know, I went down to Lennox Head in 1971 and I surfed with Nat, and I sat next to him on the hill, and it was like, seriously, it was like Moses talking about handing out the tablets of the Ten Commandments! That's how much presence and aura he had. And Drouyn, Drouyn was like a superstar, he carried himself like a superstar. He was something else. He'd go into these acting modes, and he was *ultra* flamboyant. I can remember going to a few WindanSea Boardriders meetings, and Drouyn made a late entrance, and this was even at a club meeting, a late entrance that was like . . . *acting!* I was just mesmerized by the whole aura about the guy. He was just this so larger-than-life figure. And I think this had a lot to do with the fact that he felt like a forgotten man later, because he was *such* a star. Like, he was a *mega star.*"

Rabbit describes a session at Kirra in 1971, right after Peter had his epic winter on the North Shore. Peter was so riveting that Rabbit got out of the water, parked himself on a rock overlooking the break, and watched. Rabbit not only reenacts Peter's terrific surf moves, but he wraps his words around them.

"People talk about back arches and soul arches, *noooooobody* did it like Drouyn! And he was doing stuff on the face that people just weren't doing, weren't capable of doing."

Rabbit's telling, I think, is probably more compelling than watching Peter actually do this stuff. He pauses dramatically, face torqued as if performing the maneuver himself. It's like he's describing Chuck Yeager test piloting the X-1, or Neil Armstrong walking on the moon. The crescendo, after Peter dances with this curling, heaving, charging bull of a wave, is the carving 360 he pulls, way back in 1971, a breaking of the sound barrier of sorts, a glimpse of a decade or more down the line.

"It was just so . . . majestic! That's the only word I can use. Now I actually saw something that was pure inspiration. It always stayed with me. I looked at him and I went, *That is it! That's what it feels like to be the best in the world!* And that's what stayed with me. I always drew a lot of inspiration from that one session. Probably more than any other session I've ever seen, and I'm talking about, I grew up with Michael Peterson, I mean I saw all that. But this one session with Drouyn at Kirra, it opened my eyes to what true greatness really could be.

"Peter, he always had these amazing dreams, and amazing plans. But he definitely wasn't a team player. It had to be his way. He was really like an emperor, you know, it really had to be by his doctrine. And therefore it made it difficult to pull things off. I remember one time he came to me and he said, 'Look, I've got this wave stadium, and it's amazing, and it's going to be a ground-breaking thing.' This is like in '87, '88, and he said, 'Look, I'm raising some money, even my old nemesis Nat Young has given me a thousand dollars, and, you know, would you be prepared to put in a thousand dollars?' And I went, 'I'll back you, but like, how much are you trying to raise?' And he went, 'A hundred million.' And I went, 'A hundred *million!* You could have bought Billabong for that money back then. It was like a ridiculous amount of money! So it was all grandeur, it was all way out there. There was Drouyn's Island, and there were all these amazing things he was going to do. And I loved all these plans, but you needed a team. And eventually he'd make some business decision that would put his partners off. It'd all blow up. And then I remember a few years later, he was driving cabs, and I went, *Wow! This guy was like such a superstar, and it just fell through the cracks.* And I mean, a lot of surfers have fallen through the cracks, it's just really part and parcel of surfing, it's a sad indictment of what surfing is, and the surf industry in many respects. People just fall through the cracks, and just, you know, *See ya later. Get out of the way. We're moving forward. Pfff! Who are you?* And I really dislike that about surfing. You know, this whole thing about the surfing family, and how the industry looks after its own—that is such propaganda! It is so not how it is in reality. And Drouyn's a kind of a victim who didn't help himself in many ways. Because we've all got to reinvent ourselves. That's a fact. And no one is going to look after you, and you've just got to keep this whole reinvention happening. And he would reinvent himself, but he would always reinvent himself as the emperor. And it just never . . . nothing quite stuck. You know, something deserved to. Like, he really deserved to have something really stick, really big. I don't know what happened with that Stubbies thing, that was his baby and all of that, but the next year he was gone. Like, the next year he was in exile. And that definitely embittered him. That definitely embittered him."

Rabbit's so moved by the harsh way in which the surf industry treats its former pros that he has to stand. The mic attached to his shirt falls to the floor. I fix it.

"The surf industry has a specific agenda. When you no longer sell boardshorts, well, there is someone else to fill your shoes. It's cruel. They basically hand you a gun, and say, 'Go outside, go around the back to the shed, put the gun in your mouth, and pull the trigger. But put a silencer on it 'cause we don't want any ruffles in the stock market.'"

THE FORGOTTEN MAN

ONE BALMY AUGUST NIGHT IN THE LATE EIGHTIES, after way too many beers and cigarettes and way too much nonsensical banter, the surf writer Tim Baker stepped out of a bustling Lacanau café and walked across the street. Lacanau is a sleepy seaside village in the southwest of France. During the week of the Oxbow Pro it turned into a round-the-clock rage. Tim stood there in T-shirt and boardshorts and took it all in.

At one café there was Box and Branno and Shmoo and Miller Time chatting up a row of olive-skinned French girls. At the café next door the Hawaiians and Californians huddled around tables, shouted over heads, clinked glasses, knocked back tequila shots. The third café, where Tim had been, was a scrum of Aussies in neon jerseys and rosy glows. The cafés faced the promenade. Lovers ambled. Families in matching polo shirts and boat shoes licked ice creams. Teenage girls in blue jeans smoked and gossiped on corners. To the far left a beret-topped, mustachioed man played the accordion; to the right, a cabal of kids took turns riding their bikes off a wooden ramp. Street vendors selling *frites* and *gaufres à la chantilly* added amusement-park smells. Low, honeyed light cast the scene in a beatific luster. It looked like a painting; like *his* painting.

With imaginary brush in hand, Tim scratched his chin and wondered what the frame was missing. Then it hit him.

He hijacked one of the kids' bikes, wheeled it up to the far end, stripped off his clothes, brought a lighter to his groin, and peddled down the promenade, naked, with pubic hair aflame, the surfers shouting their approval, the rest of the crowd utterly baffled.

I remember it the way I remember the cyclone scene in *The Wizard of Oz*, Miss Gulch on a bike morphing into cackling wicked witch on a broomstick. I also remember it symbolically. In the late eighties surfing was evolving into a more professional, more athletic realm. Tim was flying the flag for the sport's wild and crazy roots.

It's been several decades since Tim last set fire to his pubes. Married with two kids, he has a cozy home atop the Currumbin headland. He pushes his kids into waves at The Alley most mornings, and writes from a nearby office every day. He is the author of a slew of books about surfing: *Surfari*, *Bustin' Down the Door*, *Occy* and *High Surf* among others. A stocky, sandy-haired, bright-eyed fellow, he is gentle and compassionate, but looks the sort of bloke you wouldn't want to piss off (a scar slashes the bridge of his nose; I didn't ask).

When I was writing my *Surfer's Journal* piece I spent a lot of time with an extensive profile Tim had written of Peter Drouyn in 1997. Along with doing an excellent job of chronicling Peter's life, it depicted something I knew well: a seduction. In the course of the time they spent together, Tim found himself deeply drawn to Peter, wanting to rally on his behalf.

Over lunch in his office, Tim tells me how he'd first met Peter at the 1997 Quiksilver Surfmasters in Fiji. It was the first of a string of annual masters events, as much a reunion as a competition. They stayed on Tavarua, a small, heart-shaped island resort where breakfast, lunch and dinner are served banquet-style, and the guests carry on like one big family, with lots of drinking and table-hopping. Peter had taken a shine to Tavarua owner Jon Roseman's girlfriend.

"One evening after dinner Peter just announces that he'd composed this poem in honor of Roseman's girlfriend, and people exchange puzzled glances, and Peter just gets up and orates in this beautiful, really flamboyant, really eloquent way, except that it was this really, really bawdy, erotic poem. It was a strange moment 'cause no one was quite sure how to take it."

Tim explains that it was shocking, but that those who knew Peter might have expected it.

"The next day I came across Peter in a distraught state. I asked what happened and he said that he'd had this confrontation with Gerry [Lopez, aka Mr. Pipeline] and Gerry had just punched him. And Peter said it was because they'd deemed it inappropriate that he'd recited this poem in front of [Gerry's cousin] Victor's teenage daughter."

Tim says that there may have been more to it than that (dormant rivalries had flared in the surf; the old blokes were getting aggro), but regardless he felt sad for Peter. Peter had been really excited about the event, he'd been surfing well, and now the trip had turned into yet another bitter experience.

At the time that Tim wrote the profile, Peter had recently formed his own company, Drouyn Oceanographic Research. He'd been studying maritime engineering for the last seven years. In classic Peter style, he took it to the nth degree. "Like the Wright Brothers watching the seagulls and then saying, 'Surely we can make something like the gull,'" was how he described his research methods to Tim. With mask and snorkel, Peter would spend hours in the water studying the contours of sandbars and reefs. Westerly had shown me some of the blueprints Peter had drawn up. They were highly detailed, with Vegas flourishes. One depicted a wave stadium that included a surfer riding a machine-generated wave on center stage, a laser show, and pods of trained dolphins leaping through the scene.

Peter told Tim that much of his research was beyond the comprehension of the engineering academics at the university. He said that he'd become so proficient in the mechanics of a perfect wave that, studying nautical maps, he could pinpoint the exact locales where they'd break. All of this information, of course, was top secret. He even had a surf resort in the works, Drouyn's Island. Peter showed Tim photos of a tiny palm tree-studded isle in the Philippines. In one of them Peter stood in Speedos on a white-sand beach, arms outstretched like Mr Roarke in the TV series *Fantasy Island*. "I'm going back to the sea again," he told Tim. "A new career, an independent consultant."

But the deal went bad shortly after Tim's piece went to print. According to Peter, his Filipino business partner had burned him.

Tim's friendship with Peter continued well after he'd finished writing the article. He'd been working on a screenplay about the surf industry, and thought Peter would be perfect to play the lead.

"I saw in Peter a stifled actor/genius. It's like when you close off a hose, the pressure just builds. He was someone who I felt surf history had done a disservice to, and in some way I wanted to save him."

By this time Peter had started studying law. To make ends meet he drove a taxi in Surfers Paradise. He was rapt at the idea of a starring role.

"You could sort of see the way he does set himself up for disappointment, because with every project he'll very quickly build it up into something that's going to be huge and be a huge redemption, and when that's not fulfilled it's another crushing source of despair."

Tim worked on his screenplay, but as he got deeper into it he wondered if the story might work better as a novel. Meanwhile, Peter's excitement about playing the lead snowballed.

"When you get sucked into Peter's world it quickly becomes this thing that he is now counting on. So there was this pressure that I found a bit oppressive."

When Tim told Peter that he was putting the script on hold Peter was disappointed.

"I think it was another bitter pill," says Tim.

They remain friendly. When I met with Tim his latest book had just come out, *Australia's Century of Surf*, in which Peter Drouyn is treated very respectfully. Tim signed a copy and had me pass it along to Westerly. Westerly was pleased, and wrote Tim a thank you email the following day.

"I think for that late sixties/early seventies generation and the advent of pro surfing, I think there was the sense that something was just building and building, and it was all going to lead to something where they could all make a living. And Peter was really at the forefront of that. Peter straddled that divide between the longboard era and the shortboard revolution, and remained relevant and competitive and reinvented himself as contest director, and I think for him he'd look at his CV and go, 'Look what I've done, this has all got to be leading towards some sort of greater destiny,' and when it didn't I think it was devastating—devastating that he didn't go on to some great and revered position within surfing."

PART THREE

DYING TO BECOME

THE FINAL MONTHS OF THE FINAL YEAR OF THE twentieth century must have felt truly apocalyptic for Peter Drouyn. In September his mother died. Peter and Gwendolyn were best friends. Of all the women in his life—of all the men in his life!—no one understood him like his mother. His grandiose dreams, his fanciful ideas, his love of make-believe, of play-acting, of improvising—much of it had been passed down from her. She was his biggest fan, his unconditional believer.

And he was grieving for more than just his mother. The last decade had been a litany of false starts, near misses, and utter disasters. There were all those years of studying nautical engineering, all those sleepless nights of divine inspiration in which surfers, dolphins, and light beams slashed across the movie screen of his mind. What did they amount to? Naught! There was that dirty friggin' scumbag that burned him on the Drouyn's Island deal. There was even a Drouyn's Island Plan B, in Yemen of all places, but that too was foiled when an AK-47-wielding guard sent him home for having the wrong travel visa.

The new millennium? Well, there was his acting school, in which he taught the Method to eager students from the Gold Coast who were in total awe of Peter, couldn't believe the electricity bursting from this man. There was Golden Girls Modelling Academy, where he taught graceless, diffident teenage girls how to own their beauty (one of his students went on to become Miss Australia!). These were not exactly fiascos, but they fell way short of what he'd hoped they could be.

149

His latest dream was to become a barrister. Mal Chalmers was helping him with that. He was taking courses and studying fiendishly, with all the good old Drouyn resolve he could muster, but it was still a few years off. And driving a cab to make a buck was killing him.

He moved in with his father for a while. Then he moved out. About the only good thing in his life was Zac, who was ten—nearly old enough to turn on to all those great movies.

And surfing still sorted him out, though it could be ego-crushing. And it was getting harder and harder to find a quiet wave.

•

It's funny how the ocean calls out to you. It's not about checking wave cams on the internet, or reading the surf forecast. It's a feeling in your bones and blood, something like the way dogs sense earthquakes.

It was the summer of 2002. The sun was of a certain heat and density, the cloudless sky was of a pinprickingly rich cerulean, the air had a vague effervescence, carrying whiffs of whatever it was to his shitty little flat in Labrador, a redneck neighborhood above Surfers, the only place he could afford on his meager cabbie's pay.

He'd worked a long shift the night before, he'd been at the books all morning right through lunch, his sixth sense that wind, tide and swell were delivering arias in the form of waves—he felt no guilt in bailing on his plans to hit Woolworths and ducking out for a surf instead.

He loaded his six foot one Mad Dog thruster into his white Holden and drove south along the Gold Coast Highway in the pre-rush hour traffic, past Jupiter's Casino and its monorail, past Rubber Jungle Wetsuits (formerly the Hohnesee factory), past Miami High with its name spelled out on the side of the hill like some C-grade version of the Hollywood sign.

At the surf club he got his first glimpse of the point. Whitewash exploded up around the cove; a bottle-green wall shimmered past the pool. He passed Montezuma's where many a top-sixteen surfer got toasted on margaritas, passed the Burleigh Beach Towers with its tennis court and steaming jacuzzi, passed the patch of grass that was Ground Zero for the man-on-man format that they'd stolen from him. His eyes were half on the brake lights in front of him, half on the set of waves screaming down the point. You could always tell the surfers from the non-surfers based on whether they slowed down, how neurotically they craned their necks at the sea. A wave doubled up and heaved, the spinning tube ejaculating a ghostly spit. It enraptured Peter, washed him with adrenalin. He was so glued to the surf that he nearly rear-ended the old Kingswood in front of him.

He parked in his usual spot under the pines, hopped out, shimmied into his wetsuit top. He ran around to the passenger side, opened the door and pulled out his board. Another set caught his eye, this one slightly bigger. On the first wave a goofy foot pumped heartily but the curl dashed past him, leaving an empty blue wall that seemed almost to wink at Peter. A second wave roped, a third wave twirled.

From the trunk, Peter grabbed a bar of wax and rubbed it in circles across the deck, paying close attention to the tail, to the dents that marked his front foot, to the nose where after all these years he still loved to hang five. He tossed the wax back into the trunk, locked the doors, and stashed his key under the rear bumper.

He trotted up the footpath, down the trail lined with pandanus, and across the black boulders already scorching in the 10 am sun.

Burleigh boulders are the size of kegs and potentially leg-snapping when wet, but Peter knew them like he knew the furniture in his Wharf Road home; his feet had practically shaped themselves to this familiar dance, toes clasping ridges and puckers with koala grip. A wave heaved and shot foam up to his knees. Peter hardly noticed. His eyes were fixed on a head-high barrel corkscrewing down the point.

At the jump rock he paused, watched the water suck away, revealing shiny black rocks, darting crabs, wafts of brine, a primordial hiss. An exhalation later the ocean surged up to his knees. He lurched forward, mounted his board, and stroked for the lineup.

It wasn't epic Burleigh but it was pretty damn good, especially considering there were only twenty or so guys out. Peter slipped into his rhythm the way he always did. He waited for sets, read the angle and the taper and what he liked to think of as the wave's visage, and picked the ones that seemed to call out to him. He drew his trademark lines, off the bottom and off the top, vertical bashes in the soft sections, lateral swooping arcs in the zippy bits, power surfing, albeit at a middle-aged tempo.

Surfing at age fifty-two was something he was still trying to work out. Yes, it was humbling; the weaker paddling arms, the slower reflexes, the stuttering cutbacks, the gap between how he dreamed of riding waves and how he actually rode them widening by the year. A single hour in the surf exhausted him, demanded afternoon naps—*when did that start?* Then there were the young blokes who literally paddled circles around him, flew above the lip. Clearly they had no sense of history.

But there was a chop wood/carry water simplicity to surfing that put things in perspective. He did some of his best thinking in the water. Something about the vastness, the exultant blue, the impregnable horizon. And the afterglow, those little cells and fibers and nerve endings so grateful for their daily fix. His life was a towering, teetering house of cards and at the bottom, wedged just so, was surfing.

Peter caught a slightly overhead wave from way out the back. It went fat as it rounded the cove. He kickstalled at the top, skittered and zagged, dropped to the bottom and swooped. He climbed the gentle crumble of lip, floated over it, then darted off the bottom and across the steepening face. But the wave sectioned fast, too fast. He kicked out over the back.

Behind it he saw a second wave. It was a tad smaller but it bent into a sort of saddle, that wonderful half-pipe effect that occurs during short interval swells. He dropped to prone, sprint-paddled for the shoulder, stroked up the face sideways. As the crest redirected him he popped to his feet. He plunged down the face in a low crouch and sprung into a hard bottom turn. His lip bash was nearly vertical, punctuated with a faint arch of the back. His board stayed right under him as, mid-face, he dashed for the shoulder. The wall was velvety, delicious. For a suspended moment he just stood there, rapt, the nose of his board streaking past a thousand diamonds, the blinding white crest feathering. The wave mowed fast. He was nearing the inside section, where the sandbar sucks nearly dry and the swell bends off towards Surfers Paradise, the pocket like a slingshot. Subtly, with a thrust of his leading shoulder and a torque of the ball of his front foot, he pumped. The whoosh was mesmerizing. The curtain dumped over his back. The wall seemed to almost grow, sand clouds in its trough.

And then it was zippering away from him. He did what he always did on this inside section. He waited for the lip to nearly clock him, and with a matador's flourish, straightened out. Only this time it did clock him, square on the right side of his head, with brutal force. His face slapped the water. His left ear seemed to tear open, a deafening hum. The power was preternatural; it belonged to Pipeline, Mavericks. The turbulence rag-dolled him, pushed him deeper and deeper. Where was the bottom? Where was the surface? He tumbled and grasped and needed desperately to breathe. He felt himself losing consciousness, saw powdery white light, let go.

Then he broke the surface, gasped for air.

He coughed. Spume blinded and burned. His ear rang. His head swayed. He waved his arms, looked for fellow surfers, but there was no one. He turned around and there was another wave, about to collapse on his head. He lunged for his board, death-gripped the rails, bounced shorewards. Whitewater deposited him on the sand. For a long while he just lay there lifeless.

"This feeling is never to be forgotten," says Westerly. "Peter felt terribly disoriented, his equilibrium was shot, blood was pouring out of his ears, he thought he was dead."

This accident, which left Peter with a concussion and a perforated ear drum, "pretty much fried his brain." Westerly says that there had been many instances where he'd felt like he was in the wrong body, but this loosened something, something irreversible. Peter started staying up into the wee hours, listening to classical music, feeling things shift inside him. One night he watched a documentary about albatrosses. He was transfixed, particularly by the part about the lone albatross out at sea for days, away from its family.

The documentary finished right around midnight. Peter got into his car and drove down to the beach he'd been frequenting, a secluded, wooded area near Sea World in Southport. He parked by the side of the road, crossed the dunes, and walked along the shoreline, feet sloshing in the wet sand, surges of water licking his toes.

He felt light and bubbly. He stripped off everything but his underpants, which he hoisted up his hips, because he wanted to feel like a woman. He felt a rhythm swelling in his body and he followed it, an adagio here, an arabesque there, a graceful flapping of the arms into a series of twirls. He danced and danced and danced.

"It was like Moses parting the sea. He started dancing like a ballerina, like the Bolshoi Ballet." Westerly glows as she tells me this. I can almost see him twirling across the jewel of her eye. She sniffles. "That's when it happened."

A month or so later he was coming out of the surf at this very same beach, ambling across the squeaky sand, when he nearly stepped on a pair of women's shorts someone had left behind. They were pink with white stripes. He tried them on. They fit.

Daily visits to thrift stores followed. She found herself searching solely the women's racks. She became what Westerly calls a "phantom of the night," staying up till dawn, blaring Tchaikovsky, trying on her new outfits in the full-length mirror, striking poses, dancing, making friends with the new sensations that coursed through her.

"The creation of Westerly was totally unplanned and evolved under extreme sensitivities and vulnerabilities derived from sheer exhaustion," says Westerly. "*Raw* is a word that minimizes the feeling. *Rebirth* is the accurate way to put it. Restoration was/is the creation from rebirth."

There have been cases of a similar ilk. After a head injury as a toddler, Alonzo Clemons of Colorado discovered an ability to sculpt animals to a remarkably lifelike degree using solely his hands and fingernails. Orlando Serrell of Virginia could tell the day of the week of any given date after being hit in the head by a baseball at age ten. Anthony Cicoria, a sixty-two-year-old orthopaedic surgeon from New York, was struck by lightning; suddenly he could play the piano to concert standard. But these "acquired savants" discovered hidden talents, not new identities.

·

For a long time it stayed in the closet, or more precisely, in Westerly's home or on the beach in the middle of the night. In the mirror she saw what looked like a narrowing of the hips. Her legs, cleanly shaven, were beautiful woman's legs.

One day she was at an old bookshop near her home looking for a particular doorstop of a law treatise. After searching the shelves for a long while she finally found it. Next to it was a biography of Marilyn Monroe.

"I started reading and went, 'Oh my god, we're exactly the same!' I forgot the law book, bought the Marilyn biography, and within a couple of days I'd read dozens of them and realized how much she and Peter had in common. They both suffered panic attacks, both hated to be alone, both had terrible low self-esteem, both studied Method acting, both loved Brando and Gable, both spent two weeks in a mental institution, both tried LSD at exactly the same time. I realized Marilyn was deep inside me, almost guiding the creation of Westerly. I realized I was developing quite unintentionally into the image of Marilyn."

Marilyn took up residence in Westerly's head. Not only did she consume her thoughts, but she kept popping up, as if trying to communicate with Westerly. Turn on the TV and there she was, in *The Misfits*, a movie Peter never much cared for when he saw it as a boy. Go into the thrift store, flip through old records and there she was, in classic Marilyn giggle, hot breath almost palpable, on the cover of *24 Great Songs*. Take Zac to get his haircut and taped to the tatted, nose-ringed hairstylist's mirror was the iconic image from *Seven Year Itch*. There were sly winks as well. Marilyn died at age thirty-six. As far as Westerly saw it, that was the age that Peter died as well (by then his surfing career had declared bankruptcy). When Westerly happened to look at the odometer on her car, it read 100,036. On the Pacific Highway, headed up to Brisbane for a doctor's appointment, she got stuck behind a sea foam and white '62 EK Holden driving absurdly slow in the fast lane; 1962 was the year Marilyn died. "And guess the last two digits of the number plate: 36!"

Marilyn was elsewhere when Westerly started thinking about a name for this girl emerging inside her. She saw phoenixes rising from ashes, caterpillars morphing into butterflies, space shuttles jettisoning their boosters. But it was the wind that burnished the waves velvety smooth, the wind that had summoned Peter to attention his entire surfing life, that won out. It rolled off the tongue. It had the ring of a Hollywood starlet. Only later, long after the name "Westerly Windina" had stuck, did she realize that WW was MM turned upside down.

•

For years Peter Drouyn and his longtime friend, Mark Bennett, a doctor, would meet up at 5 am for a coffee then a surf. It was one of those rituals that cut the sting out of this getting-old business. Mark was a good man, broader-minded than the rest of these Gold Coast philistines.

She didn't overthink it. She did it in the same fanciful way that she danced down the beach in the middle of the night, or recited lines from *Bus Stop* in the mirror.

She got up at four, dressed in her Westerly girly stuff, drove to the little café in Mermaid Beach where Mark and she would meet. She waited in her car, anxious. When Mark pulled into the parking lot she got out, opened his passenger door, and plopped herself right next to him.

Soft peach-colored light hit their faces. Mark wore board-shorts, a striped T-shirt, and a totally baffled expression on his face. Before he could say anything Westerly spoke up.

"It's me, Mark. I'm a female. I'm a female."

"Is that you, Peter?" He meant it sincerely, he was that shocked.

"No, it's not Peter. It's sort of—I'm me, I'm a new person who's come from Peter. You can still see me as Peter for a little while if you want. But, Mark, I've completely changed. I am not the person that you knew. I'm really happy in my new form."

Westerly told Mark that she herself had had a hard time believing it at first, but that she was here, and there was no going back. Mark just stared at her, speechless.

"It's all good, Mark. Don't worry. Peter hasn't gone crazy. I'm more female than any female that you will meet in your life. And I'll keep changing. I'll keep transforming. I'm like a chameleon."

Westerly tells me that it took a while, but Mark got used to Westerly, embraced her even. They kept up their weekly surfing ritual, but at off-the-beaten-path spots. Mark was married. He didn't want it getting around that he was having an affair with this platinum-blonde surfer chick.

Over time Westerly observed a shift in the way Mark related to his new female friend. He opened doors for her, allowed himself to be more vulnerable. "It was this subtle shift, Westerly pulling out the more honest man in Mark," says WW.

•

In 2007 Westerly received an invitation in the mail for the Stubbies Pro thirty-year reunion. A tremor of her old self leaped from somewhere deep in her stomach, but before it could take root, it was replaced by a much grander thought: *Could there be a more perfect stage on which to unleash the miracle of Westerly Windina?*

Sleepless at 3 am, triumphant movie soundtracks on the CD player, she pondered outfits. Many nights she got up, slipped into a gown, dress, skirt, pair of shoes, and posed in the mirror. This went on for weeks leading up to the big night.

She settled on an outfit that was elegant but formal. She wore her favorite black-and-white Chanel ballet flats, a black slit skirt, a white frilly blouse and a cherry-red bolero jacket, with matching lipstick, her freshly blonded hair in loose curls, like those Burleigh barrels that rifle down the point.

On the evening of the Stubbies Pro reunion she started getting ready about two hours before Mark Bennett, her date for the evening (he didn't know that's what he was), was scheduled to pick her up. When the knock came at 7 pm she felt a squeal of butterflies. She opened the door. Mark stood there in jeans and a striped collared T-shirt, salt-and-pepper hair brushed back. He looked less surprised than scared.

"No," he said, shaking his head. "No. Definitely not."

It was far from the response that Westerly had in mind, but over a beer in her kitchenette, Mark made a convincing argument as to why this was a bad idea.

She didn't lose all of her girly things, but she toned it way, way down. Hoop earrings, silver sandals, pencil-line eyebrows—that was as much as she gave them that night. It was still enough to shake 'em up. Most of the guys were too uncomfortable to ask, they just shook her hand, treated her like a bloke, perhaps even more so, to overcompensate. The only one to outright confront Westerly was Randy Rarick, and there was no use trying to explain. She took the slithery approach, she told him what Peter would have told him: that it was an act, a way to get attention.

•

She came out on the *Today Tonight* show on January 14, 2008. She wore an orange high-cut swimsuit in one interview, and a red fifties style sweater with lots of gold chunk jewelery in another.

"What's become of Peter Drouyn?" asked the host.

"Well, he's somewhere in there," said Westerly. "He's not dead. But he's not a he or he's not there anymore. He's gone."

She was poised and dignified. The reporter continually referred to her as "he." She said just enough to get her point across, but also to keep them guessing, to plant a little seed in their heads. The papers rang the next day. Neighbors stared. People at Australia Fair, the local shopping center, did double takes.

ALL IN THE FAMILY

AFTER I'D GATHERED ALL THE MATERIAL I NEED-
ed to write my profile of Westerly in 2009, we continued to keep in
touch, via Skype (or, to be technically precise, I'd use Skype to call
her mobile phone—much cheaper than phone to phone). We'd
talk at least a couple of nights a week, usually for an hour or so.
We'd start with pleasantries before moving on to bigger concerns.

A recurring theme was Westerly's loathing of Australia. She
referred to it as "backwards-thinking and redneck." She was living
in a halfway house-type place in Grafton, and got into an argument with a fellow guest, an ex-inmate. He started stalking her.
Westerly was convinced he was out to rape her or kill her or both.
She moved into her car, slept in the forest at night.

I felt for her. I did a lot of listening. We'd usually talk in the
afternoons her time, which was around 11 pm or midnight my
time. It was like listening to late-night radio. I never knew what I
would get. One night she'd be giddy, full of humor, breaking into
song. The next she'd be so despondent, in such low spirits that I'd
hang up and wonder if it might be the last time I ever spoke to her.

"If not for Zac I'd have already done myself in," she said to me
more than once. "But I know my son needs me."

She told me she was taking growth hormones, that they were
softening up her genitals to make the surgery easier. I wondered
how much the hormones, how much the long bouts of solitude,
were contributing to her mood swings. Sadly, she said that her law
degree was all in vain, that no one would hire her. I remembered
how I'd often seen trans people pushing shopping carts filled with

their possessions down the street in Los Angeles, rendered un-employable by the "civilized world." On one side was male, on the other female, and in between this giant abyss.

Westerly saw a way out. She just needed someone to help connect her to the right producer, then she'd be brought out to America, where they'd recognize her for the Hollywood showgirl that she was. There were no doubts in Westerly's mind. She was destined to become a global sensation.

My profile of Westerly was published in *The Surfer's Journal*, as well as publications in Brazil, Japan and Australia. It was well received—by surfers, by the GLBT community. I didn't do much. I merely midwifed Peter/Westerly's story along.

"Will you help me, Jamie? Help me find a producer in America?" Westerly asked one night.

I loved the way she said "America"—so grandly and dreamily. I told her that I would.

The more she imagined-out-loud her rise to fame in "America," the more I realized she was living in an America fifty years ago, an America in which JFK was president, Sinatra was crooning "Young at Heart," Mickey Mantle was swinging for the fences at Yankee Stadium, and Billy Wilder was begging Marilyn for "more teeth, more breath, more sparkle" on the set of *Some Like It Hot*.

Westerly was determined to make it to America, and I was determined to help her. I'd write a screenplay based on her life, I thought, and it would be a huge hit! (I find that these delusions of grandeur are essential for long-form writing projects.) I told Westerly my idea. She was thrilled. I talked to my movie industry friends, shared my Westerly profile with an acquisitions man at Creative Arts Agency—everyone confirmed that Peter Drouyn's metamorphosis into Westerly Windina was a terrific story. But before I do anything else, I was advised, I should acquire Wester-ly's life rights. I hired a lawyer, explaining that I had no money. She promised to do it on the cheap. She sent Westerly an industry-standard contract. Westerly balked at it. There was the Gold Coast ingenue, and then there was this diva, a side of Westerly that felt it her Marilyn-reincarnate birthright to be difficult. Westerly and my lawyer went back and forth, but in the end, Westerly would not agree to the terms. ("He just couldn't work with other people, and all his projects went to dust," I remembered Rabbit saying.)

Meanwhile, Alan White had hired me to write a screenplay based on a profile I'd done of a pair of irreverent surfer brothers from Malibu. Alan had been a successful director of television commercials for a couple of decades, but he was dying to do projects closer to his heart. He was a surfer. In our development meetings we inevitably drifted into conversations about the colossal Ms. Windina. Most of these conversations took place in the surf, between waves, at Point Dume in Malibu, where Alan and his family live. We decided to team up on a documentary film about Peter/Westerly's transformation. And so it began . . .

Jordan Tappis was a regular foot with a seething frontside hack. After a brief stint on the pro tour, he decided to follow his first and probably more enduring love. He started a record label called Record Collection. This led him to producing films and TV programs, most of which focus on music.

Through a mutual friend Jordan met Beau Willimon, who'd written an off-Broadway play called *Farragut North*. On a visit to New York, Jordan and Beau talked about their shared interests and respective ambitions. They discovered that they had more than a few things in common. Months later *Farragut North* was adapted into a screenplay, *The Ides of March*, directed by and starring George Clooney. A year later Beau was approached by director David Fincher about resurrecting a 1970s British drama about a corrupt politician. Beau's series, *House of Cards*, would go on to become a global sensation.

Somewhere in between, Jordan and Beau started Westward Productions. One of the first projects they took on was our Westerly documentary.

I met Nick Atkins at the 2011 Quiksilver Pro New York, where I worked as a webcast editor and he worked as a director of photography. Nick had a graceful way with people. He was gentle but efficient; he earned people's trust quickly. When we were trying to think of who would be good for the Bangkok trip, his name came up. Jordan and Alan met him. They loved him.

•

So Nick I are knocking on Westerly's front door. It's November 2012. Last I saw her was when Alan and I were here a year ago to shoot the sizzle reel. She has since signed a life-rights contract, received a considerable sum of money, made huge demands regarding the showcase finale, called the surgery on, called it off, and caused us to cancel plane tickets and hotel reservations. Recently she was invited to the Surfing Australia fiftieth-anniversary celebrations. That too has become a source of drama. First she offered to pop out of a cake and sing "Happy Birthday." When Surfing Australia declined her offer Westerly called them a bunch of "counterfeits" and "right-wingers" and "hypocrites." Will she go to the gala? "Maybe," she says. "Maybe not." I'm beginning to wonder whether my betting the farm on Westerly Windina might be one of those decisions that, three years down the track, from the cardboard box I'm living in, from the taste of bile in my mouth that no amount of Scope will ever wash away, I might sorely regret.

Ah, but she charms us. Nick becomes "Nicka" within seconds of their first meeting. I'm "Jamesy." Westerly's in her Mexican fiesta dress, cha-cha-cha-ing around the living room.

"Let me show you my Marilyn room," she says and finger snaps and dances us into her bedroom, which is decorated in pinks and purples, a doll's house in the corner. Presiding over the room is a poster of MM.

"Great-looking gear," says Nick, nodding at the outfits laid out on the bed.

"That's my stuff for Bangkok," Westerly says.

"So Bangkok's on?" I ask.

"Oh yes."

Ah, but she charms us—then throws the monkey wrench. Now

I'm on the phone with Jordan and Alan back in LA, scrambling to
re-book the flights and hotel reservations we'd cancelled. Instead
of the leisurely two weeks we'd planned to spend with Westerly at
home on the Gold Coast, we now have forty-eight hours till we
leave for Bangkok.

·

Westerly has errands to run, but first she wants to take Nicka
and me to her favorite coffee place. A few blocks from her house,
Goldsteins Pie Shop is fluoro-lit, plastic seats, decor not unlike
McDonald's or KFC. As we walk through the door she's greeted
with a chorus of *Hi Westerlys* from the three women working behind the counter.

Westerly half bows. "These are the guys from Hollywood who
are making my movie," she says.

Nick and I introduce ourselves to Emma, fiftyish, matronly,
banging at the coffee machine; Toots, warm, pinkish, waving hello
from the drive-thru window; and Amy, twentyish, bouncy, blonde.

"So when are you going?" Amy asks Westerly.

"Friday midday."

Amy brightens. "Hear that, girls? Westerly's off on Friday."
Emma and Toots come over. They share a moment of solidarity—
deep eye contact, nodding heads, "So exciting!" "Ah, good on ya,
Westerly." Clearly the Goldsteins girls have been hearing about
Westerly's surgery for quite a while.

"Sorry, what would you like?" Amy asks Nick and me.

We order pies and coffees. When Westerly says, "Quarter
strength, ext—" Amy finishes it for her: "Extra hot—got it, Westerly."

Sitting at the corner table, pies poking from their paper sheaths,
Nick and I eat like hounds. Westerly pulls a to-do list from her
pocket, goes through it.

The locals who come and go, hands full of meat pies and sau-
sage rolls and day-old lamingtons, are every bit the "insensitive

culture" Westerly has complained about. A couple of twentyish blokes in grass-stained footy outfits; a greasy-haired guy in Jimmy Barnes T-shirt with a three-schooner glow and belly to match, an old couple who eye WW and her vibrant dress with disdain. Labrador, aka "Lockyadoor," has a reputation for break-ins and tweakers.

"Why do you live there?" I once asked Westerly over lunch in 2011.

"I'd've been gone a long time ago if it wasn't for Zac," she said. "He's here with his mum. I could never leave him."

From Goldsteins we go to Australia Fair, a beast of a shopping mall in Southport. Among other things, Westerly needs to get undergarments that will be, as she puts it, "sensitive to my new undercarriage." Moving from shop to shop, she says that this is what she and Zac do most weekends, cruise the mall. She points out the theatre where they see movies, the massage place where she gets him massages.

A dark-haired girl with tattooed arms walks up.

"Nice pins," she says to Westerly.

"Pins?"

"Nice legs!"

Westerly laughs. "Aw, thank you, thank you."

The girl wants to know who Westerly is, what we're doing following her with a camera. "You're so beautiful," she tells Westerly, pawing her hands. Westerly is visibly touched.

•

Westerly's beam carries to the bank, the pharmacy, Vinnies and to the highlight of the day: spending a couple of hours with Zac. Nick and I are excited to meet him. That morning I'd called Stephanie, Peter's ex-wife, to ask if we could interview her for the film. She curtly said no, that she wanted nothing to do with it.

We're at Westerly's. A blade of sunlight cuts the room. A white sheet covers her couch. She tells us that that's where she sleeps every night; for some reason she can't sleep on a proper bed. Bags from today's shopping are stacked on the kitchen counter.

"I'll just be a tick," says Westerly.

She heads out, then returns less than ten minutes later.

"Zac," she says to the smiling, pimply-faced kid in a Cannibal Corpse shirt standing in the doorway, "this is Jamie and this is Nick."

Zac greets us with a soul brother handshake. He's warm, innocent-seeming. He's a heavy-set kid, slumped shoulders, dark hair. He asks us about the movie, then tells us that he directed and starred in his own. Westerly grabs a DVD from the shelf and hands it to me. Sure enough, Zac Drouyn directed and starred in *Batman: Escape From Arkham Asylum*, a Batman-spinoff, featuring a few of his schoolmates, shot here in Labrador.

"I love movies," he says. "My favorite actor is Steve Bacic. He got his start on *21 Jump Street*."

We interview Zac, with Westerly sitting next to him on the couch. He talks about his love of indie film and death metal music, lists off a string of bands with "zombie" and "black" and "morbid" in their name. The serious questions—how he feels about his father's transition, what he thinks abut the big trip to Bangkok—are off-limits. Westerly insisted that we "mustn't blow Zac out," that it's still a very sensitive, personal thing he's coming to grips with. I should point out that before she went to pick him up, Westerly washed off all her makeup, rinsed the curls out of her hair and brushed it into a classic comb-over, removed her earrings and bracelets, and changed into sandals, jeans and a white blouse.

"Do you like death metal?" Zac asks Nick.

Nick says yeah, mentions a couple of bands.

Not a lot happens in our chat with Zac. He seems uncomfortable with the camera, with the mic clipped to his T-shirt. When we finish he jumps on the computer, puts on headphones.

"Have a good trip to America," he says to Nick and me when we say goodbye in the driveway, Westerly and Zac on their way to a final dinner together before the trip, Nick and I headed to our hotel.

He turns to his father. "Are you guys going to go to the Sunset Strip?"

Please, no, Westerly Windina, you have not! That's what's transmitted in the fleeting glances between Westerly, Nick and me.

"We'll be working on the movie, son," says Westerly. "But if we have time . . ."

·

Tony Drouyn lives a couple of kilometers from Westerly, but as Westerly tells us on the drive there, they don't see much of each other. We pass several blocks of nondescript houses, a grassy park with a skate bowl, a pot-bellied bloke standing on a ladder washing his boat, and pull up in front of a one-story brick house in a quiet cul-de-sac. Westerly, in skinny jeans, blue spandex top and her dad's navy hat, steps out of the car and adjusts the Lav radio mic tucked in her pocket. She raises stick-em-up hands, speaks in a mock cowboy accent.

"I'm all loaded up with my six-guns, I'm ready to shoot it out at the OK Corral, ladies and gentlemen, that's what this is here. Let me tell you right now, we're goin' in. We ain't steppin' back, we ain't pullin' out—*we're goin' in!*"

She giggles, leads us up the driveway, narrates to camera. "This is my brother Tony's place. And he's been here, oh, probably fifteen, twenty years. He lives by himself, and he's got the best movie and music collections in the world. He can hardly move 'cause it's all so close around him, and he's still puttin' more in. Let's go and meet him."

A dusty, rust bucket Toyota Cortina with at least one flat tire sits in the driveway.

"That's his old car," says Westerly. "And it hasn't moved for twelve years, fifteen years. Obviously he doesn't drive anymore."

We walk through a side yard of crabgrass, rubbish bins and outdoor furniture covered in leaves. The front door is obstructed by an overgrown tree. An old bicycle leans against the side of the house. Weeds grow out of the wheels and frame.

Westerly calls out through the screen door. "Hey, Tone, we're here!"

A shadow appears. "Hold on," goes a strong voice. "Hold on a second."

Tony shuffles around a bit then opens the screen door. A heavy-set man in faded blue cotton shorts and a half-unbuttoned Aloha shirt, Tony's face is big, ruddy, fleshy. He's bald up top with a skirt of fine white hair falling around his ears. Big, curious eyes are made even bigger by Coke-bottle glasses. His full lips are curled into a suspicious, ironical smile.

"Hey, Tone," says Westerly. She nods to us: "Don't mind them, just filming, Tone. Just go ahead, be normal."

Tony shrugs. "Who am I supposed to be? E.T.?"

Westerly, all cute: *"You're my brother! You're my brother!"*

Nick and I introduce ourselves.

"The boys are going to interview you," says Westerly. "I'll just wait outside."

Tony brings us into his living room. It's a claustrophobic little space, packed with books and VHS movies on every shelf, every dresser and tabletop, books and VHS movies stacked on the floor, in corners. There's not much light. The room smells stale, moldy.

Tony sits in a well-used chair. Behind him is a black-and-white photo of their mother.

"What was it like growing up with Peter?" I ask.

"Peter could be difficult. He was completely different to me. He was a total extrovert; I was a total introvert. I was a person who could barely look at people without wanting to run away. I was the ultimate introvert and he was a manic extrovert."

Tony chooses his words carefully. He speaks in a wheezy baritone. He says that it is not uncommon for siblings from the same parents to be vastly different, makes reference to the biblical story of Jacob and Esau.

"Peter was always playing up," he continues. "I don't think

Mum and Dad would mind me saying this. He was mischievous. But he rarely got into trouble for it. He sort of got away with it for being a boy with a big, beaming smile." Tony shakes his head, laughs.

"And he's been through some radical changes over the last decade, yes?" I say.

"You'll have to be more specific."

"Well, you know about Westerly Windina?"

"No, I don't. Except when people breathe sideways and let the cat out of the bag. And I hear this name, and someone says something, and I don't know anything about it. I know *nothing about it*. I'm the last one to know. It's like everyone in this place knows something that I don't know."

"But haven't there been articles in the press?"

"Not about—what's his name? Westerly Windina? There's one article, so-called, on television that I never wanted to see again and I never wanted to watch the television again because of it. It was on Channel Seven, and I nearly had a heart attack, and I think Dad nearly had one, too. But this 'Westerly Windina' thing, a swami of higher India, is it?" Tony mumbles, gets tongue-tied. "I don't know what to say about it."

Alluding to gender-bending but careful not to mention it outright, Tony explains that Peter started to "go funny" at the beginning of the 2000s. I ask if he feels close to his brother. "A bit closer than I was, definitely. He was swinging a bit too far from my reality at one stage, for quite a while, nearly six or seven years. He's been a lot better lately. He's definitely been a lot better."

Tony changes the subject to what we soon discover is one of his favorites. He says that he never saw the UFO in 1968, but that he definitely remembers Peter waking him in the middle of the night all stunned and traumatized.

"Do you follow UFOs?" he asks.

I feel like I'm letting him down when I say no. Tony tells us his own UFO story in which a "shining, incandescent light drifts slowly down to the hills." A wave of awe sweeps over his face.

"Never got over it." He says that his fascination with UFOs started when he saw the movie *Close Encounters of the Third Kind* in the late seventies. That led him to UFO literature. "I couldn't get enough of it," he says. He lists his favorite books and authors, quotes Carl Sagan, says that a nearby town was once a hot spot for UFO sightings. I get the sense that this is only a fraction of his knowledge of the paranormal.

I steer the conversation back to the brothers. Tony tells me that he was always proud of Peter, but he had too many problems of his own to be deeply involved in Peter's surfing life. I ask if the young Peter liked attention.

"Oh yes. He was effortlessly funny. He had a way of making me laugh even when I didn't want to laugh, with his faces and impersonations and funny voices."

"He seems happiest with the cameras on him," I say.

"Well, that would mean that at heart nothing has changed." Tony has a little private chuckle.

I ask if there was a moment when it became obvious that Peter would have a giant impact on the surf world. He cites Peter's win in the 1965 Australian Titles.

How did it change him?

"He got more full of himself," he laughs. "Peter was outrageously manic. I'm not afraid to say I'm manic depressive, schizophrenic—and got over it, forged my way through it, so it shouldn't worry him for me to say that. The mania part definitely helped him to get ahead. He was really energetic. He was anywhere from over-mania to super-mania. It helped him, though, because you do need it. Unfortunately, I was depressive. Absolutely depressive."

Like Peter, Tony is grateful to have found surfing at a young age.

"Surfing could be very therapeutic for people who had any kinds of domestic problems, personal problems. Parents were generally universally good back then. They were all fine and loving people, but they couldn't do anything about boys who were lost in and out of love or just having some kind of depressive time. Surfing was amazing for me. It really pulled me out of shocking depression, really awful, suicidal depression. No after effects, no side effects except tiredness."

After we finish the interview Tony shows us his collection of LPs and CDs. He explains that they're arranged by decade. "Film soundtracks down there, sixties collection all along there, seventies and eighties over there."

I notice he has a massive collection of books about the paranormal.

Westerly enters.

"Still Planet Earth?" she asks.

Westerly raves about Tony's thousands of records and CDs. "You've got everything you need to survive a nuclear blast," she says.

"Except about a ton of canned food," says Tony.

"Tony tends to store everything away like . . . what's that movie? *Blast from the Past?* It had Christopher Walken in it, and they lived underground."

"Oh yeah," says Tony. "I've seen it a long time ago. One of those replacement-personality films."

We step outside to the front of the house, Westerly and Tony continuing their movie talk. They seem at ease with each other, chummy. But that disappears when Westerly says, "Good to see you, Tone. I'll see you when I come back from America. I'll be back on the twenty-fourth."

"Hey?"

"I'm going to America with the boys."

Tony rubs his chin suspiciously. "You're going to America. I didn't know that."

"Just to finish off the film. Ah, well, I thought I'd tell you today."

"I didn't know you were going to America."

It's not a good feeling watching Westerly lie to her brother. And she does a poor job of it, averting eyes, cutesy body language. I feel even worse when Tony nods to Nick and me and says that Westerly will be "in good hands."

"I'll be in good hands. And no doubt you've had a good interview. I'm glad. I'm glad." Westerly's voice turns soft and maternal. *"I'm glad."*

"I didn't even get around to doing any impersonations," Tony says.

Tony and Westerly bounce off each other in shorthand, referencing old films and actors—James Mason in *Pandora and the Flying Dutchman*, Michael Caine in *Zulu*, Marlon Brando in *The Godfather*, Richard Burton, Stacy Keach, Daniel Craig, *Les Miserables*. They laugh, bump shoulders. Tony breaks into a soliloquy from Dickens' *A Tale of Two Cities*. Westerly picks it up, can't remember the lines. Tony jumps back in, flubs it once, starts again, and in a long, long breath delivers it with rising and falling cadences, like a stage actor. When he hits the last line Westerly applauds.

"That's my brother," she says. "That's my brother."

•

That afternoon we interview Westerly in her living room. I sit next to Nick, who stands behind his camera, mounted on a tripod, and Westerly sits in a chair about six feet in front of us. She explains that she leaves tomorrow for Bangkok, that she'll be having her operation with one of the "most famous reassignment surgeons in the world."

"It's been at the front of my mind since the sudden change," she says. "About five and a half years now."

She describes the prerequisite psychiatric evaluations she's had to do, the questions the doctor asked: *When did it happen? How did it happen? Are you happy with your female disposition? How long have you been wearing women's clothes? Consistently, or alternating between men's and women's clothes?*

Westerly explains the difference between a cross-dresser, a transvestite and a transsexual.

"I really think my situation's entirely different than any of the normal transsexual or transgender. It's totally different," she says.

"What do your family and friends think of what you're doing?"

I ask.

"Well, they think they've never seen me happier. They just can't believe how confident and how happy I am. My son Zac, it's been hard for him. It's been difficult, so I've sort of gone slowly, slowly."

She says that she has to take steps backwards so she doesn't lose his confidence.

"The beautiful thing is that I'm pretending to be a boy for Zac. That's the great inverse relationship that I now have, female looking at male as something strange."

"Does Zac know you're going to Thailand for gender reassignment?"

"No, no, he doesn't. No, that's too much for him all at once, that's just sort of throwing the snowball off the cliff and just letting it roll down wherever it hits."

"Does your brother Tony know?"

"No, it's the same with Tony. It's not good for him to know that just yet. He's not ready for it yet either."

"You're not telling your brother, you're not telling your son, and yet you want us here with cameras to document it, which means it's going to come out in a film, so there's going to be a sense of deceit to two people who are very, very close to you."

"No, no, that's not right at all. The operation, the completion, is the most important thing in my new life, the life that should have been from the start. Now you must understand that we live in a corner of the world that's so backward in this sort of thing that I'm not just going to go around shocking everyone, particularly my family."

I tell Westerly that I was shocked when she told both Zac and Tony that she was going to LA to work on the film, that I felt like an accomplice in what feels to me like a big lie.

Westerly turns nervous. She says that the solution is simply to edit out the bit where she lied to Tony on camera. "I don't want it in the film," she says, and demands that before we continue with the project, I have to sign a document stating that "We will not use the scene in which Westerly Windina tells her brother Tony that she is going to LA," or words to this effect.

"Here's the thing, Westerly. Sometimes I feel like you want to manipulate everything to fit this certain image of Westerly. But it has to be truthful."

She grimaces, shakes her head. "No, no, this is not right." She takes off the Lav mic clipped to her white blouse. "No, this is not right, Jamie. I won't go on. Honestly, I knew this was going to happen. I knew at some stage you'd let me down." She stands, walks over to the kitchen counter. "You just simply don't believe me. You don't believe in me."

"I do believe in you. I wouldn't be here if I didn't believe in you."

She walks into the kitchen, sulking. "Jamie, I just get the feeling that you're trying to complete a documentary because you're obliged to. You've now widened and expanded it to include my family as a proposition for my credibility. This is just wrong, Jamie!"

Westerly paces back and forth, she's wholly pissed off. I remain in my chair, calm. Half of me is fully immersed in the argument, the other half is amazed: we're carrying on like an old married couple!

"Sit back down, Westerly. You tell me what you think it should be."

"Jamie, I just want it edited out."

I ask how she sees the story. She says it's the story of Peter Drouyn becoming Westerly, going to Bangkok to get her completion.

"But now you're bringing my son into it. Accusing me of deceit. You're saying that sometimes you get the impression I'm manipulating. This is terrible what you're saying!"

"I'm just trying to understand who Westerly is."

"*I thought you already did!* You've had four or five years, you've had thousands . . ." She opens the kitchen cupboard, pulls out a four-inch thick stack of paper. "Look, there's only a third of the emails!"

She flips through them, reads aloud. "Here: *My story has its*

*maximum essence generated at the crossroads of time, now time
. . ."* She gives up.

"I don't think I asked you anything unreasonable," I counter,
"and you're trying to turn it into *I stepped out of these parameters.* If
I'm trying to get to know Westerly Windina I should be able to
ask questions."

She's flustered, pacing, hand on hip. "No, no, no. Jamie, if your
trying to get to know Westerly Windina is about trying to see
whether she's deceitful or whether she's partially deceitful or stu-
pid or she's making a huge mistake..." She shakes her head, sees
Nick focus his camera. "Hang on, is this being recorded?"

YANHEE HOSPITAL

YANHEE HOSPITAL IS A GIANT, LEGO-LIKE, fifteen-story building with dark-tinted windows, multiple roof decks, and a tower emblazoned with green crosses.

We pull into the drop-off area, packed with taxis and cars and motorcycles. A traffic controller—white coat, white cap, white gloves—waves us into a spot. Huddled around the entrance are valets, nurses, patients in wheelchairs and taxi drivers speaking into mobile phones. We enter through glass doors. The foyer buzzes with activity. A counter to our left is staffed with several receptionists, one of whom smiles warmly at us. We approach her. Westerly explains that she is Australian, that she would like to see Dr. Greechart. The receptionist speaks little English, but with a graceful upturned hand points toward a desk fronted by a prominent sign that reads INTERNATIONAL COORDINATOR. We head over.

The massive hall is sleek and modern, with curvy desks and counters and chairs. Nurses wear tailored sky-blue uniforms that look straight out of an S&M fantasy. A trio of young, beautiful, ponytailed Thai girls glides across our path on rollerblades. In yellow tops and powder-blue miniskirts, they resemble cheerleaders, but instead of pompoms they carry documents. Yanhee is so big, I soon realize, that the rollerblades expedite the transfer of information.

Nick and I hang back while Westerly sits down with the international coordinator, a middle-aged, earnest-faced man. With slumped posture, she scribbles notes on a piece of paper. Wheelchairs roll past. More rollerbladers. Westerly stands, bows, walks over to us. "Third floor," she says.

We ride up in a crowded elevator and step out. The first thing we see is a counter selling cosmetics and sunglasses. Behind it sits a young woman—gorgeous and unblemished. Next to her are two nurses on stools, heads tilted back. Makeup artists huddle over them, applying lip liner, eye shadow, mascara. The sign leading to the wing we're looking for says it all: PLASTIC SURGERY CENTER.

Nick and I follow Westerly into a large room. Rows of couches face a long reception desk staffed with young nurses, or young women dressed as nurses, their lilac uniforms with cute little caps like something you'd see on a Paris runway. Their posture is perfect. They too are all gorgeous and unblemished—reminders of our crow's feet and double chins and big noses.

Westerly approaches the reception desk. She's sent a few chairs down, chats with one of the nurses, turns back to us and gives a wave and thumbs-up, then follows the nurse down the hall. Nick taps away at his BlackBerry. I look around.

In front of a mirrored door that says TREATMENT 1, a lithe, thirtyish doctor talks sternly with a well-dressed Caucasian woman, a bandage covering her nose. A few seats in front of us, a pair of rotund middleaged ladies, Australian by the sounds of their accents, pore over a brochure. An elderly, silver-haired man in an expensive-looking suit greets a doll-like woman with whopping boobs. He shakes her hand formally.

"Check this out," says Nick, reading aloud from his BlackBerry: *"Yanhee's emphasis on beauty enhancement procedures is demonstrated by the fact that, of the total number of international patients that Yanhee serves, seventy-two percent receive cosmetic care, twelve percent receive care in general surgery and medicine, eight percent receive dental care, and another eight percent receive care in alternative medicine. Of the total number of cosmetic surgery procedures conducted at Yanhee Hospital, breast augmentation comprises twenty percent; face lift comprises sixteen percent; blepharoplasty comprises twelve per-*

*cent; tummy tuck, nose reshaping and liposuction comprise nine per-
cent; breast lift and hair transplantation comprise five percent; nose
implants, breast reduction, and varicose vein treatment comprise three
percent, hair removal comprises two percent, and other procedures comprise the remaining one percent.*" He shakes his head. "This place is a
bloody Frankenstein factory!"

We Google around and learn that Yanhee is popular for "medi-
cal tourism." Package deals offer flights, hotels, a few days of sight-
seeing, and a little nip and tuck before heading home.

Westerly emerges, following a nurse who looks seventeen years
old. "I've just got to go and see the doctor and have a blood test,"
she says.

"We're going to get some air," we tell her. "Meet you out front."

The scene in front of the entrance is nothing like the plastic surgery center. A rickety old man in a hospital gown plods
alongside his mobile IV drip, a male nurse assisting him. A family
stands in a huddle, their stooped postures and downcast glances
suggesting only one thing. On cue, a barefoot monk ambles past
them, a saffron-robed Grim Reaper. Passing him, heading into the
hospital, is a shiny-haired nurse, her curves accentuated by her
tight uniform, her heels clacking musically on the pavement. You
could cut and paste her to the entrance of the most hard-to-get-
into VIP nightclub in LA and the red velvet rope would part and
the asshole doorman would bow as she struts past.

Westerly appears after a half hour or so. Her face beams, her
gait is triumphant. She crosses herself. She raises her hand to her
throat. Her mouth moves as if she's speaking but no words come
out. She giggles. Her mouth moves again but still no words, followed by another giggle. Finally, she delivers the news: "I'm gonna
have my surgery on Saturday!"

•

From this moment until the Friday afternoon when Nick and I
drop her off at Yanhee Hospital for her surgery, Westerly is as up-

beat and fun as I've ever seen her. In fact, it is almost frightening what an entirely different person she becomes. That night we eat at the same restaurant as we had the night before, when she was slumped and gruff and too defeated to play Westerly, only now she is Westerly 2.0. Elbows off the table, fingers waving daintily across her radiant face, she tells stories, ad-libs funny songs, flirts with our gay waiter. The same green papaya salad and baked fish that she plodded miserably through twenty-four hours earlier is now "to die for," "look how tender and perfect . . . the best meal I've had all year . . . oh, look, the little fishy is looking at me, *hee hee!*"

After dinner we get ice cream from a street vendor. She's old, hunched over, speaks a bit of English. Westerly chats with her, places a loving hand on her wrinkly forearm. Empathy gushes from her mascaraed eyes. This is Westerly losing herself, I think, or perhaps becoming more of herself. This is the person—prerequisite of first the sex change, then the rise to stardom via the show-case finale—she aspires to be.

She pushes it too far at the massage parlor around the corner. It's nearly 10 pm, and we all three want massages, but the place has already closed. There is only one masseuse in the house, and she is willing to do one final massage for the night. With Nick and I sitting on either side of her, Westerly goes for not the sixty-minute, not the ninety-minute, but the two-hour massage. And she is not quiet about it. She moans in delight. *"Oh yes, ohhh, that is beautiful, mmmmmm . . ."* ("She fucking loved that, us like little minions at her feet," says Nick after we've dropped her off at her hotel.)

But she redeems herself a couple nights later, the night before her scheduled surgery. After dinner at an open-air restaurant, we browse a row of shops. Westerly finds a little hole-in-the-wall boutique so densely packed with dresses and tops and headless mannequins that you have to suck your belly in and shuffle sideways to move down the aisle. She tries on a pair of cut-off jeans then takes them to the owner to pay for them. A diminutive, oval-faced woman with a lookalike Maltese at her feet, she scans Westerly up and down.

"You're beautiful," she says. "You're beautiful *all the way.*"

Westerly brightens, presses her palms together and bows. "Thank you. You are too."

Later, walking the footpath, barbecue smoke from a cluster of street vendors drifting across our faces, Westerly says, "Those compliments mean so much to me. I think she's telling the truth."

Music plays in a café across the street. We walk over, poke our heads in. On stage, a band plays camp Thai pop under swirling colored lights.

Westerly raises a finger. "One song?"

Nick and I follow her in and take a seat at the edge of the stage. The all-male band members look like teenagers. They wear shiny high-tops, their thick raven-black hair painstakingly mussed. A dozen or so people are gathered at tables, more concerned with their drinks and conversations than the music. Westerly watches the band. A tinkly melody builds and, as it peaks, she rises from her chair. Her forearms cross, her hands flutter, her face creases in inspiration. She eyes Nick and me, smiles. She sways her hips and flits her hands into what looks a fusion of tai chi and hula and Juan Belmonte and perhaps geisha and kabuki and Balinese theatre, but what's really the inimitable Westerly Windina, charged by some deep, nascent inner voice. All eyes are on her. When a waiter steps in to clear away chairs to give her more space, she dances playfully behind his back. The room chuckles.

I see this stuff—Westerly with blazing confidence, Westerly giggling at the world—and in that moment I'm a full believer, I hear in my head those stories from Rabbit and PT and Jack Mc-Coy, their Dennis Hopper-describing-Marlon-Brando-in-*Apocalypse-Now* zeal. Indeed, Westerly can be everything she aspires to be.

•

Westerly does not so much step out of the elevator as she drives, hands steering her rolling suitcase through the Bangkok Rama lobby, burbling lips making the sounds of a Ferrari. She wears white ballet flats, slim-fitting jeans and a navy-blue lycra top, with a powder-blue cardigan draped over her shoulders. Her new sunglasses—knock-off Diors—add the air of a starlet.

"Check out, please," she says to the receptionist.

When the receptionist hands her a receipt she brings it to her mouth and pretends to eat it. Last night she was channelling Juan Belmonte, today Charlie Chaplin.

We get in the taxi. Passing the restaurant where she ate her *Papillon* broth and the street corner where she burst into song, she explains that she will be laid up on a hospital bed for two weeks, supine, legs spread.

"There is a wound that is going to have to heal. It takes time. It's a wound like any wound, it's a nasty wound and it's got to heal and heal properly, no complications and things—there's all little nervous bits in there. They'll try to get me on the plane by the twenty-fourth so I can see my son on Christmas Day."

She says that the psychiatrist she saw here in Bangkok told her to avoid being alone, both before and after the surgery. "He was so right, because every time I'm alone the walls start to close in. It's freakish, it really is."

"Do you have some good books to read?" I ask.

"No, nothing."

I regret not bringing some of my research material—*Sexual Metamorphosis: An Anthology of Transsexual Memoirs* by Jonathan Ames, *Conundrum* by Jan Morris. But then I don't. Westerly wants nothing to do with the transgender community. What's more, she doesn't consider herself "transgender." Later, when I write to her telling her how fascinating I find these stories, she writes back saying that she does not want to be pigeonholed. "If I were a Spitfire pilot, the only thing I would have in common with other pilots, on both sides of the warring skies, would be that we all begin and end, independently of each other."

The sky is grey and verging on rain. The expressway is nearly empty. As we pull into the drop-off area for Yanhee Hospital, Westerly draws a long, deep breath and exhales audibly. She squeezes her lips together and clenches her handbag to her chest.

At the curb we hug goodbye. "You guys have been like good friends," she says to Nick and me. She drags her rolling suitcase through the door and into the sea of patients and S&M nurses and *Swan Lake* bladers. A few paces in she stops, turns around, and gives a giant, sweeping wave goodbye.

HOME

I'M BEING TOO CUTE, HAVING WAY TOO MUCH fun, given the weight of what she's about to go through. But Westerly arouses this. In her war metaphors and mood twists and mind changes, I have lost touch with what's at stake here. Given all that she—that she and Peter—have endured, I shouldn't be so flip. But I've yet to recover from what she said just before pulling out of her first surgery. She was referring to the showcase finale, the end of the film: *"If in the event that I didn't have this operation, Peter will reappear. You see? He reappears in the end. The twist is: Westerly goes back to being Peter. And Peter just walks from the ocean with his board."*

I can't begin to imagine the fear and anxiety one would feel before irreversibly switching gender. On the other hand, I'm amazed by her tenacity, that she can still employ artifice in the face of flayed open vulnerability. I think of the villain in a Western who, shot up with bullets, manages in his dying breath to say something witty, or to spit in the face of the shooter.

Back in LA, Alan, Jordan and I discuss what might be happening in Bangkok.

"She's capable of anything at this point. I guess what I'm saying is: I don't trust her anymore."

"For all we know, she walked into that hospital, waved to you guys, and walked straight out the back door. Right now she's probably sitting in some Bangkok hotel, the joke on us."

I know. We sound heartless. But ride the Bangkok rollercoaster with Westerly and you too would suspect such things.

Three days after her surgery, I phone Yanhee Hospital. A voice that sounds like a schoolgirl in an anime film answers. When I ask to speak to Westerly Drouyn she does not understand. I spell it out several times. *D-R-O-U-Y-N.* I try "Peter Drouyn," "Peter Westerly Drouyn," "Westerly Windina." She puts me on hold. A sort of lullaby jingle plays.

The line clicks. "Patient not home," says the receptionist.

"She's not there?"

"Patient not home."

"Okay, thanks for your help."

Just before I hang up she says, "Moment please."

Long pause.

"Hello?" goes a voice like a scouring pad.

"Westerly?"

A growl.

"Westerly?"

"Hi, Jamie. How are you?"

"I'm good. How are you?"

"Oh, you know, I've been a little bit sore and stuff but I'm okay. I, uh, I had a throat, ah, Adam's apple shave as one cosmetic procedure. And so I can't speak very well through the throat."

Through a series of grunts she tells me that the doctors won't let her talk.

"I just wanted to let you know we're thinking about you."

"Ah, thanks, Jamie. I appreciate it very much. And say hi to everybody, and that the showcase finale's going to be on."

•

A week later I call again. Her voice sounds a touch less gravelly. She says that after ten days on her back, she's just started to get up and walk. "It was terrible," she says, "terrible." She sounds trembly and fragile, on the verge of tears. Our connection is horrible, and a visit from her doctor cuts our conversation short, but before we hang up she tells me that all the nurses and staff have found out about her surf star past, and "they're all really excited."

•

On Christmas Day she sends this email:

> My surgery was monumental—words aren't available and perhaps will never be.
>
> I sit here here in the hotel close to the airport on a doughnut shaped pillow fifteen days after my surgery. I'm flying home tomorrow 26th Dec. Rang Zac this morning—so happy he's fine.
>
> Actually the hole in the middle of that pillow minimizes direct loading on the "target area." Without it I still walk around like a wrestler with shoulders permanently held up—mine through pain not muscular entropy.
>
> Carrying a large wound around with an inserted catheter to boot (I couldn't stay in the hospital any longer or madness may have set in—so armed with a "Bond" like list of instructions including less a stampede of complexity for my control process but shrouded with pills, liquids jells, bandages, surgical tape, crotch pads with connectors to waist strap, washing bottled dilations and two piece syringe that remind one of the world's first "Frankenstein" needles, (they resemble the early "Apollo" mission rockets and almost as big!).
>
> Have I left out anything? Yes—probably me! The one who carries and monitors it all. I am acutely aware, same as the case in the first untested "Apollo" mission; one little mistake and it's all over red rover!
>
> So I'm somewhat a "Robot" at present—simply carrying out the physical part of the mission to its painful finality— but mentally the determination to hold on to this new life. Undoubtedly a feeling like no else. Above all—I am endeared to the magnificent free mindset that engages even my pain and with cautious checks and rechecks like a new kind of mental

science! I am simply standing in a cool rain and fresh gusty west-wind that blows away the hot misty day and its cobwebs.

·

On her flight from Bangkok to Brisbane, Westerly sits on a pink doughnut-shaped pillow, a catheter snaking out of her floral slit skirt and disappearing into her black purse. Flying time is just over nine hours, but it feels like ninety.

"It was one of the most painful things I've ever been through," she would later tell me.

With short, feeble steps she makes her way through the gate, immigration, baggage claim, customs. In that waiting area full of expectant faces she feels the stares and the double takes. She looks for Mal and Nick but they're nowhere to be seen. She wheels her suitcase to a café, sets out her doughnut pillow, and carefully takes a seat in the grey booth. After fifteen minutes or so they appear, Mal in shorts and T-shirt, tousled grey hair looking straight from the surf, Nick in nice-fitting V-neck T and that incessant camera cradled like a baby in his tattooed arms.

Without speaking a word Mal walks up and places his hand on her head. It's about the warmest, most comforting show of affection she can remember in decades. Westerly stands and they delicately hug. She looks weak and devoid of color and drugged and like she could topple over at any second, and they feel it, and she feels them feeling it. When she reaches for her medication on the table, Nick nearly leaps to help her.

They head for the parking lot, Mal beside her dragging her suitcase, Nick behind, shooting. Every little stride is a reminder of the stitches and the swelling and the hourly swabs of antibacterial ointment that sadly, for now at least, register no sensation, not even a tingle. Exiting the terminal, the bright Queensland sun washing over her like a hot bubble bath, she can't help herself. First that pulse of raw nerve endings, then the sniffles, then the tears. Mal places his stump lovingly on her back.

On the hour and a half ride home, Westerly tells them about the hell she endured: buzzing for nurses who never came, the repetitive cycles of Fox News and BBC that instead of making time go by faster slowed it down, the clock on the wall in front of her bed that scowled down at her. Of course her voice demands explanation. She shows them the tiny cut on her throat.

"I had an Adam's apple shave," she says. "I'm concerned about how it sounds. Does it sound okay, Nick?"

The sight of the Labrador exit on the Pacific Highway incites a flurry of good feelings, most involving Zac. When her little brick duplex comes into view she wants to wrap it in her arms and never let go. Slowly, carefully, with the help of Mal and Nick, she steps out of the truck. At the garage she stops and kisses the door.

Nick and Mal help her into her chair. They carry her bags into the bedroom. Westerly sinks into her sheet-covered armchair and looks around. Her keyboard, her TV, her DVDs on a shelf, her Marilyn poster, her little workstation surrounded by lipsticks and lotions. It just comes out of her:

"Home. Home. Home."

"Safe," she says through stuffed nose and quivering lips.

She looks up. *"Roof over my head."*

She sniffles. *"Safe."*

Shakes her head. *"Secure."*

She sniffles twice. *"I belong here!"*

Her face crumples. She breaks into guttural sobs.

A LITTLE PINK ROSE

THROUGH THE FIRST COUPLE OF WEEKS OF THE
New Year Westerly sends me updates.

On January 2, 2013:

> i'm sorry to say you find me in low spirits.
> i can't be faking it that's all—my voice still has not returned
> to normal after expecting it to have already done so.
> The doctor said one week then progressively better then
> two then one month—and that's up now.
> I left Yanhee hospital with a catheter inserted in me after
> an emergency operation to regain urination—after faulty cath-
> eter was removed beforehand—finally.
> My vulva complex is a good construction with mostly posi-
> tive recovery.
> I'm still in a lot of pain though—can't sit straight—must lie
> down after walking a little ways.
> So many pills and wash techniques for vulva complex
> and so on and so on until I forget which is what and what is
> where.
> Right now it's my voice I am concerned about for obvious
> reasons—without it I am finished—life as i know it.
> i have written to Dr. Greechart through his emissary and
> another very nice nursing sister who looked after me to make
> representation for me to Dr. Greechart and ask him to provide
> more answers, more specifics other than "She'll be okay,

mate."

i need friends desperately now—these next few days are crucial. i get the catheter out Friday and pray I can pee okay.

It's now time to take more pills and more pain and worry and dizzy spells from extreme extension of my nerve endings.

On January 8:

I'm finally able to sit on my behind: finally got new computer; and I'm finally not in so much pain even as to even think.

Been a terrible post-operative period: worst in my lifetime. I will get there. I will.

Can't sleep yet; at night for some reason the walls close in on me and I pray for the dawn light to appear.

Good time to call me is eleven o'clock late morning or so. Can't go anywhere yet—no driving allowed. But I risk the short hop to my GP each morning for 9 am appt.

She's happy with "V" construction's progress though my throat progress is turtle speed—very frustrating; I sound like a gasping fish with a raspy voice. They say it is improving very slowly but of course too slow for this girl.

I think and it's agreed my whole body and mind went into "Hell" for two weeks and left stony hard (major contraction of all the tissues and senses). Fear installed itself and created its own hellish pitch.

People, people who need people, that's me, that's what I need—a massive audience to snap me into order.

How sweet after all this will that be and it will shower more dramatic spontaneity through my performance.

On January 11, I call her via Skype. She sounds better, says she's on the mend, that she's surprised by just how much she's undergone with regards to the procedure. She shifts from her normal voice to semi-gravel to full Tom Waits whisky gravel. She whispers the latter. It hits me right in the eardrum, weirdly erotic, like a tongue gnash.

"The construction is coming along nicely. It was very sore and swollen when I first went to the doctors here in Australia, but now everything's melting away to a more natural, flatter appeal. It blends, it bonds. It gets smaller and smaller, which is what you're looking for, rather than being a boy where they want it bigger and bigger . . . This is quite a road to go down, adjusting to the realities of having this new undercarriage, and the pain that goes with it."

She says that Zac knows, that she and Stephanie, Zac's mother, have sat down and talked with him. She says that Stephanie has been helping her out.

"They realize that because I went through with it, I obviously needed it. That punched a hole in their suspicions. Now they're walking towards me with open hands because of the pain and suffering, it's a weird thing."

"Have you told your brother Tony?" I ask.

"Well, in the beginning Zac was a bit upset because they found out on the Internet. I was going to do it slowly, gradually, but it happened like a bang. So Zac went with his mother and told Tony, and Tony was, you know, he went into a sort of a little bit of a volcanic experience, and was a bit negative about the whole thing." Westerly says that in the end Zac was good about it.

I ask about Surfing Australia's fifty-year anniversary gala.

She's vague, noncommittal: "If Peter gets an award you can shoot the audience clapping and we can use that with the showcase finale," she says.

There's a phone call in which Westerly tells me she's been wading in the ocean, that the saltwater is healing her vulva complex, that the hard shell is softening, opening. "It's like a sea anemone, like a little pink rose flowering open."

There's this email on January 22:

not feelin' the best right now—pain in my groin—doctor says new cervic muscles growing just like a woman—only mine came late and all at once—it's painful—like in a male hernia pain I think.

I think that's surreal—fancy the naturally required female birth element of cervic muscles (right and left sides) necessary for bearing children and other personal stuff happening now, as well as all the other external and internal elementary body parts and shapes that have grown. There's a lot of weird things goin' on. I think my doctor and her nurse assistant are fascinated and seem more like intrigued scientists at times.

THE GALA

IT'S THREE WEEKS TILL THE FIFTY-YEAR GALA. I call Westerly to see if she plans on going (she'd been waffling since she received the invite a few months earlier). She says she'd like to, provided she can get a dress made—paid for by us filmmakers, of course. She says that there's a tailor nearby who can do a good job. We wire her $500, send a guy to film the exchange. Westerly has gone to great lengths in designing her dress. It's white, lamé, Marilynesque.

We filmmakers make a big deal of the fiftieth-year celebrations. We email back and forth with the reps, seeking assurances that we have permission to film. They are concerned Westerly is going to do something outlandish, and extract a promise from us that there will be no funny business. Later, in interviews with surf luminaries at our hotel on the day of the gala, we're told about a surf event at which Westerly hijacked the microphone and spouted vitriol at surf industry top brass (the same story Nat Young told me). We assure everyone that nothing like this will happen, that Westerly has given us her word that she'll be on her best behavior. (She hasn't, of course, and there's a big part of me that would welcome a scene, not only because it'd be good for the film, but because this buttoned-up civility, this *What will the mainstream think?* mentality is precisely what bothers me most about present-day surfing. I wonder what the Westerly equivalent of spitting the winkle is?) Surfing Australia CEO Andrew Stark welcomes our involvement. And why wouldn't he? Tickets cost $220 a pop. We've purchased ten to ensure we get our own table.

We fly together, Nick, Alan and I. We depart LAX at night, arrive in Sydney in the early morning, and go straight from the airport to our hotel, The Star in Pyrmont. We check in, unload our gear, and go back to the airport to meet Westerly and Mal. Westerly wears sandals, skinny jeans, an orange terry-towelling zip-up sweater and a cute little sailor's cap that adds a certain Gilligan air to Mal's Skipper. Mal wears sneakers, shorts and a polo shirt. He is as he always is: solid, unconditionally supportive to WW. Westerly seems tired, detached. Her voice sounds more gravelly in person than it does on the phone.

Across the baggage claim from us is five-time world champion Stephanie Gilmore. She has classic surfer girl looks: bronze skin, long, salt-matted blonde hair, perpetual bright smile.

"She was on the flight with us," says Westerly. "Seems like a nice girl."

Westerly's bag arrives. Mal scoops it up. One-handed, he carries two garment bags and drags the large rolling suitcase out of the terminal. Westerly walks alongside him, purse over arm, make-up case in hand. From behind I can't help but notice the ruffle of white underwear poking over the top of her jeans. It's not the girly, frilly sort but more dude butt-hugger.

It's a bright and balmy February morning. A southerly wind carries a faint whiff of ocean. The muted roar of airplanes fills the sky. Waiting in the parking lot for Nick to bring the car around, Westerly runs through her voice exercises. She burbles her lips like a cartoon fish, as if trying to talk underwater. You can almost see bubbles rising to the surface. She counts out scales:

"1, 2, 3, 4, 5"—her flitting fingers rising up.

"6, 7, 8, 9, 10"—her flitting fingers dropping down.

"I have to be very careful," she says. "I've been to three specialists—two doctors and a speech pathologist. My voice will eventually recover okay, but I've got to be very careful. It's like a clashell."

Nick pulls up in our rental van. We hop in, pass the Park & Fly, the golf course, a flock of taxis. In the Cross-City Tunnel Westerly pulls out a fresh box of lip glosses she'd bought especially for tonight.

"Like any little girl, you've got to try your toys quickly," she says, applying a shade called "Bonbon" in a tiny hand mirror.

She puckers, grins, kisses. When finished she muscles the whole thing back in the box. "See, it already looks two years old," she says, holding up the frayed package. "I do that to things."

•

We go straight to Star Cosmetic Medicine in Pyrmont. Along with the dress, Westerly managed to convince us to pay for her hair, makeup and manicure. Situated in an old mansion, the Victorian decor clashes with the sign at the top of the creaky stairs: DERMAL FILTERS, ANTI-WRINKLE INJECTIONS, LIQUID FACELIFT, CELLULITE AND BODY CONTOURING.

A sunny Asian woman greets Westerly, leads her into the salon, ushers her into a reclining leather chair. Before her butt has even touched the seat a second woman zips out. She takes Westerly's left hand, begins filing away at her nails.

Cruel lighting fills this room of white walls and white furniture. Tinny pop music plays on the stereo. Wafts of toxic nail polish remover spank us in the face. Westerly is the sole client—she's fawned and fussed over.

A third woman sidles up to her with a quiver of false eyelashes. Westerly scans them. With her free hand she makes a curling, flicking gesture.

"How long do you want them?" asks the woman.

"Fairly long."

She pulls out the longest lash in the quiver.

"Oh, no," says Westerly. "It's gotta be longer."

The woman disappears, returns with a new quiver. She pulls out a giant lash. Westerly nods in approval.

"Every time you fall off and hit the water at speed you lose at least three lashes," she tells Nick's camera.

Cuticles are pushed back. Gels are glued and filed. Falsies are attached. Westerly giggles at the queenish luxury of it all. When the ladies have finished they bring her a small, circular hand mirror. Westerly lights up at the sight of her lush, curly lashes. She twinkles her long red fingernails in front of her face. She smiles fabulously.

•

We head to The Star hotel, check Westerly and Mal in. Anabel, a hair and makeup artist and longtime friend of Alan's, meets us in the lobby. Anabel has long dark hair, wears thick glasses, black jeans and a black top. She and Westerly head up to Westerly's room—it's sleek and spacious, with a great view of the Harbour Bridge. Westerly showers, climbs into a white terrycloth robe with hotel insignia, takes a seat in the dressing room. Anabel does her makeup with masterful detail. Westerly's lips are painted a fetching coral. A beauty mark is drawn in the same spot as Marilyn's. Anabel moves on to her hair, teases it into a small tower of platinum blonde meringue. It looks airy and creamy, like something you'd dip a finger in to taste. The cherry on top is her crystal chandelier earrings, all sparkle and old world glamour.

Westerly slinks into the bathroom and comes out a few minutes later in her gown. It's stunning—antique white with lace overlay, mermaid cut, a high slit up the front.

"Oh, Westerly!" gushes Anabel. She helps with the zipper. "Hang on." From her case she grabs a tube of glitter lotion, slicks it on Westerly's tan shoulders. Westerly moans the way she did during her Bangkok massage.

Anabel steps back. With head tilted sideways she inspects Westerly from top to bottom. She tugs a bit of gown, fingers a bit of hair, then slaps her hands together.

"You're gorgeous," she says. "You're an absolutely *gorgeous, gorgeous lady.*"

Westerly's nearly in tears. "Thank you for making it happen for me."

"Pleasure."

Westerly has a private moment in the mirror. She dips her chin, purses her lips. Her mouth curls into a big, toothy smile that bursts into a Marilyn giggle. She sneaks out from behind the dressing room and poses and dances and cha-chas for Nick's camera. Anabel cheers her on with a *"purrr-meow!"* She looks truly dazzling. If there's a pinnacle of Westerly's femininity, at least in terms of physical appearance, this is certainly it.

•

The deck of Doltone House, venue of the Surfing Australia fifty-year gala, is bathed in an orange glow. Guests arrive either by foot from the hotel two blocks away, or by taxi from the drop-off spot below. They ride up an elevator to the second floor, hang a sharp right, and run straight into the red carpet, partitioned off by velvet rope. If you're "someone" the host ushers you onto the red carpet, where a blonde anchorwoman conducts interviews as large cameras, moving and still, fire away. If you're not, you're funneled around the back of the jockeying lensmen.

True to its name, the last fifty years of surfing are represented. There's puckish Bob McTavish and his much-taller wife, Lynn, clinking glasses with a debonair Nat Young. Bob is sixty-nine but his eyes sparkle like a mischievous teen's. Nat is sixty-five. He looks regal, a surfing Kirk Douglas. There's casually dressed Rabbit Bartholomew chuckling with equally casually dressed Barton Lynch. They look cheeky, like they might be plotting a water balloon attack. There's Peter Townend, in signature pink shirt. There's Layne Beachley and her husband, Kirk Pengilly from INXS. There's a veritable scrum of former world champions: Tom Carroll (1983, 1984), Pam Burridge (1990), Damien Hardman (1987, 1991), Joel Parkinson (2012), Stephanie Gilmore (2007, 2008, 2009, 2010, 2012).

There are more Aussie surfing greats gathered on this deck in Darling Harbour, with a postcard view of the Sydney Harbour

Bridge, than perhaps ever in history. It feels dreamlike, the heroes of my former life all suffering the gravity of time with their receding hairlines, their shivering dewlaps, their happy paunches.

I sound cruel. But when a single roundhouse cutback at Bells in 1977 or a kick-stall tube ride at Duranbah in 1982 burns into your brain and lives there, magnificently, for more than three decades, it's hard to face the fact that your teenage gods are made of flesh and blood, that they are subject to the same cruelties of ageing that you are. I'm reminded of Willy Wonka's grand entrance. The clock strikes ten, the door to the chocolate factory opens, and out hobbles Willy Wonka/Gene Wilder, a fragile old man with a cane. The applauding crowd stops. Charlie's smile fades. All we hear are Wonka's feeble steps. Then he halts, lurches forward, and rolls into that glorious somersault.

This is Wonka minus the somersault.

This is so many things that I don't know where to start. First: what the dream of the Wheaties box was to my 1980s, the red carpet with logo-splattered backdrop is to today's surf culture—which is to say that instead of surfing coming up with its own unique way to celebrate its heroes, it has adapted one of the tawdriest clichés of celebrity culture. It does not glamorize the evening. It creates an awkward, hierarchical, vampirical, E! channel vibe that seems counter to what good ol' Aussie surfing—and surfing globally— was founded on.

The overflowing bonhomie—or, more truthfully, buried hatchets—is striking. Mark Richards killed Cheyne Horan's world title hopes not once, not twice, but three times. Damien Hardman took down Gary "Kong" Elkerton in an epic clash in the Coke Classic at Manly—the winner would claim the 1988 world title. In the twilight of her stellar pro career, women's surfing icon Pam Burridge would have seen seven-time world champion Layne Beachley as a retirement-accelerator. Now they all have a good laugh about it. Arch rivals become old war buddies.

There's a strong sense of family. An argument could be made that this group shares more in common with each other than their actual blood relatives. All came to surfing at a young age. All won a contest and stood on a dais and clutched a trophy before they had any idea how dramatically this would affect the course of their lives. All found through surfing a way into themselves. A glimpse at their own potential.

A few years back I interviewed Kelly Slater on the North Shore. He'd just won his tenth world title, and in his blazing blue-green eyes I saw something that was not there five years prior. It was an intensity; a burning, unwavering truth; a physical manifestation of his pursuit and realization of giant dreams. Kelly had used surfing to access his inner Superman. It had spilled out—he is someone who holds himself to tremendously high standards in all aspects of his life. As a result, it was almost hard to meet his gaze.

•

A white taxi pulls up to the curb and out steps a dashing Mal Chalmers—black suit, maroon tie, dark glasses. He holds the door wide open. First one high-heeled foot, then another, then the entirety of Miss Westerly Windina steps grandly onto the footpath. A white bolero jacket drapes over her forearm, a white clutch in her hand. She looks every bit the Marilyn reincarnate she aspires to.

With Mal at her side she walks to the elevator, rides up one floor, and steps out. Alan is right there to meet her, camera in her face. In a breathy whisper she says, *"Definitely resurrected, Alan."* She continues on, and of course she's fed to the red carpet, handed over to the blonde with the microphone.

"Winderly Westerly. You. Look. Fabulous. Are you inspired, your dress, by Marilyn Monroe, let me guess?"

With hands clasped demurely, Westerly shimmies her elbows. Flashbulbs pop. "Perhaps," she whispers.

"And you have got the raspy voice, you've got a bit of laryngitis, because you're such a socialite, you've probably been talking all night?"

Westerly raises her fingers to her throat. "It's a shame that I've lost my voice for tonight," she says. "I'm just so happy to be here with all these lovely people."

By this time the entire deck is gaping at Westerly. Every photographer has bolted over. Elbows and lenses bang against each other to get the shot. Westerly smiles, laps it up. If Surfing Australia had indulged her, if Westerly had been given free rein with the choreography, this is the moment when the sub-red carpet fans would blow and Westerly's gown would climb her thighs to deafening *oohs* and *aahs*.

She shuffles off the red carpet and onto the deck. There's a suspended moment in which she stands alone, hands held together nervously. "They are ruthless," Westerly once said of her surf peers. "I hope I don't run into her . . ." said Rabbit. "She's a drama queen!" said Sultan of Speed Terry Fitzgerald. Her email to Surfing Australia proposing that she pop out of a cake and sing "Happy Birthday"—was it all a way to self-sabotage, was it all to avoid the raw vulnerability she emits right here, right now?

Ah, but Stephanie Gilmore is so beautiful! Perhaps feeling acute "girl code," perhaps reflexively doing what Instagrammers do, she skips up to Westerly.

"May I have a photo with you?" she asks.

They smile shoulder to shoulder. Barton Lynch walks up, gives Westerly a warm hug, the two share a laugh. Layne Beachley approaches, they shake hands, fall into a cheek-to-cheek kiss. And suddenly everyone wants a piece of her: Nat, McTavish, Rabbit, Tom Carroll . . .

•

The dining room of Doltone House is elegantly decorated, with historical surfboards and iconic photographs creating a museum-cum-ballroom effect. A voice over the loudspeaker asks us to take our seats. The show begins.

MC Mark Beretta welcomes us. "Surfing Australia was formed

in 1963 to guide and promote the development of surfing in Australia," he says. He explains that the event will be televised, that there will be periodic intermissions which will be filled with commercials, and that when they cut back to the show, he'll give us a cue, and could we all applaud and cheer loudly.

Andrew Stark runs us through a list of Surfing Australia's recent accomplishments: they published a book of Australian surfing history, created commemorative stamps, formed the Vegemite Surf Groms National Junior Development Program, opened a high-performance center, launched a TV program. If surfing straddles the fence between sport and lifestyle, Surfing Australia is clearly pushing it towards the former.

Deputy Prime Minister Wayne Swan talks about often seeing three generations of family in the water. "It is more than a sport," he says. "It is something that goes to the very core of our culture. It is part of our way of life."

Hearing these speeches, looking at the Betacams and monitors, I now understand why the Westerly-popping-out-of-a-cake idea was never even a possibility. Surfing will be on its best behaviour tonight. Australia is watching. Prime Minister Julia Gillard is more than watching; she appears via video feed. Big Brotherishly, on every camera around the room, she welcomes the surfers, says how intrinsic surfing is to the fiber of the Lucky Country, adds that she hopes to one day get out there and 'ave a go herself. She even throws in surf slang: *sick, goin' off, pitted.*

As an American, it's surreal to see a head of state talking surf slang. Our Kelly Slater has taken the sport leaps forward, but it's still a long, long way from the White House.

Awards are handed out: Joel Parkinson wins Male Surfer of the Year, Stephanie Gilmore wins Female Surfer of the Year, Jack Freestone wins the Rising Star award, Jamie Mitchell wins Waterman of the Year. Shuffled between these are the Ten Most Influential Surfers, delivered in threes. The winners' speeches are preceded by a short video clip that does a fine job of reminding us of their contributions. Bob McTavish, progenitor of the shortboard revolution, is number ten. Mark Occhilupo, after drug problems and a long stint on the couch, in which he grew to 240 lbs, came back at age thirty-three to win the 1999 world title. He's number nine. Wayne "Rabbit" Bartholomew, celebrated for many things but, above all, service to the sport, is number eight.

Number seven is Layne Beachley, number six Tom Carroll, number five Bernard "Midget" Farrelly, number four Michael Peterson, number three Nat Young, and number two Simon Anderson.

Between these clumps of awards are fifteen-minute breaks. During one of them I head up to the bar. In line I run into my old pal Ross Clarke-Jones. Ross and I traveled together on the late eighties tour. He's one of the few surfers from my generation to keep it going. A fearless big-wave rider, a lunatic behind the wheel of a car, a hard-partier with the constitution of a grizzly bear, he and tow-partner Tom Carroll are the stars of the TV series *Storm Surfers*.

"What's his trip?" he asks, as if the question has been nagging at him all night.

"Westerly?"

"That's just fucking weird, mate," he says, genuinely troubled by the fact that there's a transgender woman in our midst.

Ross is not the only one. Half a dozen or more of my old surf buddies come up to me with baffled expressions, demanding an explanation for Westerly. One asks if he's "had the snip." I tell him that I believe she has. "Well I hope he's saved it," he says, "so that way he can go fuck himself!" I feel torn between my past and present. This sort of narrow-mindedness was the norm during my competitive surfing years. These are not bad people; they just get uncomfortable when things stray too far from the simplicity of surfing. I often forget that people see Westerly as a freak. To me, she's probably the most human person in the room. I correct their pronoun misuse.

Some wonderful things happen during these little intermissions. A good-looking blonde in a toga-like dress zeroes in on

Westerly, sits down next to her, repeatedly tells her how beautiful she is, how hot, how gorgeous, all the while running her fingers along the top of Westerly's hand (ecstasy?). While this exchange takes place, dozens of Peter's old friends come over to say hello to Westerly. They literally line up, waiting their turn to sit next to her, have a chat. At one point Nat Young, Rod Brooks and Brian Singer, founder of Rip Curl, approach her all at once, almost pushing each other out of the way to get in close. Nat gives her a big kiss on the lips. This draws a squeal of delight from the blonde.

"Everyone wants to fuck you!" she says at way too loud a volume.

After more awards, more drinks, more canned applause for the TV program, Mark Beretta announces that they're going to give out the award for the number one Most Influential Surfer. I've not had a sip of alcohol, but in the staggered way they've been announcing the awards, I've completely lost track of the fact that we are down to this moment of truth. I've also lost track of the nine surfers who have already won. I jog through them, count them on my fingers. A spurt of optimism overcomes me. *Westerly is going to win!* Then a Mark Richards off the bottom/off the top swoop arcs across my mind. Four-time world champ. Consummate professional. No, MR has not yet been honored tonight.

As they declare Mark Richards the Most Influential Surfer in Australia I turn to Westerly. "If Peter was not invited onto the stage, and not included, Westerly Windina immediately walks out," she'd said in Bangkok. But she doesn't. She brings her hands together in applause, a faraway, vulnerable look in her eyes. If story arcs are supposed to reveal change in a character, this taking of the high road, perhaps more so than the new "vulva complex" between her legs, is precisely that for our dear Westerly.

•

"Can we get the Hall of Famers to the stage?" asks Beretta. Up they go—Mark Richards, Doug "Claw" Warbrick, Barton Lynch,

Rabbit, Phyllis O'Donnell, Cheyne Horan, Damien Hardman . . .

"I wasn't even sure whether I should go up there, because Peter wasn't there, you know," Westerly would say later. "Things started going through my head. And I thought, *Hang on, they think I'm Peter, so I have to go up there, out of respect for Peter and out of respect for everybody here and out of respect for myself.*"

A beautiful group cavorts onstage, and for a minute it's a study in mannerisms, body language, warmth versus cold, the spotlight accentuating smiles, back pats, back problems.

The video monitor shows a lean blond girl dancing across the surf. Her numerous achievements are listed: five-time world champion, won her first title during her rookie year. Mick Fanning talks about her big moves, how she maintains great femininity on the wave. "Ladies and gents, put your hands together for Stephanie Gilmore, the thirty-fifth inductee to the Surfing Australia Hall of Fame."

Gilmore takes the stage with a giant smile. She looks mermaidlike in her tight, long green sequinned dress. As she finds her way into her speech about the great characters of surfing, how they've shaped the history, the line of Hall of Famers all take a step back, allowing Gilmore her moment. All but Westerly, that is. Hands clutched, beatific smile, she basks in the spotlight, on the four feet of height that elevates her above the rest of the room.

I still can't tell whether Westerly was trying to steal a bit of spotlight, distinguish herself from the pack, or if she was in fact in the pack, but so luminous and alluring that, beautiful as Gilmore is, we just couldn't help but look at Westerly.

•

The next day I talk to some of Westerly's peers about the night. Peter Townend remembers being on stage with his fellow Hall of Famers.

"If you look at the photos, Nat is standing right behind Westerly, and it looks like Drouyn could be his date. It's hilarious!" He bursts into laughter. "When I saw him come up on stage I went, 'This is just Drouyn doing his thing. This is the attention-grabbing Drouyn we've known since the sixties.' I mean, Drouyn's always been a bit of a drama queen."

"She was definitely looked at by some as the freak of the night, and I could see the elbows going in like, 'Look at that! Look at that! Oh my god, did you see that?', you know?" says Barton Lynch. "But I think she got up there and she did her thing and it was great to see her there and a part of it and just without fear. You know, some people are paralyzed by the judgment of others, literally can't move because of what they think other people think. And Peter Drouyn sort of crawled his way out of caring what other people think, and Westerly Windina is sort of the metamorphosis of what he is and feels she wants to be with the future, and there he was, she was, and they were livin' it large. I think it's good to rattle the cage, mate. It's epic."

"Everybody just sort of ate it up. You know, nobody turned a head at Westerly's presence at the occasion or on stage or anything. Westerly was as welcome up there as Pete would have been," says Nick Carroll.

Even Westerly was pleased with how it all played out: "All I can remember was a sea of faces going like this . . ." She makes a stunned face. "They didn't move! I thought, *Wow, this is amazing, the impact of this is what I've been waiting for. It's working.* And I felt incredible. I didn't want to leave. I was stuck to the floor."

BOBBING AND WEAVING

THE MORNING AFTER THE GALA I GET A CALL from Fred Pawle, online editor for *The Australian*. He says that he's writing a piece about the event, and according to everyone he's spoken to, the highlight of the night was Westerly Windina. He asks me a few questions, about the gala and our documentary, and asks if I could put him in touch with Westerly.

By the time Alan, Nick and I arrive on the Gold Coast that afternoon, Westerly has already spoken to Fred. She's buzzing; everything is coming together exactly as she'd hoped. At dinner that night (Mexican, stale chips) there's a strong sense of team spirit between us, the awards night having provided some kind of resolution. For Westerly personally there was great reassurance, perhaps closure, in having her peers accept and embrace her as a woman. And for the film, for the narrative to which we are trying to find a shape, this return to the world that had both launched and spurned Peter felt like a proper ending.

Since we'd started the project Westerly had wanted to meet Jordan and Beau, the producers (she loves saying "producers"). When I tell her that Jordan is arriving the next morning she's elated. When it is revealed that he'd been on a fishing trip to New Zealand and rerouted his ticket to the Gold Coast, rather than flying from LA specifically to meet Westerly, she's less elated.

Nonetheless, Jordan arrives, it's a happy meeting, he and Westerly take an instant liking to each other. We go for coffee at Goldsteins. Westerly is thrilled to show us off for the girls there. She turns it on for Jordan, ad-libbing and metaphor-mixing and

Marilyn-giggling. We order our coffees and grab seats in the back, sprawled like teenagers just let out of school in the plastic booths. Westerly has lots of questions about the film, and even more about the showcase finale. Jordan assures her that we will sit down and have a proper meeting to discuss it.

"Promise?"

"I promise."

Westerly, in skinny jeans, orange top, teal blue sparkly sweater, Gilligan cap and dark sunglasses, beams little-kiddishly. With a froth moustache she says, "I've got to show you where it happened!"

"Where what happened?" asks Jordan.

"Where I saw the UFO."

•

UFO talk turns to Tony, and suddenly we're saying goodbye to the Goldsteins girls, hopping in the rental van and heading over to Westerly's older brother's house.

"Shouldn't we ring first?" asks Alan.

"Tone never answers his phone," says Westerly.

The sky is low and grey. Labrador looks flat, shadowless. We pass the tailor where Westerly got her dress made; the bakery where Alan and I, on our trip a year and a half earlier, ate chicken sandwiches on buttered brown bread; a tattooed, singlet-clad Maori who looks like the last sort of bloke Westerly would want to run into.

We park in front of Tony's house. It looks exactly as it did when we dropped by three months ago. The broken-down Toyota has not moved. We wait on the footpath while Westerly goes to the door. Tony comes out looking disheveled, caught off guard. His faded blue shorts are splotched with bleach stains. His Aloha shirt—a fruit and flowers print—is buttoned only halfway up. He does not look thrilled to see us, the film crew. He stands at the edge of the driveway with a fist on his hip, a scowl on his face.

"This is Jordan. He's making the film," says Westerly. "And they just want to see what's left of the family."

"Hi, Tony," says Jordan, with California warmth.

We all say hi.

"They were going to ask you if you wouldn't mind coming back to Wharf Road," says Westerly, "and to the laneway where the UFO was."

Tony scans our little posse. Jordan and I flank Westerly. Nick stands behind us, filming. Alan stands behind him.

"No, you do that," says Tony, raising a dismissive hand. "That's your thing."

"No, no, no. They just wanted to do, ah, it's like a going back in time. Just to walk over the ground, you know. Like a documentary thing."

Tony grimaces, swipes fingers. "Could I leave it? You do it. It'll just make me depressed. It'll really make me depressed."

"All right. Okay. That's all right. I understand," says Westerly.

"Did you guys grow up in this neighborhood?" asks Jordan.

"Not this one, no," says Tony. "There wouldn't have been anything here. It would have been swamps and trees." Tony softens, talks about the local area. Westerly moves to stand next to Tony—Drouyns on one side, documentary team on the other.

I ask about the two of them in the surf together.

Tony snickers. "Him champion, me zoob. Something like that. Ah, me trier, him confident. Me idiot, him winner."

"Can you show us your board?" asks Jordan.

We follow Tony up the driveway to his garage. He rolls up the door to reveal a clammy mess. There's stuff piled everywhere, the smell of mildew.

"How did it get like that?" asks Tony.

Amid the clutter of boxes and bags he senses something not right, a box not as he'd left it.

"It must have fallen over," says Westerly.

Tony straightens out the box, tries to reach the surfboard.

Westerly points out a wet, decaying spot on the ceiling. "See,

Tony's got water coming . . . I'll get it Tony."

Westerly brings the board out to the driveway, rests it on its tail. "You stand there," she says to Tony, nodding to the spot stage left.

"Your board?" Tony asks Westerly (translation: Yet again stealing the spotlight, little brother).

"No, you stand there. He just wants a picture of the both of us."

Peter and Tony pose for the camera, the board—a nine-foot-something longboard, beaten up, flouro orange pinstripe—standing between them. Their differences are vast. Tony is almost twice as wide as Westerly. He wraps his meaty arm around the board proprietorially, his free hand clenched tightly at his waist, his wide stance overtly masculine. Westerly is lithe and dainty. She stands slightly away from the board, hand delicately touching its rail, almost pushing it away. Both smile awkwardly.

"Did you shape that, Westerly?" asks Jordan.

"Peter did," answers Tony.

Jordan asks Tony what it was like surfing with Peter when they were kids.

"I had more of a problem than Peter did," he says. "I had a kind of a social problem. And the surfing was perceived by me as being a way out of the problem."

While Tony elaborates, Westerly, head bowed, studies her fingers. She looks mournful.

Tony points to Westerly. "Him, big man, athlete, good-looking one. Me, kind of, ah, 'Is that Tony over there in the corner, pulling the blanket up over his head?'" Tony laughs at his younger, sad self. Westerly chuckles nervously.

Now that everyone's getting along, I ask Tony if he'd like to join us for lunch.

He thinks about it. He bows his head and considers. Then, in the most palpable illustration of one thought triggering another, he whips his head to the side. His face flashes with purpose. *"Oh, shit!"* he says, passing the board to Jordan. "Could you just hold that a minute? I just remembered there's stuff on the stove."

Tony bolts for the house. Nick, ace director of photography, follows.

Tony tears open the swinging screen door, maneuvers through stacks of books, enters the kitchen where a pot of something burns on the stove. Baked beans? He turns off the burner. The pot is black and smoking.

"I think I'll have to leave it," he says.

Tony's kitchen resembles the drop-off bin at the Salvation Army. Pots and bottles and condiments litter the counter. Empty water jugs teeter atop garbage bags bulging with God knows what. It's a kitchen straight out of the TV show *Hoarders*.

Tony stands in the doorway, wheezing.

"You okay?" asks Nick.

"I'm relieved to see Peter alive."

"You were worried he wasn't going to live?"

"I was just worried by . . . does he still have his lower part attached?"

Nick says nothing.

"Oh," says Tony, peering out the front door at Westerly. "I'll leave it at that . . . 'Cause that's the thing that makes it impossible for me to be happy." He paws his chin. "I don't know what this is about, but Peter coming back looking like a woman I'm afraid is too much for me. I honestly thought he'd come back looking different. I can't stomach it." He clenches his teeth. "I can't stomach it." He wheezes. "And nobody seems to want to tell me what the truth is." He turns to Nick. "What is the truth?"

Jordan stands behind Nick. "Do you want to ask Westerly?" he says.

"*Westerly.*"

"I'll go get her."

"*Her.*"

Jordan heads out the door. Tony, shuffles, paces. To Nick and me: "See, that's what worries me. That . . . is . . . what . . . worries. . . me. *Her. Westerly.* And you people talk as if I'm mad."

Westerly approaches the door. Through the screen door, hand

on hip, Tony asks, "You still have everything on you?"

"What?"

"Do you still have . . ."

Westerly presses fingers together like a meek old lady. "Have what?"

"Look." Tony steps back. "Stephanie came around here just after you'd gone and said you'd taken a detour to Thailand to have your gender reassignment."

"Hmm."

"Oh, don't look at me like I'm a bloody idiot."

"No, I did, I had it. I had it. And I'm still the same person."

"No, you're not."

"I am, okay?" Westerly brings fingers to throat. "My voice box has gone a bit because of—"

"Ah, look, just leave. Please, just leave. I've had enough. Just, please leave."

Westerly walks away. Nick, standing inside the house, poking his camera into the scene, follows.

Tony grumbles amid the boxes. After a minute or so he steps outside. His face is an exasperated grimace. His hands are balled into fists. He less walks than shuffles.

"Now this is to somehow justify him. Everything he's doing is going to fail. I kid you not."

He passes rubbish bins, rounds the garage, mumbles something about Westerly conducting a scam, tells Nick to be careful of the broken glass on the footpath, continues.

"The whole thing is starting to spook me. What's going on?"

Nick asks if he's okay.

"No. No, I'm not." His face quivers. "No, I'm not because I can't handle it. I just can't handle it. I don't know if he's telling me the truth or not. If he has, then all plans for his re-establishment on this earth to do something significant are gone. I don't think it'll grow. I wanted to say it when you came around here the first time, but I was in a kind of hallucinatory state, I was too shocked at what I was hearing in my mind."

"What did you want to say?" asks Nick, camera duly trained on Tony's face.

"I didn't know. I was in a hallucinatory state. I have a mental illness, a shocking mental illness. For at least fifteen years. Badly. I mean schizophrenia, voices. It's taken me all of that time to get better, despite him and his nonsense." Tony points a contemptuous finger at Westerly. "Despite it! And he still won't tell me the truth."

•

Westerly has moved out to the van. She sits on the tailgate with sad posture, head down. Jordan and I are there, half consoling her because she seems genuinely hurt, half being diligent documentarians.

"To me, Tony is one of those people who sort of gives up somewhere along the line. But not this girl here. I've found out. I've found out who I am and what I am. And nobody's going to take it off me. No matter what he says about me, it means nothing, because over the years Tony's had this sort of thing about me—Peter the superstar, Tony the nothing—which is selfish."

•

We never wanted to fall into this reality television-style filmmaking but it's happened. While Westerly sits on the tailgate of the van, talking less to Jordan and me than the actual camera, Tony stands by the side of house, barely out of earshot, talking to Nick and Alan. But when I look at the footage later, he too seems to be talking more to the camera than to them.

"His wife, or ex-wife, Stephanie came around and said he hadn't gone to America, he'd gone to Thailand for gender reassignment. I nearly hit her!" Tony sounds deeply distressed. "He's my brother, for god's sake. He comes back today, to my relief, and then he looks exactly the same. And the first thing I do is look to see if he has any bulge down there."

Tony breathes heavily. He looks as if he could shudder into cardiac arrest at any moment.

•

"Maybe I'm not human. Maybe I do come from somewhere else," Westerly muses on the tailgate. She speaks softly, wags her head from side to side. She looks down. "I know I'm not crazy." She looks up. "Whatever planet I come from, maybe if I could take Zac back there it might be better."

•

The raw footage reveals what must be a decades-long story between these two. Despite being out of breath, Tony looks like he could turn physical. Westerly, on the other hand, is demure—she's given up. Was it always this way? At the height of Peter's powers, was Tony still the boss behind closed doors?

•

Tony walks around to the garage to put his board away. Jordan has already done so. Tony rearranges the box that was not as he'd left it, remarks that it was "probably Peter scrabbling around and looking for something." He catches his breath. "I'm just disappointed that he came home looking and sounding, attitudinizing, exactly the same as when he left. And I thought he was getting better at one stage."

•

"If Tony looked hard enough he'd see a lot of our mother in me. And it'd be so nice if he said, 'Gee, you look like Mum . . . You should've been my sister.'" Westerly laughs. "It'd be so nice, but that's not going to happen."

She shuffles, checks her nails, sighs, makes a fish-lipped gurgle. "It's been a hard life," she says. "Losing my mother was, for Peter that was just, life just finished there. She was the only one that understood him." Westerly looks over to Tony. "Dad was always more Tony's side."

•

Tony's rant seems as if it's been brewing for decades. It is less angry and spittle-laced than a recognition of how ridiculous the whole sibling rivalry has been.

"I should have been Peter," he says, pointing down the driveway at his little brother. "Forget about Tony having any rights at all. There's almost a kind of irony, there's almost a kind of crazy irony. Tony is still kind of running around trying to pick up pieces of Peter and kind of pretend it's food so he can kind of stuff it into his mouth and go, *ahhhh*, to get by on it until Peter sorta throws another crumb somewhere by way of his name . . ."

Tony laughs at himself.

"My heart and mind are utterly broken. Because I know things. And, ah . . . I'm just disappointed. I'm terribly disappointed. It seems I had some kind of proposition in my mind that could've worked out if Peter had changed, and not just come back as another version of this . . . happy-go-lucky character. But seeing he's come back exactly the same and even worse, I may as well get with it. He's my brother, he's—I don't know—a eunuch."

Westerly, halfway across the overgrown lawn, says, "See ya, Tony."

"Bye."

She walks over. "Nice to see you."

Tony does not look at her. "Well, I'm glad you're back. I'm glad you're back safely and—" He looks at her. "Been back a while, have you?"

"I've been back two and a half months."

"So, were you here for Christmas, or—"

"No."

"All right, so you came back . . . What's now? February. End of February. Ah, if you've been back for two and a half months you must have been here for Christmas?"

"Tony, no. I came back two days after Christmas. So it's about eleven weeks."

"Oh, Happy New Year, just in retrospect."

"No, Happy New Year to you too. Happy New Year. And I was going to—obviously you had a birthday that I missed and I'm sorry . . ."

"That's right, I had a birthday. I got older."

"I was in hospital, so I was—"

"Much older."

"I was going to give you a card and I will and anyway I look forward to seeing you again and bringing Zac around and talking about the movies and things. So we're going to go over the UFO ground, back in 1969, and . . ."

Tony seems perturbed by the mention of this. "I'll tell you about the experiences I've had one day. It could frighten the living daylights out of you. My whole unconsciousness was turned into consciousness, didn't matter what area of the brain it was. *You will listen*, right. *You. Will. Listen.* And then I ended up talking out loud and it didn't matter what kind of framework was in you, I, we, brother mother father cousin sister, ah, you know, every aspect of human . . . It's a madness."

Westerly tries to calm Tony down, says that people talk to themselves all the time.

Tony angrily proclaims that he has never been able to communicate what he means when he talks about hearing voices. He imitates them.

"Excuse me, I'd like to talk to you. My name is Cliff Robertson and I'm an actor and see you now. And I'm Humphrey Bogart, and see you now. And I'm James Cagney. And I'm President Abraham Lincoln and I'm, we are all talking to you at once, coming from multiple lines of channel demarcation across a galaxy that is infinite. And we are all ex-

people on earth, and we are all fire-and blood-infused people overseas that is up there beyond and we are all talking at the same time like an infernal, incredible, interplanetary, intergalactic, interuniversal tele- phone connection—a kind of mind relay system which just goes on and on and on, talking, talking, talking, the whole universe is alive with people talking—"

Westerly, almost maternal: "Tony . . ."

"And it comes into my head—"

"Tony, Tony . . ."

"And it drives me mad."

"Don't worry, now come on."

"And it's all because of an awoken unconscious. The big thing these days: *Well, let's liberate the unconscious.* Believe me, you don't want to. It's just *full of blood.*"

Tony sniggers. Jordan seizes the moment, offers a handshake goodbye.

"It's full of blood," says Tony, shaking it.

We all thank him, shake hands. Tony follows us to the van. "The fact that we even have pi r squared, there's a recurring num- ber, I say is insane. I mean it's everything we make is inclined to fall apart—"

We get in the van, shut the doors, roll down the window. Tony sounds like he could go on for hours.

"We'll leave it with pi," giggles Westerly. "Pi always!"

We wave, drive away.

•

Small talk in the car—about the bright sun that's just broken through, the beautiful board Peter made Tony, the fish-and-chips place Westerly can't wait to take us to—only highlights the seri- ousness of what just took place. The most honest response is the one that comes from Westerly.

"I think I might like to have a surf," she says.

I know this one all too well. The ocean washes away, resets.

So we go back to Westerly's place to grab her board. But all it takes is a step into her Marilyn room and the showgirl overrides the wounded brother/sister.

"This one? This one? Or this one?" she asks.

Westerly holds up three swimsuits. One is day-glo checkerboard, distinctly eighties, with a little skirt that makes it look more suitable for ballet than the beach. The second is red, and fifties-style. The third is a black shiny halter-top.

Nick likes the red one. I like the day-glo. Westerly goes with the black.

She slinks into the bathroom, emerges twenty minutes later in swimsuit and hot pink shorts, pearl-colored sandals and her dad's navy hat, with full makeup and hair poking from hat just so. She looks great.

"Ready, guys," she says.

We exit into the garage. She loads her board into her grey sedan. Nick asks her to do it a second time so he can shoot it from a better angle. Westerly goes all Marilyn and hyper-effeminate. When the board's loaded she turns to camera.

"We're going to the beach, and I'm going to surf as good as Peter did. Watch me! Watch me!"

We drive past the fish-and-chips shop, the bottle shop, the seedy hotel where we nearly stayed but Nick's brother, who works for Channel Nine news, advised us not to on account of the recent murder that took place there ("It's where all the crims stay," said Westerly). We pass Goldsteins Pies, pass the broadwater, turn left, loop around the bay, pass the Italian restaurant where Westerly and I first met, pass Sea World.

We drive down a narrow spit, flanked by the Pacific on one side and the broadwater on the other. We park, trot down a dirt path that cuts through the thick, dead-looking foliage and over the sand dune. The ocean is a shimmering aquamarine, the sky is robust and cloudless, the blindingly white sand squeaks underfoot. Aside from a lone fisherman a hundred meters to our right, and the odd pair of joggers who bounce past, the beach is empty. The waves are small and slaphappy. They lack the clean shape of the point breaks. As a result there's not a single surfer as far as the eye can see.

"I like it here, away from all those thugs down in Coolangatta," says Westerly.

She shuts her eyes and takes a deep, audible breath. I'm unsure if this this is to savor the natural beauty or to prepare for method surfing.

We were here a year ago, Westerly, Alan, and I, to shoot the sizzle reel. On the drive over she told us about an osprey that hangs out in the trees, how the two of them have a sort of relationship. Alan and I exchanged skeptical glances. Though I loved her stories of communicating with dugongs and albatrosses during her euphoric session at Uluwatu in *Drouyn and Friends*, I wasn't sure I believed them.

Westerly led us along the dune to a big tree trunk that was almost human shaped. It had two arms; one extended out to a sort of hand. Its striations and knobs were like something you'd see in an Ansel Adams photograph. Westerly used it as a rack, leaning her board against it, hanging her bag from a branch. Alan and I surveyed the choppy waves. Westerly, making a visor with her hand, studied the pines.

"There," she said, pointing to a shadow amid the branches.

"I don't see it," said Alan.

"It's looking right at us," whispered Westerly.

Indeed it was, a brown osprey camouflaged by the brown foliage. Westerly flapped her arms and cawed loudly. The osprey seemed unimpressed. She ran down the dune, across the beach, and out to the hard-packed wet sand, flapping and cawing. Alan and I watched. Had there been people around we might've apologized for our insane friend. Then the osprey flapped off the branch and glided in the direction of Westerly, its gaze, as far as we could tell, aimed downward. Westerly flapped and cawed. The osprey did not flap and caw back. It soared right over Westerly's head and out towards the ocean, dipping low over the breaking waves as if to get a hit of those negative ions we surfers get so jacked up on. Then it arced regally, breathtakingly, in a wide half-circle and headed back towards Westerly. It arced back again and again and again until sure enough, it was circling over Westerly's flapping and cawing head.

•

Today there's no brown osprey, but there's Westerly at the water's edge, board propped in the sand next to her, doing what is definitely her pre-method surfing routine. She touches toes, stretches shoulders, and spins arms with mannered puffs. Sinew and muscles pop. She has the physique of someone half her age, save for the leathery, sagging flesh.

She grabs her board, skitters through a wash of foam, drops to prone, and strokes horizonwards. There are many subtleties that reveal great surfers. One is the way in which they get from beach to lineup. Westerly does not paddle in a straight line, she angles, zigzags, senses eddies and currents and rides their momentum. She arrives in the takeoff zone with dry hair.

Twinkling surface, legs straddling board, back erect and chin raised so as to get maximum elevation, Westerly studies the looming swells. They are not long lines but rather A-frame wedges, chopped into pieces by last night's onshore wind. She sees something she likes, paddles out to meet it, jockeys into the precise position that will line up her entire ride, like a first move on a chessboard. She wheels around, strokes twice, and pops up to feet. Her stance is wide and sturdy, knees bent and bandied. Her arms are delicate, balletic. She swoops off the bottom and darts across the steep face, taking an expertly high line, flirting with the tapering lip. As the wave flattens out she steps back and stomps the tail, heaving her upper body into a slashing cutback, arms like wings, hands relaxed, fingers held just so.

Now she's going left, soft bobs and weaves with the shoulders, muted ducks of the head as if trying to read the sandbar that will in turn command the wave's next move. Whitewater surges at her. She banks off it, rides its momentum to the right. Then another surge, this one aimed left. She redirects accordingly. It's a dance and a flow and a sort of lovemaking. She moves gracefully, with quintessentially WW flourishes. She makes it look easy, but it's a showy easy, as if at any moment she might clasp her hands behind her back. She weights and unweights, applies the accelerator pedal of the front foot then the brake/steering wheel of the back foot. Her technique is perfect: front arm pointing her way forward, shoulder and torso naturally following, knees bent for balance, for propulsion, for shock absorption.

The wave hits deep water, backs off, turns fat and slow. Westerly responds by leaning forward, stretching her front foot over the nose, a hang five. The wave gets even slower and nearly doesn't want to carry Westerly along with it, but she sees the shore break in front of her and imagines herself there, ventriloquizes her body mass there. She mounts a sort of hump, inching up, up, and over the ledge. Just as she crests it she leans back to keep from nose-diving. The whomp of shore break shoots her forward, a burst of speed. She rides it out until her fins hit the sand, steps off, looks to us to ensure that we're filming, waves to camera, redirects her board seawards, skitters through the shore break, and paddles back out to the lineup.

It's inspiring to see fifty-plus years of surfing so palpable. She is not gymnastic and lightning-reflexed like today's top pros, but she emanates ocean knowledge, a sixth sense of right place/right time, both in the lineup and on the actual wave. She graciously rides every breaker from as far out to sea as she can catch it until her fins hit the sand, the surfing equivalent of eating every last crumb of food off your plate. She looks like she's having tremendous fun. At the end of her rides you can see the ear-to-ear smile, almost hear the inner whoops. She makes me realize just how feminine good surfing is. When the rider utilizes the wave's sweet spots, it is not an act of grunts and clenched muscle, it's light and yielding and fluid.

Westerly's final ride is her best. With the incoming tide the waves are backing off, making it harder to connect the dots to shore. She finds the perfect line. If you were to track her path starting from where she took off it would look like a switchback road down a steep hill. In the shore break, a frothy lip cascading just behind her back, she pulls one of her trademark soul arches, gorgeous, matadoresque. Stepping off on the sand, she raises a fluttering hand above her head and dips into a majestic bow.

I MUST HAVE AN AUDIENCE

ON OUR LAST DAY IN AUSTRALIA WE MEET WESTerly at her house at 10 am. She's with Zac for the day, and the plan is to hang out with the two of them, film them doing whatever they do. We're also hoping to speak with Stephanie.

Jordan and I ride with Westerly over to Stephanie and Zac's house. Westerly is in her toned-down outfit: sandals, jeans, white blouse, hair in a simple comb-over, no makeup. Zac and his mother live in an apartment unit only a few blocks away from Westerly. We pull into the driveway, get out, knock on the door.

A short, dark-haired woman opens it. It's hard to make out much more than that as the lights are off in her place and she doesn't open the screen door, and she hangs back, out of the brightness. Westerly introduces us. She's polite but cold. She tells Westerly that the plan has changed, that Zac is at a friend's house, that they won't be together today. Westerly is visibly disappointed. Jordan ever so politely explains that he is one of the producers of the film, that we've flown over from Los Angeles to work on it, that Westerly's family is a key part of the story, and that we would like to interview her.

"No, I'm not interested," she says. Her tone is guarded, suspicious.

Jordan tries to explain more but she cuts him off, repeats that she's not interested, says goodbye, and shuts the door.

"I told you," says Westerly in the car on the ride back to her place.

That night, Westerly comes over to our hotel to discuss the show-case finale. We meet in our ninth-floor unit overlooking the sea. Westerly has clearly spent time putting herself together for this meeting. Her makeup is perfect, her hair is pinned to the side with a turquoise barrette. She wears black heels, jeggings, red cummerbund, navy blue blouse, and a black leather jacket just like Brando's in *The Wild One*. I get the sense that she did not drive along the Gold Coast Highway to get here, but rather Sunset Boulevard; that she did not pull into our drab hotel, but rather the Beverly Hills Hotel, where a valet named Buzz helped her out of her '55 Lincoln Capri. I love Westerly for this.

We offer her a drink. She opts for a glass of water. We sit in the living room, Westerly perched with half a butt cheek on the sofa, Alan, Jordan and I across from her.

Jordan explains that as the president of Record Collection, he is very familiar with organizing tours for bands. He says that it's way too soon to plan city, venue, date (what Westerly has been demanding from us), but that he'd like to hear Westerly's vision for the actual performance.

"Jordan, we've already got an outline, and that is a stage presentation." With her fingers she mimics taking the stage. "You've got a spotlight following me out to the stage. A grand piano, color pearl, preferably. An older man, who knows songs from the fifties, a classical guitarist sitting on a stool. Maybe an electric guitar as well."

She says the guitar should have a Western feel, and the pianist gives the Hollywood feel. She says that all the musicians from the fifties had pianists, that's where songs originated from.

"My thought," she continues, "and I'm talking keeping costs down, so I thought piano and guitarist, and, you know, a couple of spots, a big one on myself, an old-style microphone, very much a *Casablanca* feel about it, very *Some Like It Hot, River of No Return.* I would change costumes a couple times for particular songs."

"Do you envision this in front of a live audience or in a studio?"

asks Jordan.

"I was hoping for a live audience, forty or fifty people in the front row. Make it look like there are a lot of people."

I tell her that a live audience means that she's got to nail it first take, whereas the studio's more forgiving.

"I want applause," she says.

"Peter loved an audience, didn't he?" says Jordan.

"It's been a part of Peter and me. There were many times Peter was in front of a large audience. He was scared. He always got panic attacks. With Westerly there is no such thing. He's there." She points to her head. "I want to do it for him."

Jordan prefaces his speech with: "You're not going to like this." He tells Westerly that the truth of the matter is that big cities like LA, New York and Chicago are so full of clubs and concert halls and live performances that it's nearly impossible to make any kind of splash with an unknown performer, and that it'd be very hard to book her a gig. Alan and I suggest that a better idea might be to do the showcase finale in a studio, shoot it, and launch a viral video that would in the end draw way more viewers.

Westerly shakes her head. "No, no. What's important for me is to have real people watching me, a real audience, so that that gives me the energy to blow people's minds. I must have an audience."

Jordan asks if she's been rehearsing.

"No."

"Do you have any musicians in mind?"

"No."

Jordan says that the way it works is a singer will find the musicians he/she thinks might be suitable for the material, they'll meet, run through some of those songs, and see if there's chemistry. He asks Westerly if she's done anything of this sort. Westerly says that there are no musicians here on the Gold Coast. Sydney maybe. Melbourne yes. But definitely not here.

We bat around the idea of doing her showcase finale in Australia. Westerly's not keen, and begins to explain why. Jordan stops her, says that the first thing she should do is send him an email listing all the songs she'd like to perform, how she sees them in terms of accompaniments, lights. He says that she should also start thinking about musicians. Westerly can't wrap her head around this last part. She makes it clear that she'd expected us to handle this, that she'd simply show up to rehearse with a readymade band. When Jordan says it doesn't work that way, that she should go on the Internet, search for musicians, check out their work, Westerly, disgusted, says, "Well do you have money for me to do this?"

The meeting falls apart. Jordan delivers the truth as kindly as he can. Westerly looks crushed, her gaze way, way off in some sad distance. It's as if we're killing her dreams.

A MESSAGE, A REVELATION

THERE IS MORE MEDIA COVERAGE FOR WESTERLY in the wake of the Surfing Australia gala. *Tracks* does a feature on her. *Surfing World* does a theme issue on "The 50 Most Intriguing People in Surfing Today"; Westerly is voted number one. They send an excellent photographer to shoot her. Her piece opens with a full-page black-and-white shot of Westerly in her gala gown, chandelier earrings, hair and makeup sparkling, big glowing smile on her face. In the Q&A she says how disgusted she was that Peter was not included in Surfing Australia's Top 10 Most Influential Surfers, that she felt sick when she got back to her hotel that night (she was in a buoyant mood with us). The interviewer, Sean Doherty, asks Westerly about the documentary:

If the producers could see my vision they'll make a fortune. You've got someone like Peter Drouyn, who's completely screwed, who you could make sixteen films on, then you've got Westerly, who's another film altogether, an incredible mysterious drama. The way she's suddenly appeared as a connection to the great goddesses of Hollywood in the fifties, with her infantile nature, is a little girl developing her own mind.

Sean asks how the movie ends:

Then you have the showcase finale when I come out of the dark into a spotlight on stage in my beautiful white dress with a white piano with a flamenco guitarist on a stool and we'll sing a few of my favorite songs . . . It will be a miniature variety show that will prove to everyone she's made it. She'll blossom on stage. I know that something is going to happen that is going to blow the world away. And why would I be wrong? Why can't I say that when what's happened up to now has all come true? Why can't I say that? She's achieved what she's wanted for years and years and years while she's had to go through the tragic life of Peter.

"Is this Peter's showcase finale as well?" asks Sean.

This is what Peter wanted too. Peter wanted showbiz, so it'll be like a double whammy in a sense. I don't look 63, I look 36 and I'm going to look even younger by that stage, and I feel all this mystery is going to reach its pinnacle at the showcase finale. That showcase finale could be a message, a revelation. Maybe Westerly isn't human. Maybe she's a spirit from somewhere else. Maybe she's something more . . .

•

I remember our first fight. This was after I'd finished fact-checking my profile, we'd entered our late-night-radio-Skype-call phase, she'd been bombarding me with self-portraits, and it was Christmas and I was with my family, and I just didn't have time to respond to each email, each photo.

She turned nasty, accused me of abandonment, rudeness, insensitivity.

I might have had a couple glasses of wine. I quoted Henry Miller: "The world is infinitely fascinating—we just need to get beyond ourselves to see it." (More like I misquoted him.) She wrote back saying she understood now. "I won't write again and I definitely won't send any photos."

•

226

Westerly's voice did not improve. She forwarded us the tempestuous email exchange she'd had with Dr. Greechart's assistant. Like so many things in Peter/Westerly's life, it became yet another combustive ending. And though her voice was a travesty and I was genuinely sympathetic, it was sad to see this ongoing pattern emerge so early in Westerly's post-op life.

She found a doctor in Brisbane who was certain he could fix her voice. The surgery would cost about $5,000. Westerly asked us to pay for it. When we told her that we'd used our entire budget filming in Bangkok and Australia she didn't hear us. "It's the right and moral thing to do," she wrote, "everyone I've talked to about it agrees." As gently as we could, we told her that we were in the business of making movies, not funding surgeries. She threatened legal action, said that the project was over, that we should send back all her materials immediately.

It was absurd. Perhaps even more absurd was the fact that we eventually caved, wired her $5,000 against her royalties, with the caveat that she sign a document stating that she would never ask us for money again.

The surgery didn't work. For whatever reason, Westerly was not getting the voice she wanted. And of course she did ask us for money to fund the second surgery she had planned. And called the project off several more times.

THE PILOT AND
THE NAVIGATOR

I FLY INTO THE GOLD COAST ON THE MORNING
of February 19, 2014, rent a car, and drive to Labrador to meet
Westerly at her new home. It's exactly as she'd described it when
she was giving me directions—a red-brick duplex, windows covered with sheets. I park on the street, pass her sturdy brick mail-
box—the same kind she'd posed on like a pin-up girl at her old
house—and knock on her door. Faint music. The clack of sandals.
The door opens, then the screen door. Westerly looks vibrant. Her
jeans are pulled down to her ankles, a towel is wrapped around her
waist. Up top she wears only a white bra.

"I'm just on the toilet," she says. "But come in, sit down."

We hug. I peck her cheek. She shuffles back to the bathroom.
Her towel hangs low and loose, sacrum and a hint of ass crack
visible.

The living room is bare and cold, as if she's still moving in. The
white walls are blank. The blue granite floor is clinical, sterile. Two
armchairs are aimed at a flat-screen TV, which plays the score to
the movie *Glory*. In front of them is a coffee table stacked with
DVDs, shoes, moisturizing lotion and the smooth rocks she col-
lects from the beach. The chairs are draped with panties and bras.
Across the room is a small desk topped with a laptop and a framed
photo of Peter and Zac. Next to the laptop is an exercise book with
Showcase Finale Program written in bold letters across the cover.
Her keyboard crouches in the corner. The L-shaped kitchen counter is scattered with sunglasses, jewelery, hair clips, a vanity mirror, boxes of prescription drugs, a tube of 7-Day Rich Repairing

Lotion, a packet of tissues, and a birthday card to Zac. Hanging on the wall is a calendar with a black slash across every day that's passed. Pinned next to it is a sheet of paper with *WW Big change! No worry attitude* written on it.

The bathroom door swings open and out walks Westerly in black panties and white bra.

"Jamie, how does my body look right now?"

I scan her from top to bottom. She's put on weight.

I manage a "Great."

"Ah, Jamie, say it like you mean it."

"You look fantastic, WW." I remember our game. I laugh. "It's really great to see you."

"Great to see you too, Jamesy."

She says that over the last few months, she's had only Mal to tell her she looks okay. "It's like Steve McQueen and Dustin Hoffman in *Papillon*—'*How do I look? I feel pretty good but I need someone to tell me how I look.*'"

She slips into her blue jeggings and an orange top.

"So how have you been, Jamie?"

I tell her I've been okay, a bit anxious, a bit emotional.

She giggles. "Ah, that's okay. I'm as sensitive as sixty-five baby lion cubs fused together standing at the edge of a cliff."

·

In my rental car, on the way to breakfast, I ask if she's been going to Goldsteins.

"Haven't been there in months," she says. "The girls there just turned on me."

We go to a café along the broadwater, an indoor/outdoor place owned by a friendly Chinese family. At the counter, Westerly orders a toasted ham and cheese sandwich and a latte, "quarter strength, extra hot." We take our number and find a shady table. The sun is warm and inescapable.

"I've been contacted by the ABC to do a segment on *7.30*," says

Westerly. "It's one of the most respected news shows in Australia."

I tell her I know all about it, that I spoke to the producer on the drive from the airport to her house, that he told me he'd talked to her, and that he wants to shoot Nick and me filming her rehearsing the showcase finale at the Cambus Wallace, a bar in Nobby Beach. Westerly explains that this was her idea, that her voice is not yet ready for the showcase finale, but that they could pretend for the cameras.

"Do you think it'll be okay?" she asks with a worried face.

"It's a rehearsal," I say. "There are no failures in a rehearsal."

Breakfast arrives. Westerly, all lipstick-mottled teeth, speaks to the toothy Chinese waiter in Mandarin but he seems to have no idea what she's saying.

Her sandwich is simple—white bread, a few slices of ham, goopy melted cheese. Westerly takes a bite, moans. "This is so nice," she says, as if it were a three-Michelin-star meal. I'd forgotten this side of her, how when she's up even the littlest things take on a dazzle.

"You haven't said a thing about my voice," she says.

"Your voice sounds wonderful, Westerly."

"You're not just saying it?"

"I'm saying it. I'm not *just* saying it."

.

On the ride back to Westerly's she tells me that she's meeting with the *7.30* people that afternoon. Her new place, I realize, following her directions, is only a short walk away from her old place. The single-story homes are washed out in the bright midday sun. We pass a pre-teen kid practicing ollies in a driveway, the park where we interviewed Mal a couple of days before Westerly and I flew to Bangkok for her surgery. A hatchet-faced, possibly meth-tweaked woman in stonewash denim dashes blindly across the street.

"She wasn't looking so good," I say.

"There are a lot of them around here," says Westerly.

I hang a left into Westerly's driveway, park, get out, walk around the back of the car and open her door. Westerly steps out, clutching her handbag with both hands.

"It's really good to see you, Westerly. And listen, I know some heated emails were exchanged over these last few months, but emails can be deceptive. You seem to be in a great place. I'm glad to see it."

"I'm just happy my voice is finally coming good," she says. "That third surgery was the charm. I just have to be careful not to overuse my voice."

Westerly tells me about her most recent laryngeal surgery. Dr. Broadhurst, the specialist in Brisbane, had done two surgeries, but Westerly was not satisfied with the results.

"I thought, *If I don't have a voice that fits the person, that* belongs *to the person, I'd rather be dead.*"

Dr. Broadhurst consulted with another specialist, and proposed to Westerly that they try something that had never been done before. The idea was to use a local rather than general anesthesia so that Westerly could remain not only conscious throughout the surgery, but alert enough to be able make sounds in various pitches, so that Dr. Broadhurst could calibrate accordingly—like tuning a piano.

"I've poked my finger almost into his nose and said, 'Look into my eyes.' I said, 'Matt'—Matt is Dr. Broadhurst—'Matt, we've failed on two missions, we're not failing on this mission. But if it just so happens that we're so shot up, our fortress bomber has just lost three engines, it's on fire, smoking, everybody else is dead, you're the pilot. No, I'm the pilot and you're the navigator, you've got to navigate us home and I will get us there. *I will get us there!* So don't say no to me now, I want us to do this. I would rather the plane crash than not to give this the best go we can. So if you want to keep me awake, keep me awake.' And he said . . ." Westerly laughs, can hardly get the words out. "Like, I was almost threatening him. And he looked at me and he said, 'Okay, we're going to do it, we're going to do it. I'm the navigator.'"

Westerly describes herself laid out on the operating table, neck sliced wide open, vocal cords exposed.

Dr. Broadhurst is pulling them up to the hyoid bone, just below the chin, he's cut the vocal cords, shortened them by seven millimeters. He has a round silver plate with little holes in it; it's like a little button that you sew onto your clothes. He's got that ready to anchor the vocal cords against the hyoid bone, once he found the right pitch, and he had little screws that the nurse would hand him and you could feel the drilling, he was screwing them in with a screwdriver. So I'm singing, "*Eeeeeee.*" "That's good." "*Eeeeeee.*" "A little higher." I am just in sheer agony. Fingernails went to the other side of my knuckles. It was like someone in the Vietnam War who'd just been shot up and was having his guts sewn together. And this went on for three hours! I nearly passed out. It was only when I thought about my son and the showcase finale . . ."

Westerly's neighbor exits her house. She's an elderly woman in a power chair. She greets us with an enthusiastic hello. Westerly introduces me as the producer of the film. Her neighbor is kind, jovial. She motors off. Westerly tells me they get along well.

"Wow, Westerly. That's a hell of a story."

"Can you believe it?"

Westerly and I make plans to meet for breakfast the following morning. We hug goodbye. I drive off. Minutes later, my cell phone rings. It's Westerly.

I grab it. "Hey, WW."

"Listen, Jamie, I got it wrong," she says in this lovable, earnest third-grader voice. "I was the navigator and Dr. Broadhurst was the pilot. I had it mixed up."

"I knew what you were trying to say."

"Yeah, I was the pilot and Dr. Broadhurst was the navigator."

LATE AND TAKING PILLS

I ARRIVE AT WESTERLY'S AT 9 AM. SHE COMES TO
the door in a bathrobe, smiles, points to her cheek. I kiss it. Of
course she's a long way from being ready and we're due to meet the
ABC people at 10:30.

She tells me she's excited about the day. Pointing to her throat
she whispers, "I'm going to try to talk very little. Have to save my
voice." She wears that familiar appeased and exhilarated mien that
comes when the spotlight is aimed solely on her.

She steps into the center of the room. "How do I look?"

"You look great, but you're not dressed. What are you going to
wear?"

She gestures towards her armchair. Draped over it are at least
half a dozen dresses, blouses, pants, a few jackets, several pairs of
shoes and a couple of hats.

"I thought I might give them a bit of variety," she says.

She slinks into the bathroom. She can be so charming, that
sweet place where her imagination and ingenue vulnerability co-
alesce, Norma Jean just forming into Marilyn. It's when she's got
JFK squeezing her from one side, Darryl F. Zanuck from the other,
a cavalcade of paparazzi on her tail, two months' worth of unre-
turned fan mail on her nightstand, and the pharmacy's closed and
the champagne's run out that we run into trouble. Actually, it's
precisely the opposite. She aspires to all of the above. It's when
the reality of her life gets too real that she starts throwing monkey
wrenches in the works.

She exits the bathroom. She wears silver heels, skinny jeans, a turquoise blouse. Her makeup is immaculate, her beauty mark twinkles. She does a sort of demi-ballet bow.

"Looking great, WW."

"Thanks, Jamie."

I check the time. I remember all the traffic along the Gold Coast Highway due to train construction. Yesterday it took me a half hour to move about five kilometers.

"We should probably get going," I say.

She's at the kitchen counter, rifling through her packets of prescription drugs. She snaps one out, pops it in her mouth, washes it down with a gulp of water.

"Like Marilyn," she says. "Late and taking pills."

She giggles at her herself. She shuffles through the unpaid bills spread about the kitchen counter, digs through her case of DVDs, prattles on about composers and scenes, grabs her showcase finale notebook off the desk and reads me her latest entry. She does exactly what she should not be doing, given that we're late. I wonder what the hell she's doing. And then I don't. I know; I do it too.

"Listen to this one, Jamesy, this is just . . ." She cracks up. She seems almost drunk. There's a nasal, frayed twang in her resigned giggle.

"I don't think it's a good idea to be late, WW."

She says something, I don't catch it exactly, but the gist is that lateness is in fact part of the WW show.

"We really do need to get going," I say.

A little girlish panic sets in. She starts putting together her handbag.

I walk over to the clothing spread about the chair. "All these coming with us?"

"Yeah, I thought it'd be good to show 'em we're professional."

I scoop up the clothes, load them in the car.

Back in the house, Westerly rushing to gather up her things, I fall into that familiar role: *Sure you've got everything? Let me help you with that bag. Don't forget your keys.*

The day is bright and hot. Traffic is minor. Riding shotgun,

Westerly fiddles with her makeup. She does her vocal exercises. *E-e-e-e-ee-ee-ee-ee.*

"Sometimes a little massage on my neck and shoulders helps relax my vocal cords. Would you mind giving me a little rub before I sing, Jamesy?"

"Of course not."

We arrive at the Cambus Wallace. Nick and his girlfriend Jessie—tall, blond, beautiful—are there to meet us. Westerly and Jessie hit it off; Jessie offers to help Westerly get dressed. I unload the car, bring Westerly's things into the ladies' room.

The ABC crew arrives. David Lewis, the segment producer, is brown-haired, fresh-faced, affable. His cameraman and boom operator are equally pleasant.

We ask Westerly how she'd like to do this. She says she wants to sing from a stage. We move some tables around, set up an open space in the center of the bar, and slide two benches together, creating a makeshift stage that's easy to light and easy to pull good audio. Westerly steps upon it, checks that it's sturdy. She breaks into song—a Bobby Darin tune. It feels strange to be rehearsing this showcase finale after all the talks and fights and strong-arming. Westerly looks extremely happy with her two feet of elevation.

Westerly says she'll need a little time to change and put herself together. David suggests that in the meantime he interview me.

I take a seat on a barstool, they arrange the lights, the boom, clip a mic to my shirt. David asks what drew me to Westerly's story. I tell him that I love the surf world, but it can be narrow-minded. I feel an affinity with Westerly, her plight. "I think it's an important story to tell," I say. I tell him about the documentary, the team making it, the incredible ride we've been on with Westerly.

Westerly comes out in silver heels, aubergine cocktail dress, fifties earrings and bracelets. She takes the stage, breaks into a Judy Garland song. She has a jazzy, lounge style. Fingers snap. Heels click. She sings "River of No Return." My role as director feels staged. If anything, Westerly's directing me. Nick, next to me, films away. He too is just sort of following The Miracle. At one point she hits a high note and her voice cracks. She tries to hit it again—cracks. Again—cracks.

With cameras rolling she steps off the stage and sits in a chair, relishing the attention, loving the fact that she's got all of us in her thrall.

"Jamie," she says coquettishly, curling her index finger. "Would you come over here and give me a little massage?" She points to her shoulders. Yes, the cameras are still rolling.

I think: *You passive aggressive monster! You serial belittler! You're actually going to do this?* I say: "Sure! With great pleasure, WW!"

I massage Westerly for *7.30* and its however-many-million viewers. She shuts her eyes, moans.

•

Westerly sings for a good half hour. More than once I note a "what the hell kind of weird game have I walked into" look on David the segment producer's face. Westerly preens. Delicately, almost bash-fully, David tells her that he's got what he needs, that we're good. Westerly seems a tad disappointed that we can't keep going, but she stops, steps off the stage, grabs Jessie, and heads back to her dressing room.

I nearly break character, say something like, "She's a real hand-ful," to David. Instead I throw the question back at him: "What drew you to Westerly?"

"Same as you. I think it's an important story to tell," he says.

The cameraman disassembles his tripod and camera. The boom operator takes down the lights and puts away the boom. The snap-ping shut of cases, the click of latches.

"Thanks for all your help, guys," says David.

The cameraman and boom operator come over. "Yeah, tha—"

Westerly walks up. "I was going to do my comedy sketch," she says, in a new outfit, clasping her showcase finale notebook.

"We've already put our gear away," says David.

"It's really funny. You'll just die laughing. You can't leave without seeing this." Westerly wears a "pretty please" look.

David reminds me of me when he says, "Sure. We can do that," and instructs the crew to pull out the gear.

Westerly's comedy sketch is a load of fun, cut from the golden years of Hollywood. She's campy, cute, exaggerated facial expressions. There's an awkward moment when she looks at us with a *where are your laughs?* face. This is the vulnerable, amateur WW shining through. David and his team are fly-on-the-wall, which means that as far as the viewer knows, there's only Westerly, Nick, Jessie (who by now deserves a title: stylist? personal assistant?) and me in the room. But Westerly doesn't see the bigger, TV audience picture. She wants laughs and she wants them now.

SATURDAY WITH WESTERLY AND ZAC

IF WESTERLY'S GOING TO INDULGE IN MARILYN'S habit of showing up late, then I think it's only right that I counter this by showing up early. On Saturday morning I arrive at 9:45 for our 10 am meeting. I knock on her front door. She materializes in the kitchen window, waves, points with her finger that she's on the phone. She appears to be deep in conversation, but no, thirty seconds later the door opens and there she is, silver/gold sandals, jeggings, black stretchy top, pale yellow cardigan, lemon meringue hair.

"I was just leaving a message for David at the ABC," she says. "I was thinking about that last scene I did, from my comedy sketch. I told him that I thought it might be nice to add some canned laughter at the end. What do you think?"

"If it were me I'd tell you a flat out no."

She looks at me nervously. "There was no laughter."

"Yes, Westerly, but it was a rehearsal. They were filming a rehearsal, so Nick and I were the only people in the room. If you're rehearsing you're likely telling the joke over and over—it's not falling on fresh ears. Canned laughter would be totally phony."

Westerly's visage tells me she does not like what I am saying, but she accepts it, or perhaps she's just picking her battles.

We get in her car, drive over to Zac's. Normally he's waiting in the driveway, but not today. Westerly looks concerned. A few minutes later he comes out.

His gait is slow, hunched over. He wears black sneakers, camouflage cargo shorts, black Black Veil Brides T-shirt and a black

NY cap. His eyes are squinty. He's lukewarm with me, a bit shy.

I offer my hand. "So good to see you, Zac."

He shakes it. "Hi."

He sits in front, I hop in back. He tells Westerly that he'd been waiting, insinuating lateness on Westerly's part. To be fair, Zac might be playing the same game I am, because my phone says it's exactly 10:30.

"Sorry, son," says Westerly.

Few words are spoken in the three or four suburban blocks between Zac's place and the gas station where Westerly pulls in front of a pump. She turns off the car, fumbles through her purse.

"Do you want me to pump the gas, Westerly?"

As soon as it leaves my mouth I wonder if "Westerly" was the right way to address her in front of Zac.

"Yes, please. Six dollars."

I pump the gas. Westerly hands me three two-dollar coins. I run in and pay the dolled-up blonde cashier.

We head north on the Gold Coast Highway, pass Goldsteins where Westerly no longer goes, pass KFC, pass Bob Jane T-Marts.

I ask Zac about his T-shirt. He explains that it's a glam rock band.

"I've been listening to death metal bands from the Gold Coast," he says, and rattles off a list of them, adding details about their sound, their songs.

Westerly dives in with the names of Scandinavian metal bands, and the two of them slip into a father-son shorthand, Westerly almost interviewing Zac on my behalf.

WW: You like Depravity.

Zac: You mean Devastated. I've been really into Eye of Solitude.

WW: What's your favorite right now?

Zac: Harvest of the Moon, they're from the Gold Coast. I've been listening to the old stuff. GF93. From Italy. I was listening to their stuff since high school Year 12. I got into a lot of metal stuff that was made for the Internet.

Zac speaks slowly, with a softness on his consonants, as if rolling the word in his mouth a while. He takes his time, thinks about what he's saying.

"My favorite actress is Sapphire Wolf," says Zac without prompting. "She's a cosplayer, metal head, and model. She's my favorite actress on YouTube. My favorite actor is Patches Metal. He's from the Netherlands. He's got his own band that he plays in, kinda like stoner rock, a cross between stoner rock and blues."

"I'll have to check them out," I say.

We pass the bait and tackle shop, a park full of kids.

"Do you like cosplay, Jamie?"

"That's the Japanese kind of costume play-acting?"

"Yes."

"I don't know all that much about it."

Zac jumps back to Patches Metal, says that he shaved his beard. "They asked him why he did it, he said, 'Because I felt like it.' And I'm into AlphaOmegaSin. A lot of these metal YouTubers, they have rants and blogs, they have different opinions about different things. I'm starting to figure out YouTube."

We pull off the highway into Australia Fair. Westerly tells me that Zac had a band called Impact, that he was a great singer and songwriter, that they recorded a CD. Zac chimes in right over the top of Westerly. I catch only the last part: "Yo PD, the shit rises."

"What does that mean?" I ask.

"Like *LA*PD, but *Yo*PD the shit rises."

"What are your songs about?"

"Mostly lyrics about sensitivity and negativity, about childhood problems. They always say I sound like Jonathan Davis from Korn or Marilyn Manson."

Westerly tells the story of Korn coming to town, Zac meeting the band members, getting signed copies of their CD, giving them copies of his. Zac perks right up at this.

We find a spot in the parking garage, park, step out.

"Sorry bro, I'm shit in the morning," says Zac, with a raised soul-brother hand. We shake. He's apologizing for being slow to warm to me, I think.

We amble into the bright lights of the mall. Families stroll past. A pair of grandmas stares at us. Wafts of fried food. Sportsgirl. Coles. Best and Less.

A good-looking goth girl in black skirt and black Doc Martens walks past. Zac follows her with his eyes. He looks at me. We exchange fellow-lecherous-male looks.

"I'm a chick magnet," he says (I think he means that he's magnetized to the chicks, rather than vice-versa). He launches into a list of his girlfriends from primary school onward. He says he had a girlfriend in high school, but she moved with her family to New Zealand.

"Do you have a girlfriend now?" I ask.

"No," he says. "Living the single life."

We find a coffee shop. Zac takes a seat at a table; Westerly and I go up to order. We have what Zac's having: white chocolate mocha, no cream.

I sit down with Zac.

"The best thing about school is getting up to mischief," he says.

He does this often, offers random observations about random things. He'll also pick up on topics left behind several minutes and several topics ago, as if he's been thinking hard about them.

"My dream girl is Sniper Wolf," he says with a bearish grin.

Westerly arrives with our drinks, places them on the table, goes back for stirrers. She sits, passes the stirrers around.

"I don't need one," Zac says, eyeing the white chocolate shavings floating atop the foam. "I like to let it melt slowly."

"That's right son, you do," says Westerly, stirring her drink.

Zac sips carefully, joyfully.

Over coffee it is decided that next we'll go to the massage parlor.

"I like grunge," says Zac, as we make our way across the mall. "It came out of Seattle. In the early nineties." He lists off a bunch of bands, comments on their guitar tunings, playing style. Clearly he knows this stuff well.

Westerly compliments him on his knowledge. This seems to be their way; Zac's mind jumps from topic to topic, and when something triggers an observation—a CD, a T-shirt—he plunges in with lists, factoids. Westerly is loving and encouraging. It's beautiful to see. Rarely is she so focused on someone other than herself, rarely does she listen so well.

We enter China Dragon with its mint green walls and soothing, barely audible music and smells of oils and tonics. William, the serene-faced man at the front desk, greets Zac. While they talk, Westerly tells me that this is their regular spot, that they love Zac. "They're all so nice here," she whispers. "I get Zac ten minutes, but they usually go extra, fifteen minutes, sometimes twenty."

Westerly introduces me to William. "This is the producer from America. William knows all about you, all about my anxieties."

William and I shake hands.

"Is Spring or Cherry here?" asks Zac.

"Spring," says William.

Zac is led down the hall, ushered into a curtained-off stall. Westerly and I take a seat.

"Is this a happy ending sort of place?" I ask Westerly.

"Stop it, Jamie," she says Marilynishly, a hand slapping my thigh.

A few feet in front of us is a large woman straddling a massage bench, her face buried in a sort of padded guillotine. A wiry old Asian man massages her neck. A Muzak version of Foreigner's "I Want to Know What Love Is" plays. Westerly opens her purse on her lap, pulls out a roll of bills clasped together with a rubber band.

With a straight face I say, "I want you to buy me a massage."

She takes me seriously, starts counting her money, mouthing numbers. I delight in this for a few seconds, Westerly in reflexive maternal mode, leaping to fulfill my request as if I were Zac.

"I'm joking, Westerly."

"Oh!" She giggles at herself. "I'm such a girl." She says that her maternal ways have grown since her surgery, that the nurturing instinct has never felt more natural.

Westerly sticks her head in the guillotine for a ten-minute massage. When it finishes she does a *la-la-la-laa-laa-la-la*. "Listen to my voice now, it's higher, just from the massage."

Zac returns looking happy and relaxed. Westerly pays William, shakes his hand and everyone else's in the place, and tells them to watch *7.30* on Monday evening.

We take the escalator downstairs.

"Richard Greco and Steve Bacic are my favorite actors, you can't go wrong," says Zac.

Westerly tells me that these are indie actors who never had the success that was expected of them. "Zac loves underdogs, don't ya son?"

"My favorite movie director is Rob Zombie. I'm a big fan of his work. *House of 1,000 Corpses. Devil's Rejects.* The acting's awesome."

Westerly looks at me resignedly. "This is our Saturday and Sunday ritual."

We amble out of the mall and back to the car. On the sidewalk, under a row of trees, Zac moves in close, puts his arm around me. "I'm really having a good time with you, bro."

•

We drive to Broadwater, park, walk along the bike path that lines the water. Grey clouds smear the sky. Wind ruffles the pines, our hair. Wake waves from passing boats lick the shore. Zac and Westerly sip from bottles of water.

"Eh, Jamie," says Zac. "Kate Winslett's my favorite actress."

We pass a row of pandanus trees. A kite surfer glides past. Across the broadwater is Sea World. As rollercoaster riders loop the corkscrew, we can almost hear their screams.

Zac turns to me. "Is Kate Winslett naturally blond or brunette."

"Not sure," I say.

"Heard you and Dad are going to be on ABC," he says.

"Yes. In fact we're going to watch it together. Want to join us?"

"It's a weekday. I'm all booked out on weekdays."

Earlier I'd asked Westerly if Zac might like to watch *7.30* with us. She said that it was highly unlikely, that Zac's mother is not exactly a champion of Westerly's desire to be in the public eye.

Talk turns to movies. Zac interns at a local video store. It's unpaid work, but Westerly gives him money in proportion to the hours he puts in. Zac's job is to check in and file movies.

"Sniper Wolf Lila," says Zac. "She lives by herself, has a pet dog. She's from Phoenix, Arizona." He turns to me, all hopeful. "Jamie, is there any chance you might be able to contact Sniper Wolf for the movie?"

Westerly tells Zac that America's a big place, that it may be difficult.

"Is there any possibility you can get in touch with Greco and Bacic?" he asks.

Before I can answer he goes into a long, gushing rant about Steve Bacic—born in Croatia, raised in Canada, joined the cast of *21 Jump Street* in its fifth season. He's a walking Wikipedia, this warm and whiskery Zac. At the conclusion he says. "Bacic would be a perfect villain in the movie my dad's making. My part's the son."

It's surprising to hear Zac speak of the film this way. He makes it sounds less like a documentary and more like a feature. Later, Westerly will tell me that he explained it to Zac in this manner.

We near the car. It's almost time to drop Zac off at his mom's. I ask what he plans to do the rest of the day.

"Sit on my desk chair and look stuff up," he says. "I might look up what movie Steve Bacic has in pre-production."

A wonderful image forms in my head: Westerly at her computer, reading about Marilyn's hassles with Bobby and Jack, Judy's laryngitis bout during her Vegas show; and Zac, just a few blocks away, alone in his room, studying all his favorite indie actors. Like father, like son.

WESTERLY WHISPERING

THE *7.30* SEGMENT IS A COUP FOR BOTH WESTERLY and the movie, and in Skype meetings with Alan and Jordan we've agreed that it would be great to film Westerly at home, watching herself on TV, the camera framed tight on her naked face.

So here we are at our little Chinese-run cafe (Westerly loves to find a place and stick with it), a briny wind on the broadwater. In front of Westerly is a quarter-strength, extra-hot coffee, and a ham and cheese sandwich that looks ordinary but Westerly insists is "So nice."

Not so nice is her outright refusal to be filmed while watching herself on TV. I've been delicately trying to convince her, but she won't even consider it.

"Marilyn or Judy or Montgomery Clift or James Dean would never let the studios film them watching themselves on TV," she says.

"But you're an extraordinary case, Westerly. This is not you acting in a film. This is about your transformation and your emergence, and we've been through a lot, we've seen you rubbed raw with self-doubt. This *7.30* popped up unexpectedly and it's a huge validation."

She tries to chime in.

I raise a finger. "*And . . . And*. Marilyn and Judy and Monty are actually sitting in our Malibu Studios right now with Darryl F. and Billy Wilder, smoking cigars, drinking champagne, toasting this great news about *7.30*—and they've just sent a telegram that reads: 'Dear WW, *stop*. Congratulations on your recent coup. We raise our glasses in your honor, *stop*. Now quit being selfish and get with the whole letting-us-film-you thing, *stop*.'"

She half giggles.

"And by the way," I add. "Darryl F. is Jordan and Billy Wilder is Alan."

She insists that she does not want to be filmed watching herself then launches into a diatribe against feminism and feminists that is too complex and convoluted to try to reproduce here, but the gist is that she thinks the feminist movement killed off a lot of natural and wonderful feminine attributes. "I loathe feminists!" She says it twice, tells me to write it in my notebook.

"Westerly's mission," she proclaims imperiously, chin raised, a single triumphant finger held at eye level, "Westerly's mission is to rid the world of all its false gods. That's the miracle of Westerly."

•

Now we're in the car headed to Westerly's appointment with her therapist. She's hit a sort of grace note, pointing out spots along the way—the Lyric Theatre, the shortcuts she takes at rush hour, the cinema where she and Zac see movies. She's such a cartoon of what it feels like to be human, such a funhouse mirror. When she's anxious or insecure you can almost see its blockage, its tightness on her lips, its furrow on her brow. That repression of spirit—on small levels or big—seizes the whole WW apparatus and enterprise.

We park in a massive lot across from the office building where Westerly's therapist practices. She micromanages my parking— *"Left here, Jamesy! No, not that spot—over there! Yes, yes, no, the one there, yes!"* Stepping out of the car, crossing the street, entering the building, riding up in the elevator, she explains that she's been seeing her therapist regularly since her surgery, that she likes him, that he was a big support through all her vocal cord nightmares.

Just as we're stepping out of the elevator my phone rings. It's Alan. I'd emailed him and Jordan earlier in the day telling them that The Miracle refuses to let us film her watching *7.30*.

I answer. "Westerly's standing right next to me," I say.

"Let me speak to her," he says.

"Good cop/bad cop" is a term we've used a lot these last couple of years. A new one that's cropped up is "Westerly whisperer," a riff on "horse whisperer," made popular by the film starring Robert Redford.

Westerly, phone up to her ear, does a lot of nodding. She looks at me, points down. The two of us get back in the elevator, ride it to the ground floor, walk out to the treet. I take a seat on a step, scribble notes. Westerly paces, nodding, smiling, giggling even. After a few minutes she walks over to me, hands me the phone.

"Hi Alan."

"All set," he says, and we go over the details of how we want to shoot Westerly watching Westerly.

When I hang up there's not a hint of resistance from WW. In fact, she's looking forward to us shooting her.

Some fine-ass Westerly whispering.

•

Westerly observes none of the somber, mind-your-own-business decorum that's typical of therapist's offices. She prances into the waiting room, funky sunglasses on, and announces herself to the receptionist, charms her. Her laugh has evolved into a stoner giggle. We sit for a couple of minutes, flip through *Women's Weekly*, then she's called. I spend the time writing notes. Patients arrive, sit down, whisper into phones, read magazines. There are half a dozen or so psychologists sharing the office.

An hour later I hear Westerly's giggle from way down the hall. "Jamesy," she shouts across the room, "come meet Dr. Morris."

I walk over. Westerly introduces us. Dr. Morris is bearded, South African, wears a checked shirt and a psychedelic tie. A bit of WW seems to have rubbed off on him—he too is giggly, all jokes. I wonder what goes on on that couch. Westerly the person and Westerly the performer: is there a clear line separating the two?

KIRRA REUNION

ON A HOT SUNDAY AFTERNOON I DRIVE PAST
Burleigh Heads, past a pie shop that Mike Perry swears is the
"best on the entire Goldie." I turn down a narrow tree-lined street
that leads to a blinding glimmer of ocean, hang a right, and hit a
stop sign that faces straight into a giant mural of Kirra tubes, in
procession, as seen from the side angle—this would have been a
serious turn-on when I was in my twenties and endlessly horny
for waves. The mural is on the wall of Kirra Surf, a massive surf
shop topped by a twelve-story, $89 million apartment complex. I
turn left, ocean on my left, more surf shops on my right, and find
a parking spot that looks out to the Kirra surf break. The waves are
nothing like the ones in the mural. They're twinkling and efferves-
cent, but only waist-high.

I cross the street and enter the Kirra Beach Hotel. Its airy, modernist decor (a recent makeover) defies the pub's rich fifty-year
history. Huddled around a group of tables are the Kirra legends—
grey, rotund, leathery, but strikingly vivacious in their sixties and
seventies. There's Terry Baker, former club president of Snapper
Rocks; there's Billy Stafford, first Queensland Junior State Champion in '64; there's Kerry Gill, upstanding Kirra Surfriders member for half a century. This Kirra reunion was put together by Peter
Townend, a Gold Coast native who's lived in Southern California
since the early eighties. Peter recently came back to Australia to
attend his brother Duncan's funeral. All the old crew was there
at the service; it was great to see them. Peter thought, *Why wait
for the next funeral, let's clink glasses while we're all still kicking,* and

rounded everyone up.

I find Tim Baker, who's standing at a table alongside Peter Turner, founder of Kirra Surf, former Deputy Mayor of the Gold Coast. Peter's showing Tim some old photographs of Gold Coast surfers. They're black-and-white, the boards are long, the line-ups nearly empty. Peter—navy blue Aloha shirt, sharp jaw, warm smile—launches into an account of Coolangatta before all the development, before the Duranbah groynes, before the dredging that created the Superbank. With conductor hands he describes the way the sand fills into the points. Talk drifts into the politics of the local breaks.

"I haven't been vocal about it since 2006," he says.

He and Tim discuss the $700,000 the government had given the surfers. Peter points out that it's elitist; the money was used to create breaks suited to the advanced rather than novice surfer. He thinks it should have been put towards building new breaks to facilitate the recent surge of neophytes. "Overcrowding is our biggest problem," he says.

Surfing is inescapable on the Gold Coast. You can't walk into a bar or café without finding surfboards and surf memorabilia hanging from the walls, much of it celebrating the local champions. The town's collective gaze is aimed seaward. I think about this in relation to the former pro surfers. All those articles in the local papers, all those pats on the back from the community—the more prevalent it was in one's heyday, the more it must hurt when it fades away. A couple of tables over from us stand Rabbit and PT. To their left, hanging from the wall, are surf posters of them from the seventies: PT in an impossibly cool soul arch, arms like wings, the curling lip tickling his pelvis; Rabbit standing in a heaving tube, mouth agape with stoke, eyes and index finger pointed at camera. It must feel great being honored everywhere you go. It must also feel constricting, a life in the past tense.

I grab a Bundaberg ginger beer from the surfer-looking bartender and join Rabbit and PT. Rabbit wears a madras short sleeve shirt, boardshorts and sandals. His hair is slicked back like an albino raven's wing. PT wears a red Hurley tee, boardshorts, and his signature pink sneakers. Both sip beer. Rabbit is in the middle of one of his animated stories, his hand is curled up into a tube much like the ones in the Kirra Surf mural.

They greet me warmly. We talk about the surf, how it's supposedly on the rise, Rabbit says he had a fun wave yesterday afternoon. Up walks Andrew McKinnon—grey Billabong tee, boardshorts, sandals, baseball cap atop his silky, peroxide white long hair.

After more chat about rising swell, a default subject among surfers, Andrew turns to me and says, "Drouyn made Queensland surfing." He sweeps his arm around the room. "He's why all this is happening." He takes a sip of lemonade. "You know, Jamie's working on the Drouyn story," he says to the group.

Both Rabbit and PT say that we'd already talked. They ask me how it's going. I give my stock answer: *She's probably the most fascinating person I've ever encountered. She's unquestionably the most difficult.*

"Remember Drouyn's speech about the Six Sisters?" Andrew asks Rabbit and PT.

Chiming in on top of each other, they tell me about Peter's epic speech at a Burleigh Heads fundraiser some years back. Peter described the Gold Coast's point breaks—Burleigh, Currumbin Alley, Kirra, Greenmount, Rainbow Bay and Snapper Rocks—as the Six Sisters. He went into vivid detail about their respective personalities and moods and nuances, his intimate relationship with them, how they helped shape him into the surfer he became. He described them as if they were ex-lovers from his youth.

"Drouyn was one of the greatest orators ever," says Rabbit. "I gave that a ten out of ten. It was a perfect speech! He hit all the right points with the right tone, with the right pause, with the right vocabulary. And absolutely nailed it. And took me on a journey."

"What about his speech to Roseman's wife in Tavarua?" says Tim Baker.

"It was more than bordering on the erotic," says Rabbit. "We all felt he went way too far again."

"I just have this vague recollection of 'damp mosses' and stuff like that," says Tim.

"It was deadset like something out of *Lady Chatterley's Lover.*"

"I remember the '69 State Titles at Snapper. Drouyn was losing in the final, and this was '69, he was our Queensland guy, and he storms out of the water before the final was over, comes up the beach, and he had the most knock-dead-looking blond chick laying on the beach in a bikini, she gets up begging him to stop and he just brushes her aside, and, you know, just keeps going and she's begging him to stop, and he goes up to the car, puts the board on the top, straps it down, and just peels rubber out of the parking lot! That's the first impression that I have of Drouyn, and I've never lost it."

Rabbit, PT and Andrew recount with chutzpah, laughter, sweeping hands. Tony Dempsey comes over. Tony is sixtyish, fit, grey hair parted in the middle, grey goatee. Back in the Hohensee days he worked with Peter Drouyn. They were close for many years. John Allen joins in. Andrew introduces us, says that John worked with Peter back at the factory.

Andrew and John describe the famous Hohensee fire, a story I'd heard from Westerly. "Hono had a showroom and factory on the Gold Coast Highway at Mermaid Beach," says Andrew. "He had this fire one night in early '66 that blew up the factory. Hono was blown out the shop front window clutching onto two brand new boards he made for Peter."

Andrew enacts it. They share a laugh.

"Peter was never much of a shaper," says Rabbit, with rolling eyes. "His boards had reverse rocker." He makes a convex shape with his hand. "But that's how good he was. He had this cutback, this wide-stanced cutback, just full-blown power. That influenced me a lot."

"There was that 1966 Aussie Titles," says Andrew. "And the day before he and Nat were out at Burleigh, and Peter was better than Nat. Nat was copying Peter's turns. And Nat was like God at that time. And we all thought Peter was going to win. And he didn't. Nat won. Nat was doing Peter's turns. So the next day Peter's out at Burleigh. He's just changed his style. He's changed into Phil Edwards."

It has the tone of a wake, this circle of six men, drinks in hand, all reminiscing about Peter Drouyn. I only wish Westerly were here to see it.

"Has Peter ever told you about his Six Sisters speech?" Tony asks me.

"No," I say, "But these guys just did."

"My mate picked him up that night. He was in a dress. My mate said, 'No, not tonight, Peter.' He went in and changed, toned it down." Tony takes a sip of beer. "So he's up there giving his speech, he's wearing these long earrings, Turkish slippers, pantaloon pants. There were some kids there, much younger, before Peter's time. One of them goes, 'Who's the poof?' I said, 'That's Peter Drouyn.'"

COMFORTABLE IN HER SKIN

PETER DROUYN HANGS FIVE ACROSS A HEAVING blue wave, his ripped body tucked into a crouch, his splayed fingers like arrows pointing the way forward. The camera pulls back to reveal Westerly sitting alongside David Lewis of *7.30*, watching Peter surf on a laptop.

"So, Westerly, what do see when you watch Peter surfing?" asks David.

"Oh, I see an incredible guy who's just got amazing power," gushes Westerly. *"Look at the way he accelerates that board . . ."*

Westerly watches Westerly watching Peter on TV from the armchair in her living room. She wears skinny jeans and a yellow cardigan. Her hair is pinned up and over with barrettes, makeup impeccable. She sits in a feline position, legs tucked under. Nick and I stand behind his camera, mounted on a tripod. Nick's girlfriend Jessie sits at Westerly's desk. We are curious to see how *7.30* will handle Westerly's story. There are interviews with Mal Chalmers and Tappa, a longtime Gold Coast surfer. There's me saying that I've interviewed three or four dozen of Peter's peers and contemporaries and all say that Westerly is happier than Peter was. It's a seven-minute, well-researched segment that ends the way Westerly hoped it would: with her on our makeshift stage at the Cambus Wallace, singing and dancing and kicking up her heels.

"For now Westerly Windina is feeling comfortable in her skin, expressing her femininity through song and dance in the hope of becoming a performer."

She's delighted. We're delighted. And what we miss in all our excitement is the show following *7.30: Australian Story*, featuring Cate McGregor, formerly Malcolm McGregor. Lieutenant Colonel McGregor is the highest ranking of six transgender people serving in the Australian Defence Force. She underwent gender reassignment in 2012. She offered to resign but her boss, the Chief of Army, Lieutenant General David Morrison, refused to allow it. She is now a prominent and widely respected officer who attributes her acceptance to her colleagues' support and Australia's "live and let live" pragmatism. In an interview, Cate McGregor says that a feature on Westerly Windina in the *Sydney Morning Herald* in 2011 helped give her the strength and conviction to go ahead with her surgery.

The following morning Westerly will receive emails and phone calls of encouragement. She'll be hailed as an inspiration, get invited to speak at a conference about transgender studies. I'm ecstatic. This is what I'd hoped for all along. I begin to think that this might be her showcase finale: Westerly as icon and activist. I express this to her carefully.

"I love all your plans to be a performer, Westerly, and you should pursue them with everything you've got. But inspiring people to embrace their own uniqueness, to push away those narrow confines that make us feel guilt and shame for simply being human—I can think of no greater gift to the world."

"I know what you mean. It's nice to hear that, Jamie. But Westerly is a performer above all else."

"I know, but stages come in many forms. You could really help people. It's almost like the place you go once fame and wealth prove their hollowness. Like Brigitte Bardot, she was an actress and singer, and then she devoted herself to animal rights."

"Another blonde," laughs Westerly, and changes the subject.

FREE FRICTION

DEREK HYND RIDES BOARDS WITH NO FINS, which means that instead of a firm, reliable connection with the wave, he slides all over the place, sometimes riding backwards for a spell, often twirling into 360s. On the one hand it's completely childlike, an eight-year-old sliding down a snow hill on an inner tube. On the other it's laden with big metaphor: life is out of control; *wanna make God laugh, tell him your plans.*

Derek personifies both extremes. In the water he is playful, fishlike, a slave to the slide. On land, over a cold beer, he pontificates and philosophizes, he is the quintessence of the thinking man's surfer. His boards are sculptures, albeit functional sculptures. Like Michelangelo's "Every block of stone has a statue inside of it and it is the task of the sculptor to discover it," they are forever works-in-progress. He'll start with a big plank, test pilot it in the surf, make mental notes, hack away at it with chisels and files, ride it again, make more mental notes, make more hacks, and on it goes. They're crude. Grooves and gutters and channels feed out the tail, beads of resin stripe the rails. If Fred Flintstone had surfed his boards might have looked something like these.

Derek does not own a cell phone, so when I arranged to meet him in Byron Bay it's done via email—

> Looks like a tiny surf but a surf nonetheless.
> See you at The Pass at 3pm —
> I'll be under the shady trees on the new grass by the boat ramp.

255

I'll bring a board—of sorts.

•

Located about an hour's drive south of the Gold Coast, Byron Bay
has long been a hippie enclave. In the late sixties, the Vietnam
War kicking off, the shortboard revolution in full flight and hits of
L dissolving on the tongues of many an ace Aussie surfer, a movement known as "Country Soul" emerged. Disenchanted by city
life, surfers moved to the northern NSW coast, settling in old cottages in chiefly Byron but also Angourie and Lennox Head. The
living was cheap and stress-less. The waves were so good you could
center your whole life around them. Much has changed in the last
half century—crowds, real estate hikes, retro hipsters making a
travesty out of the whole thing—but vestiges of genuine Country
Soul still exist around these parts.

I found Derek perched on a low wood railing under a pandanus tree, eyes fixed on The Pass. Waist-high waves of light turquoise crashed against the headland and winded down the point.
There was something anachronistic about the scene, every surfer
on a longboard, wetsuitless, riding in hood ornament fashion. It
looked like the late fifties.

Derek's greeting was the same coldish one I've known for nearly thirty years. No hugs, no exuberant *great to see you*s, little eye
contact, just a "Hi Jim" (he calls me Jim) and a limp handshake.
"It's not looking so good," he said, referring to the waves.

His hair was long and tangled. He wore a white T-shirt that
draped loosely over his wiry torso, black knee-length boardshorts,
and no shoes. He has the short, knock-kneed legs of a lead guitarist, say Hendrix or Prince, who mid-solo drops seamlessly to the
floor.

In front of us a couple of bush turkeys pecked at the grass.
A few seconds later a goanna, gnarled and ancient-looking and
about two-feet long, dawdled past. It took its time, paid no mind
to us sitting just a surfboard's length away.

"He's a local," said Derek. "I haven't seen him in at least two years."

It crawled across the grass and across the boat ramp as if it were a crosswalk. A sunburned surfer, exiting the water, stopped and watched. After the goanna disappeared into the bushes he continued on, looked at us.

"We don't get much of that in England," he said with an English accent.

"That was the Byron Bay version of The Beatles' *Abbey Road* cover," said Derek.

The English surfer laughed.

Dozens of surfers strolled past, many of them pretty girls—nearly all knew Derek. He walked me up a grassy path to a little side street.

"This is where I get out of the sun," he said.

He opened his van, a mustard yellow Toyota HiAce that looked like it had seen some hard miles. It was parked under a canopy of trees full of squawking birds. He opened the rear gate. Out hopped his cattle dog, Hi-Lux. Derek made a high-pitched sound. Hi-Lux wagged its tail and nuzzled into Derek's calf.

After a couple hours I followed Derek back to his house in nearby Suffolk Park. Traffic was heavy with board-topped cars. The light was golden. We passed a braless, dreadlocked woman on a flower-strewn bike, an old purple school bus that looked straight out of Woodstock, and several bearded hitchhikers. We turned into the driveway of a two-bedroom prefab house and parked in the crabgrass backyard. Derek, it turns out, lives not in the house but in an adjacent shipping container that doubles as sleeping quarters/surfboard laboratory. He unlocked the bolted door, flicked on a light. It was densely packed. Two-thirds of the windowless shoebox consisted of stacks of pillows and rugs topped with a tatami mat—his bed. The other third was a mess of boxes, tools, wetsuits, and boards short enough to stand in the corner of the low-ceilinged space. From the roof hung his longer boards.

"You can sleep in here," he said, opening the rear down to ventilate the space.

"Where are you going to sleep?"

"I'll sleep in the car," he said, pulling a mosquito net from behind one of the boards.

He made up my bed then went outside to set himself up in the van. I followed. The sun had just gone down, the backyard was cast in shadow, you could smell the ocean just a few blocks away. He pulled the boards out. Underneath was a cushion.

"You sure you'll be okay sleeping here?" I asked.

"I do this all the time," he said.

He arranged pillows and blankets, hung the mosquito net over the cushion. He pulled out a rolled-up kilim, spread it out on the ground, and fed Hi-Lux on it, scraping every last fleck of food from the tin. I asked him where he got Hi-Lux. He looked up to the stars.

"When Tony Abbott became prime minister I had to go for a drive to find out if Australia still existed. I had to go out and touch the earth."

He went on a tirade about how horrifically conservative Australia has become. He delivered his words in a way that felt final, indisputable. He talked about his cross-country trip.

"That's where I picked up this girl," he said, nodding at Hi-Lux. "Hi-Lux was a junkyard dog in Halls Creek, in WA. She slept under the shade of a Ford Hi-Lux."

When Hi-Lux was finished eating Derek strapped a surf leash to his collar.

"We're going to go on a little walk-y, Jim. See you in the morning."

They walked off into the darkness. I lay down in Derek's bed. It was awfully hot in the shipping container, despite the fan on full-blast. The smell of resin and surf wax reminded me of my teenage bedroom. I kept a little wooden box full of wax on my desk (banana or coconut or, later, in the mid-eighties, bubble gum). My boards, stacked regally in the corner atop a pillow to protect the tails, were forever being fixed with marine resin—the nicks and chips and spider dings. Marine resin has a strong, brain cell-killing chemical smell. I thought about Derek's passion, how he can talk at length about a single ride he'd gotten ten years ago, how at age fifty-six he still travels halfway across the world to chase a swell. I thought about Westerly Windina. She may loathe the surf culture, but she's the first to admit that the act of surfing has served her immensely well throughout her transition. I looked up to the brightly colored boards hanging above my head. They were like a mobile in a baby's crib. I was tempted to touch them, spin them, suck on a tail.

•

In the late seventies Derek was ranked in the Top 16. His knock-kneed carves and zingy 360s featured prominently in surf magazines and movies. He had a reputation for being a shrewd, merciless competitor. He was vying for a spot in the Top 5 when the tour rolled into Durban for the 1980 Hang Ten International.

Derek held a solid lead in his crucial quarterfinal against the gentlemanly Mike Savage of South Africa. He took off on a glassy waist-high wall and proceeded to tear it apart. In the shore break, as the wave dashed across a shallow bank, he pumped his orange and yellow twin fin with all his might. Suddenly he was on dry sand. He jumped off running, as if from a skateboard, his urethane leash stretching taut behind him. When he turned around the tail of his cocked board leapt at him. He saw a flash of orange and yellow and felt a horrific pain in his left eye.

Knowing that he was seriously injured, but knowing also that if he held his opponent off the good waves he could still win the heat, Derek paddled back out. He sat as close to Savage as possible. Savage was forced to look at him. The ooze running down his face was not blood. And while another man might have responded to Savage's recoil by going into shock, Derek was hoping it would work the other way around. He moved in closer. Only after Savage and water photographer Paul Naude screamed at him to go in did he do so.

Derek was rushed to the hospital and taken straight in to surgery. He had severed his optic nerve. There was no recourse. Two days later he stepped out on to the street with a patch, countless stitches, and a glass eye.

He returned to competition the following year and finished seventh—the first one-eyed surfer in ASP history. Disillusioned by poor judging and a system he was at odds with, he retired from competing, but continued on tour, this time as a coach/journalist. As a coach he employed a heavily tactical approach, and took great pleasure in watching lesser surfers outsmart giants. As a journalist he wrote snappy, contentious pieces that often enraged the pros in question. His column in *Surfing World* was called "Hyndsight" and bylined with a Cyclops logo.

I met Derek in 1986 on my first trip to Australia. He was an anomaly amid the pro surfing community. He read fat Russian novels, had friends outside the "Bro-muda Triangle" (you get sucked into the surfing whirl, you never get out). For a couple years he was my coach, but mostly he was a mentor, feeding me books, reading me aloud his dispatches from the pro tour. Had the Peter/Westerly story emerged during Derek's writing heyday, I suspect he'd have been all over it.

For a few years Derek drifted away from actual surfing and into the marketing side of things. He worked on advertising campaigns for Rip Curl, came up with the IS Tour, an alternative contest circuit. For a while he worked from an office in suburban Warriewood, had an actual desk with memos and a calendar and a Rolodex, kept regular office hours. But his pilgrimages to Jeffreys Bay in South Africa—one of the world's great waves—won over. He started experimenting with strange and vintage boards, putting in marathon sessions, finding oneness with the water. His hair grew long and unkempt. He wore shoes less often. The weight of adulthood seemed to wash right off him.

In 2006, in what might be seen as a kind of surrender, he started riding finless (or, as Derek insists, free friction). I'm fascinated by Derek because he challenges my perceptions of the surfing life. Most of the pros that have had successful middle years have done so by, as Mark Richards put it, "expanding their horizons." I moved to New York because I was beginning to feel surfing's diminishing returns. I can remember reflexively running to the beach every morning in my late twenties and feeling a sense of dread. If the surf was good and my friends were there it was uplifting, but on flat days my empty life was reflected back at me.

Derek, meanwhile, has burrowed his way deeper into it; a kind of regressing that has miraculously almost de-aged him. He is the only surfer of his generation who is actually improving. In a YouTube video that got a lot of play a few years back, Derek flies across the freight-train waves of Jeffreys Bay, drifting sideways at long length, spinning drawn out 360s that last for several seconds, exulting in his rubbery, pouncing low crouch. It inspired me and it sparked the seedlings of midlife crisis. When I heard that Derek and a twenty-three-year-old had fallen in love, a surfer girl, an occasional finless rider in fact, I thought, *Ah, makes perfect sense.*

•

We woke at dawn, drove to The Pass. Hi-Lux rode on my lap. Along the way we passed a golf course, a jam-packed corner café, a towheaded grommet peddling swiftly on his bike, board under arm. The sky was pale blue, the trees aglow in amber light.

"It's jazz, Jim," said Derek, a way of introducing what was to be my first free friction surf session. "Good friends of mine basically lead the Australian Chamber Orchestra. Anyway, the deputy chair, her brother, Osmo Vänskä, came up with the Far Field Theory, which is the physics construct of what happens at the point of infinity when it is reached by particles. There's a mass scattering, before everything is in chaos. Just before the wall is hit, everything comes in and enters in perfect harmony. So that's the feeling of free friction surfing to a great degree. And I think it applies to life and death also."

261

We parked in Derek's spot, got out. The air smelled fresh and earthy. A symphony of birdsong played overhead. Derek opened the rear gate, pulled out his eleven six, handed it to me. It was a faded lemon yellow color, plankish. The tail had crude channels and grooves carved into it.

"Let the board lead, just give over to it," he said. "May be wise to ride prone on your first couple to get the feel."

"Aren't you coming out?"

"I'm going to take Hi-Lux for a little walk-y first."

•

I took to free friction surfing fairly easily. The rudderless feeling was akin to sliding down a snow hill on an inner tube ("If free friction was an Olympics sport, it'd be in the winter Olympics," said Derek). With a fin(s), the nose of the board is always pointing the way forward. Not so on Derek's board, which would just as happily go sideways or backwards. The waves worked in my favor: waist-high, super-forgiving crystalline rollers over a shallow sandbar. Derek's thick, long, heavy board mowed across the flats like an ocean liner. Rides carried on for what felt like minutes, a surging swell backing off then reconnecting, the wall wrapping machine-like down the point.

Derek paddled out. I watched him high-line along a tiny peeler that grew. He rode so low it was more like sitting. As the wave sectioned he aimed the nose at the crumbling lip and drifted sideways at great speed. It reminded me of the rock 'n' roll slides we did on skateboards in our early teens. I felt a burst of vicarious stoke, let out a whoop that sounded more like a giddy-up.

A few minutes later Derek paddled up. "Tell me about your best wave, Jim," he said, prayer hands rested on the nose of his board. The surface was all shimmers and diamonds. Derek re-pressed a smile.

"Well," I said. "I took off on what was a tiny little foamy thing, and it reeled along the sandbar, and I dropped to low tuck, almost parallel-stanced. And the tail released, and I wanted to grab onto something, like when you're sliding down a steep hill, you want to grab a shrub or a branch or something. But that's what's so cool about the feeling, it challenges all those learned reflexes. And then the drift let up and I was mowing forward, still in a low crouch. And no bullshit, Derek, I farted! I let out a full-on fart! I don't think I've ever farted while riding a wave before. And then I thought, *I just farted while riding a wave,* a sort of meta-moment. And then it got steep again, and the drift kicked back in, and I slid my way shoreward, almost backward, for the rest of the ride. You know that famous Shaun Tomson quote about time being suspended when you're in the tube? Well time is definitely suspended when you're riding finless."

"Free friction, Jim."

"But the magic was that weightless, giddy feeling. It's like when you go over a hump at high speed in a car, it's kind of orgasmic."

"Daytona 500," said Derek, elbows on board, hands a pair of blades. "The leading car, the green car, at best a meter behind the four others. It's doing about 199 miles an hour, and it lost it on one of the speed banks, and it started going like that." Derek's hand slides sideways above the water. "From half a mile away I could see it put a faint gap on the rest of the field, in losing all the friction. That made me just go, *Fuck! How was that? I wonder what it'd be like to drift a board?*"

We surfed for a couple of hours. The water was bathtub warm. The sun was hot on our backs. Every out-of-control sideways drift on Derek's board felt like a lesson from a Zen master.

·

A few nights earlier I'd told Westerly I was going to Byron Bay to visit Derek.

"Oh, he's on that whole finless thing," she said with a scowl.

"Yeah, it looks fun, doesn't it?"

"You know, Peter was riding a finless board a long time ago.

And that Derek Hynd actually saw him riding it, and asked him about it. But he doesn't mention this in the articles, does he?"

We were standing in line for a counter meal at the CSi. Hungry diners shuffled around us. I'm not sure what came across on my visage, but I know what I was thinking: *Is there any breakthrough in the last fifty years of surfing that, as far as Westerly's concerned, Peter wasn't responsible for?*

"You don't believe me, Jamie?"

She looked broken. Her lips curled downward at the corners—the tragedy half of the tragicomic mask of the theatre.

"It's not about whether or not I believe you, Westerly."

"So you think Derek Hynd is the first to ride without a fin?"

I shook my head in exasperation.

"So that's it, you don't believe me. In other words, I'm lying."

I was about to let loose on her. I remembered something a friend once told me: "The greatest compliment you can ever pay someone is the truth." A thousand hurtful words formed in my head.

"That spaghetti Bolognese looks tasty," I said, pointing to the food counter.

She got the message.

I thought about bringing this up with Derek. I was curious to hear his take. But the day was perfect and we were in a good mood. And besides, any surf historian knows that the ancient Polynesians rode without fins for centuries, so what was the point?

.

I spent three days with Derek in Byron Bay. Each morning was the same: drive to The Pass, park under the trees, surf in the soft, balmy, cradling waves, discuss the giant philosophical and spiritual connotations of free friction wave riding on the walk back up to the car, hang about Derek's van for a while, usually sitting directly on the warm pavement.

Derek would change out of his wetsuit and wring it out at the bottom of a steep driveway. He'd watch the rivulets of water (rivers, metaphors, nothing is without higher significance when you're with Derek), follow them as they wrap around grooves in the cement, cheer on the little surges.

One late morning, dripping wet from a long surf, ambling back up to the car, Derek asked what it was like hanging out with Westerly.

"She can be self-absorbed," I told him.

"How so?"

"Well, since I arrived it's been all about her voice. She believes that it's divined that she'll become a famous singer, and so every conversation begins and ends with her voice. It's as if she's Judy Garland and tomorrow night she's got a sold out show at Carnegie Hall."

Derek talked about Peter's surfing achievements. "The breakthroughs at Sunset, the big wave at Bells in '67—I think he went right down through Winki and walked all the way back, making the comeback post-Wayne Lynch as the ultimate visionary."

We walked in the shade of trees, cars stacked with boards passing slowly on our left.

"You couldn't get a greater pinnacle than the Stubbies. That was enough to step back and be satisfied for life," he said.

I told Derek that Westerly's both proud of and embittered by Peter's surfing history, that she often doesn't want to talk about it.

"Westerly Windina," said Derek. "In Australia, on the eastern seaboard, the westerly wind rules all. It's as if she's saying, 'Hear me, for I am the westerly wind blowing.'"

"I didn't know this."

"Yeah. The westerly's a clearing wind. It clears away all the humidity."

"Sounds like our girl."

"Does she still surf, Jim?"

"Oh, yeah. Really well. Perfect positioning, great style. And she rides every wave right up to the sand."

Derek laughed. "Perhaps Peter's sex change is the ultimate

metaphor for draining himself in the sand."

We arrived back at the van. Derek opened the passenger door and out climbed a very happy Hi-Lux. He scratched her back, soothed her with that private language they share. Hi Lux's tail wagged. She licked Derek's salty hands. He looped the surf leash through her collar and fastened it to the side mirror. He grabbed his towel, dried off.

"What does Westerly dream about? Are her dreams female?" he asked.

"That's a really great question. I once asked her about her dreams in an email. She said that they were a chaotic mishmash of nightmare and confusion, or words to this effect. She said that she hadn't been able to properly dream because of all the negative attitudes toward her. She spun it around to the showcase finale, said that she needs disciples who believe in her. I didn't push it any further."

I explained to Derek what the showcase finale is, how it came about, the comical proportions it's taken on. He listened intently, head canted slightly sideways, brow creased. With his knotted hair and wiry frame he camouflaged into the trees behind him.

"Could he get it up?" he asked.

"No clue."

A cockatiel shrieked from a high branch. Dappled yellow light showered down on Derek and Hi-Lux.

"Maybe he fucked himself out and couldn't get it up anymore." I laughed.

"What?" he said, serious-faced.

"Fucked himself *out*," I said.

"He very well might have."

"I've just never heard it put that way."

Derek wrapped his towel around his waist and shimmied out of his boardshorts. He picked up his eleven six and slid it into his van.

"How big was his dick?" he asked.

"Never saw it."

"Well, it's not too late to ask the surgeon, Jim."

Derek grabbed his other board, shorter, narrower, a pleasing, soft sky blue color. He ran his hands over the grooves in the tail. He talked about his commitment to friction free surfing, how he's been willing to give everything else up in order to explore it.

"I can really relate to Westerly in that respect, to fully embrace a concept and run it from the conceptual to the completely physical and then beyond to as far as it can possibly go." He slid the board in the van. "Surfing has become the most conservative activity. The herd mentality has just imploded the lifestyle." He shrugged, held out an upturned hand. "Where is everyone? Where is the individuality that spawned the Stubbies? 'Cause without a lot of people thinking that way, the Stubbies never would have been born."

Derek scooped up his wetsuit, shuffled over to the steep driveway.

"The age of explorers is perhaps somewhere in the nineteenth century. I don't know what happened to society to dumb it down so much. Maybe it was sport. Maybe it was family. Maybe drugs have dumbed down people's need to explore, which is an irony. At any rate, it's always interesting to find another explorer out there, because they're increasingly rare."

He held his wetsuit above his little raceway and wrung it out. The saltwater streamed down the pavement. It bumped into a rise and bifurcated, one rivulet much thicker than the other.

"Ah, look Jim, it's on, it's a race." He cheered for the little one. *"Go, go, go, go, go!"*

IS IT A FILM OR IS IT REAL?

I DROVE AWAY FROM DEREK WITH ALL SORTS OF questions. Had I gotten it all wrong? Was there no greater joy to be found than surfing? Was it too late for me to move to the northern NSW coast and surf my life away? I was drunk on free-friction surfing. My rent-a-car could slide sideways at any moment and I would relax with it.

I felt a renewed love for the culture that had been such a big part of my life. Westerly's stories about Peter Drouyn were riveting. More than once I'd driven away from her house dancing in my head, pulling over on the side of the road to scribble down some detail. I couldn't imagine a more flavorful character to write about. And Rabbit, Mark Richards, Cheyne Horan, Barton Lynch, Nat Young—these were surfers I'd grown up admiring. My interviews with them had given me little glimpses of my thirteen-year-old self, of discovering this world I could live in, this identity I could wear.

I remembered a conversation I'd had a while back with 1983/1984 world champion Tom Carroll. He'd recently gotten sober from a drug addiction that surfaced after he'd stepped down from pro surfing. He likened the transition to SAS or commandos trying to come back from tours of duty to humdrum domestic life.

"Unless you're extremely grounded you'll always be chasing the high, you'll always be getting this overspill of energy from the adrenalin side of things," he said. "That full-body satisfaction of being top-of-your-game, the one in the spotlight, the center of attention—that's what you see as the Holy Grail."

I drove down a winding road lined with gum trees to the Pacific Highway, and headed north. Popcorn clouds sprinkled a rich blue sky. The hills were so green they looked Photoshop-enhanced. I thought about Westerly. Does she consciously self-sabotage? On the morning that *7.30* filmed her at the Cambus Wallace, was her lapse into her Marilyn lateness/pill-popping schtick a way to somehow evade the fact that she wasn't going to blow our minds with her golden voice and hysterical comedy sketches? Were her incessant demands regarding the showcase finale a way to ensure that it never actually happened, so that she could blame us rather than herself if she never became a superstar?

During the months between the Surfing Australia fiftieth-anniversary gala and now she'd become insatiable. No amount of attention was enough. It was as if the buzz of the awards and the *Surfing World* shoot and the *Tracks* profile had worn off, and she was jonesing for her next fix. At the time we were editing the film, in the cutting room eight to ten hours a day. She'd shoot off an email in the morning. If it wasn't replied to within six hours there'd be a second one accusing us of neglecting her, and if that wasn't replied to there'd be a third, totally hysterical one. They were long, with lists of questions that numbered in the twenties and thirties. She wanted to know every last detail of the showcase finale. For the 10,000th time we'd tell her that it was too soon to say, that we still needed to raise our "finishing funds." She called us abusive, threatened legal action, called the project off at least half a dozen times. It was sad to watch. I stopped liking her.

Then one lazy and depressing Sunday afternoon I watched Marilyn sing "River of No Return" on YouTube and felt a rush of affection for Westerly. I thought about how much movies had shaped me. I remembered Mel Gibson in *Mad Max* lying on a blanket with his wife, talking, laughing and kissing, and how in my vulnerable, terrified first exchanges with girls, as long as I acted the way Max did, or at least imagined myself as Max, I was somehow protected. I remembered how Martin Sheen's narration in *Apoca-*

lypse Now had got so much airtime in my head that it began to fuse with my own inner voice, and how this helped make my humdrum high school existence more tolerable. I remembered watching *The Life Aquatic with Steve Zissou* days before my dreaded fortieth birthday. Zissou, played by the fabulous Bill Murray, lived an adventurous Jacques Cousteauesque life at sea, documenting the marine world, hunting the elusive jaguar shark. *That was not unlike what I did as a surf journalist! That jaguar shark was the search for the perfect wave!* With Zissou riding on my shoulder, my small, hand-to-mouth, sleeping-on-couches surf journalist lifestyle took on a romantic luster.

I told Westerly about my happy brush with "River of No Return." She was right there with me.

"If it all comes together—the acting, the direction, the costumes, the editing, the script—a movie does transport you into another world where you want to go," she said. "And it's not many people who can transport themselves. Some people—dare I say, people like myself and yourself—we can actually feel like we've been in that movie, in that period. It's like we have walked into that saloon and sat down and listened to her [Marilyn]. And it reminds us of other people, it reminds us of people we know, it reminds us what we would like to do ourselves, particularly if we are creative artists, if we are born with the creative itch."

.

When I met with Cheyne Horan on the Gold Coast he told me this story about Peter Drouyn. In 1978, at an awards banquet for a contest (in Florida or Japan, Cheyne couldn't remember), Peter was called to the stage. The room was packed with all of the Bustin' Down the Door-era greats. Sitting at a rear table, Peter got up and made his way down the aisle to hoots and applause. Halfway there he slowed, raised a hand to his chest, steadied himself on a chair, and toppled over, taking the chair and a tablecloth stacked with drinks with him. He balled up in a sort of fetal position, gasping for air. His peers ran to his aid. He choked, squeezed the leg of a chair with his hand, and lost consciousness. Someone ran out to the lobby to get help. Peter wasn't breathing. The paramedics arrived in minutes. They rushed in with their defibrillators, raced to him, and dropped to the floor to apply CPR. At that moment Peter hopped up, smiled, and gave a terrific bow.

•

Mike Perry, an American expat who lives at Currumbin, has known Peter for forty years. He remembers a day in the late seventies when he was at Duranbah checking the surf. A small scallop of white sand flanked by a groyne on one side and the rocks of Point Danger on the other, the waves were onshore and there was no one around save for a couple of girls sunbathing on the far end of the beach.

"Drouyn pulls up, and we chat, and we realize the surf's out, and he sees the girls and he says, 'Tell you what, let's pretend we're in the French Foreign Legion. We're going to sneak up on these sheilas.' We hit the sand a half mile from where they were. We started belly crawling, and we're sneaking around in the sand, hiding behind little tussocks and grass and that, and we're crawling along, and he's going, 'Can you feel it—you know, the fear? Are you feeling it?' And I'm going, 'No.' And he goes, 'You gotta feel it, man! You gotta feel it. This is it!' So we're crawling along, and he gets right up to these chicks and he jumps up and he goes, '*Yeeee-aaahhhh!*' And they nearly shat themselves! They freaked out. And that was it. And we walked away. And I went, 'That was unreal! That was like a session. That was just so much fun!'"

•

The actor in Peter and Westerly: so strong, such a big part of his/her identity. I thought about Westerly's willingness to play-act 24/7. There were times over these last few years when she was in serious mode, or even angry mode, and if I came at her as a character, as Billy Wilder, say, or journalist Richard Hamill from the *Chicago Tribune* raising his hand and asking Marilyn a question at some imagined press conference, she never failed to play along, there was no such thing as a "not now, Jamie." I loved her for this. But of course there's going too far with it. "Without a platform to showcase my talents I'll just be Peter with a vagina!" she'd said to me before we left for Bangkok. Was Westerly's need to be a performer bigger than gender? I know that's impossible to answer, that not even Westerly knows the answer, but it's fascinating to think about.

I drove over the bridge that crosses the Tweed River. Sapphire blue and twinkling, the Tweed is the waterway that washes the sand out at Duranbah. Southerly currents drag it north to create the fabled Superbank, perhaps the Gold Coast's biggest fun resource. Right around the off-ramp for Currumbin I noticed the sky turning overcast, the air much cooler than it had been an hour ago. By the time I got to Westerly's it had started drizzling.

•

I knock on her door. Westerly opens it. In skinny jeans, navy blouse and turquoise cardigan, she's all sparkly eyed and excited.

"Come, come, look at this," she says, and waves me over to her desk.

On her computer she pulls up a self-portrait. It looks much like the hundreds of self-portraits she's sent me over the years. A hand rests sassily on her jutting-out hip. Her lips are pursed in a rose-colored kiss. She wears something Marilyn-ish, or maybe a bikini.

"Can you see it?" she asks.

"What?"

"It's Westerly's essence. This photo captures it like none of the others."

"It's a nice photo," I say.

"Okay, Jamie," she says, disappointed that I'm not more enthusiastic.

We move into the living room, sit opposite each other in the armchairs. A movie score—triumphant, perhaps a battle scene—plays on the TV.

"Before the showcase finale," she says. "I'd like to do some vocal training. It's a really common thing for performers to do this before a big show, to fine-tune their voices if you will. So I thought it'd be good to set aside some money in the budget for this."

"Yeah, that could be a good idea, Westerly."

"Will you suggest this to Alan and Jordan?"

There's an insistence in her tone, a prickliness.

"We're still a long way off from that, but when the time comes we can definitely talk about it," I say.

From her handbag she pulls out a piece of paper and looks at it.

"Oh yeah. Jamie, you know I've written a novel, *The Albatross*. Will you show it to your publisher?"

Westerly told me about her novel a couple of years ago. I'd yet to read it.

"Why don't you send me a chapter," I say. "I'll read it and we can take it from there."

"So you're saying you won't help me?"

"No, I did not say I won't help you. I said let me look at it and if it seems like something my editor would be interested in I'll pass it along."

"You know with the vocal training, Marilyn had this sort of thing."

"I'm sure she did."

"It's really important. Really important to budget some money for this."

At this point I'm nearly shaking my head in exasperation. She reads from what I now realize is a list of business matters she wants to take up with me.

"Alan told me he'd take my script to his producers. Do you think he'll do this?"

Yes, she's written a movie script as well.

"I'm not sure, Westerly. That's between you and Alan."

"So you're saying he won't?"

I've been here before with Westerly. She's digging around for a nerve. She wants to poke it, grind her lacquered fingernails in. And maybe she already has.

"I'm saying that it's between you and Alan."

Her frown is a mixture of despair and contempt.

"Let's go eat, Westerly, c'mon."

We get in the car and drive to Broadwater. It's grey and raining. Westerly directs me to a fish-and-chips place located right next door to the café that we've been having breakfast at this last week. We park in front, get out. A briny wind whips across the water. The plastic tarp that covers the terrace of the fish-and-chips place flaps like a sail on a rough sea. We walk up to the counter, peruse the menu, go with the barramundi, add two Bundaberg ginger beers.

After a few minutes we're handed our dinners, wrapped in butcher's paper to keep them hot. We head over to the adjacent food court. A dozen tables and chairs are lined up in rows, but there's absolutely no one around except us. We sit at the table nearest the broadwater. Rain patters the roof. Cool wind blows our napkins away. The barramundi is lightly battered and fried. The chips are steaming hot and salty. We add vinegar and ketchup, eat with our hands.

"It's a really normal thing for a singer before a big performance, just simple vocal training, a few days leading up to it, just so I'm hitting my notes."

"I do think it's a great idea, Westerly."

"So you'll promise me that we can put this in the budget for the showcase finale?"

"Absolutely not."

"I'm not asking for anything unreasonable, just for you to send an email to Alan and Jordan and tell them that you think the vocal training is a good idea. Will you do it?"

"We already went through this, Westerly."

I shake my head. She shakes her head. The excellent fish and chips are soured by the bad conversation. I've felt this before from Westerly. There's something pent up in her that wants release. I take a sip of ginger beer.

"Westerly, we're on for the showcase finale. You know that. But here's something to think about. Your story is riveting. Your story can inspire people in the best possible way. Have you ever thought about doing a one-woman show? You tell the story of Peter becoming Westerly, and you shuffle into it all the singing and dancing and comedy sketches?"

"But my story is in the documentary."

"Yeah, but I think there's a life for your story beyond the documentary. Movies become plays. Plays become movies. You've made it clear that you need to perform, that you need a live audience. This would give you that, and it would bring in narrative."

"You're saying the singing and dancing and comedy is not enough?"

"Not at all. But I do think that the straight, unembellished story is totally mind-blowing. It's like the Rolling Stones, Westerly. They have their new album, which they're promoting and they hope the world will love. But the crowd wants all their classics. So what do they do? They give 'em "Satisfaction," "Jumpin' Jack Flash," "Sympathy for the Devil," "Wild Horses," then they throw in a tune off their new album. Everyone's happy."

Westerly looks at me with pure hurt. A piece of fish is tucked away in her cheek. She hasn't chewed for something like sixty seconds.

"Well, let me ask you this then. Do you believe that the showcase finale is the most important part of the movie?"

"I think the showcase finale is your thing. And we'll film it. And we'll support you to make it the best showcase finale we can—pending whatever budget we end up with, of course. But the story we've been invested in all along is the transition from Peter Drouyn into Westerly Windina."

Westerly holds her hand up like a blade. "I'm asking yes or no, do you think the showcase finale is the most important part of the movie?"

I don't want to hurt her. I can't keep bullshitting her.

"It's always been your thing," I say.

"Yes or no? If you say no then you don't know me. Nobody knows me. You just don't understand who I am. And you don't understand where I've come from. And that's going to blow the movie anyway, because you don't understand the reason why I'm alive, why I'm here, and that it's all about show business. It's not about surfing at all. You know, surfing can go to the dung heap, but Westerly was meant to perform."

"Westerly, I like what I've seen you do at your house, and in our rehearsal the other day."

"What you've seen is just a dying hors d'oeuvre, it's nothing compared to what you will see and hear. I'm under a lot of pressure. I'm still rehabilitating. I just need you guys to believe in me and to believe that the showcase finale is actually part of the resurrection; it's part of the whole thing you see in front of you. It's the finality to the movie. And to me it's logical to say that people will say, 'Well there she is performing, finally she's performing. And she is beautiful.'"

"I don't doubt that."

"You can't doubt it. You have to believe. For the movie to be successful you have to fully believe in the miracle of Westerly."

"You know, that's how Charles Manson got his start, Westerly."

"Aw, Jamie." She shakes her head, brings her thumb and index finger to her forehead as if I've given her a headache, pinches her lips, scowls.

An icy silence hangs over the table. The fish and chips suddenly taste cold and rubbery. The clicks and hisses of mastication rise in volume, as if manipulated by a sound engineer in a movie to ratchet up tension. The butcher's paper, spread like giant maps in front of us, is smeared with grease and vinegar and ketchup and salt. Westerly is barely eating.

"Maybe we should call it a night," I say.

"Yeah, good idea."

We fold our papers into wads and toss them in the rubbish bin. Westerly's heels clack across the cement floor. Out on the street the rain has stopped but the wind continues to whip. The night sky is black. A sliver of moon hangs over the high-rises of Surfers Paradise. I open the door for Westerly and she steps into the car. I take great caution to make sure both of her feet are in before shutting the door.

We ride home in silence. Past the murder motel, the bottle shop, the grassy park with a skate bowl. I pull up a couple of steps from her door.

"See you, Westerly."

"Yep," she says despondently. "See ya, Jamie."

She gets out, walks to the door, enters the house. She does not look back.

HOPE

THAT WAS NEARLY A YEAR AGO. SINCE THEN, AT the time of writing this, we've had little communication. A few months back Jordan, Alan, and I tried to put on a showcase finale. The idea was to connect Westerly with The Windy Hills, a respected, soulful rock band whose members all live reasonably close to her. Westerly would send them a song list, they'd first rehearse on their own, then together as a band, then play a gig, at the Byron Bay Community Centre. *Westerly Windina and The Windy Hills* as a double bill—seemed serendipitously perfect. Not only that, but Westerly would be assured a solid turnout—The Windy Hills have a big following in Northern New South Wales.

Things went bad fast. First Westerly barraged us with long emails demanding all sorts of things, including money. And the demands came with deadlines: *"5 pm your time, after that I say goodbye."* Then she referred to The Windy Hills as "a garage band of musician hobbyists," and came up with at least a dozen reasons why the plan was unworkable. It was disheartening all around. I got the sense that she was more comfortable playing the victim (*"the Americans screwed me, that's why I'm still stuck here on the Gold Coast, undiscovered"*) than making an honest attempt to step on stage and dazzle a crowd.

But that's no way to end this.

When I think back on my four-and-a-half years with Westerly Windina, several scenes stand out. There's Westerly dancing across the water on her surfboard and her terrific bows at the shoreline, bows so glorious they beg for a cascade of red roses to fall from the sky. There's Westerly flapping her wings on this same beach, she and an osprey "talking" to each other, her claim that she talks to animals validated, the sense of entering into a fairy tale, a children's book. There's Westerly's worried face the day we were supposed to pick up Zac in front of the video store at exactly 4 pm, Zac not there, Westerly in maternal panic, only to realize she'd mixed up the days. And there's Westerly and Zac chatting about Scandinavian metal bands on the ride to Australia Fair.

But the image that sticks in my head comes from the one night I slept at her house. This was after our long CSi dinner when she told me her story about going to London to audition for drama schools. It was around ten, I was driving to Byron Bay in the morning, my plan was to stay in a hotel. Westerly insisted I crash in her spare room. She went to great efforts to make it nice for me; fresh sheets, three pillows, towel and washcloth, a glass of water. The room had become her new "Marilyn room." An assemblage of dolls smiled at me from the dresser. Marilyn, hands to chest, giggled from the wall. It smelled of perfume. There were lots of pinks.

I'd showered, arranged my things for the morning, and was about to turn out the light when I heard a gentle knock.

"Hi, Westerly," I said through the door.

"Jamesy, I thought you might like to watch this."

"What is it?"

"One of my favorite scenes."

I put on pants and a T-shirt and joined her. All the lights were out save for the glow of the TV. Westerly wore a lily-white nightgown.

"Sit," she said, pointing to the armchair next to hers.

She aimed the remote, pressed play.

On TV, in voiceover, Morgan Freeman delivers his final lines in *The Shawshank Redemption*. Freeman plays Red, a contraband smuggler serving a life sentence in prison. After forty years, he gets paroled. In the scene he's fresh out and back to the world.

"Get busy living, or get busy dying," he says, pocketing a penknife, looking skywards. *"That's goddamn right."*

Out of the corner of my eye I watch Westerly. She wears a beatific glow. She mouths the words with Morgan Freeman as if she's done it a hundred times before.

Freeman closes his packed suitcase, puts on his hat, heads to the bus station, buys a ticket.

The colors from the TV dance across Westerly's face. She raises a finger.

A bus travels down a rural highway. Freeman stares out the window.

Westerly leans towards me, eyes glued to the screen. "Right here," she whispers, pointing to the screen. "Right here."

The camera moves closer on Freeman. His voiceover kicks in: *"I find I'm so excited I can barely sit still or hold a thought in my head. I think it is the excitement only a free man can feel, a free man at the start of a long journey whose conclusion is uncertain.*

"I hope I can make it across the border.

"I hope to see my friend, and shake his hand.

"I hope the Pacific is as blue as it has been in my dreams.

"I hope."

I turn to Westerly. She turns to me. Tears well in her eyes. Her mouth quivers from smile to frown. She holds out her hand. I take it.

Onscreen the credits roll.

ACKNOWLEDGMENTS

Four years after I met Westerly, my wife was killed in a bicycle accident. She was my confidante and best friend. Like me, she saw the beauty in WW. I am endlessly grateful for her love and support. Thank you to Westerly, for your strength and resolve. For mirroring back the good and the bad. For being so nakedly human. Thank you to Zac and Tony Drouyn, to Mal Chalmers, Peter Townend, Rabbit Bartholomew, Nat Young, Bob McTavish, Derek Hynd, Andrew McKinnon, Tony Dempsey, Barton Lynch, Jack McCoy, Phil Jarratt, Drew Kampion, Luke Kennedy, Mark Richards, Randy Rarick, Derek Rielly, Tim and Kirsten Baker, Mike Perry, John Witzig, Geoff Darby, Nick Carroll, Tom Carroll, Bruce Channon, Vaughan Blakey, Cheyne Horan, Paul Daly, Warren Delbridge, Lee Kennedy, Owen Ravenscroft, Eisa Davis, Sean Doherty, Andrew Kidman, Michelle Lockwood, Peter Maguire, Charles Bock, Garth Murphy, Matt Warshaw, Julian Chavez. Thank you to Scott Hulet and *The Surfer's Journal*. To *Surfer, Surfing, Surfing World, Tracks*, Morrison Media/*Deep*, Warner Bros. Entertainment Inc., and Len Freedman Music for permission to reprint articles, movie dialogue, and song lyrics. Thank you to Virginia Lloyd, Geoff Dyer, and Atlantic Center for the Arts. To Jon Roemer and team at Outpost19. To Jane Palfreyman, Rebecca Kaiser, Ali Lavau and crew at Allen and Unwin. To Ryan Harbage, Kathy Daneman, Thad Ziolkowski, William Finnegan, Simon Prosser, Craig Taylor, Paul Theroux, DV Devincentis, Peregrine and Catherine St. Germans. To Alan and Kate White, Jordan Tappis, Beau Willimon, Nick Atkins. Thank you to Mom, Dad, Steven, Jenny, Gage, Sabena. And a big thanks to Kim, for taking me by the hand exactly when I needed it. For hope.

Jamie Brisick is the author of *We Approach Our Martinis With Such High Expectations; Have Board, Will Travel: The Definitive History of Surf, Skate and Snow;* and *Roman and Williams: Things We Made.* His stories have appeared in *The Surfer's Journal, The New York Times, The Guardian,* and *The Sydney Morning Herald.* He is the recipient of a Fulbright Fellowship. A former professional surfer, Brisick lives in Los Angeles.